Michael Matt   ı
London, Englan   1
eight years at S(g
with police depa¡   l.

Once called 'The Indiana Jones of policing', Michael is no stranger to adventure. In the past he has escaped from Timbuktu after local thugs threatened to kill him, spent a year in and out of hospital after catching a tropical disease, been rescued from a murderous mob in South Central LA, broken out of a disused mountaintop hotel in China after being locked in its basement by guards, survived a trio of tornados in South Dakota, and has even eaten grits for breakfast (though he remains traumatised by the taste to this day). *Sidekick* – probably his most extraordinary adventure to date – is his fourth book.

ALSO BY MICHAEL MATTHEWS

Non-fiction

We Are the Cops
The Riots
American Ruin

SIDEKICK

The Incredible True Story of How a British
Police Officer Became a Real-Life
American Superhero

Michael Matthews

SILVERTAIL BOOKS • London

'Being a superhero is a little bit of theatrics, a little bit of police procedure and a little bit of tactical, black-ops, commando style shit.'
– Midnight Jack. Rain City Superhero

"Wear a costume if you want, but when you cross the line and start doing law enforcement, that's dangerous territory for you to be on because you could get hurt."
– Mark Jamieson. Seattle Police Department spokesperson

For my mother, Gracinda (aka Cindy)
who always enjoys hearing about my weird adventures.
It doesn't get much weirder than this.

SIDEKICK

Introduction

'Mick, it's PJ.'

PJ was Phoenix Jones, a Seattle based Real-Life Superhero I know – bear with me on this – but hadn't heard from in a while.

'I'm putting the Rain City Superheroes back together,' he told me.

For a moment, I sat in silence, wondering how to respond. The Rain City Superheroes Movement – or RCSM – were a group of men and women who dressed up in superhero outfits of their own design and patrolled the streets of Seattle, fighting crime and helping people in need.

No, really.

A few years before, I had been researching Real-Life Superheroes, after a New York cop I knew had told me about them. I was in Manhattan, looking up at the skyscrapers and jokingly mentioned to my cop friend that I was always expecting to see Spiderman swinging through the concrete canyons.

'We've got superheroes,' he said.

'The cops? That's a bit modest, isn't it?'

'No. Well yes, but no. I mean *real* superheroes. There are a couple of guys who dress up and fight crime on these streets.'

I looked at him sceptically. 'Really?'

'You think I'm joking? Look it up, you'll see.'

I looked it up. And what I saw both appalled and delighted me. There really were superheroes in America – comic book-type superheroes who dressed up in costumes and went around fighting crime. They wore masks and capes and gave themselves incredible names such as Mr Xtreme, Urban Avenger and Master Legend.

How had these guys gone unnoticed? How had I not heard of them before? Every night these mysterious men and women would don their outfits, pull on their masks, clip their utility belts in place and set out onto the mean streets of America. They hid in the shadows, watched from the rooftops, and protected the public from those who would do them harm. And although they didn't have any real superpowers (although – rather worryingly – some claim they do), what they lacked in that department they, seemed to make up for in both enthusiasm and lunacy.

It was crazy. It was dangerous. And it was wonderful.

I quickly became fascinated with them, both as individuals and the entire folly of their enterprise. But then my fascination became an obsession. I began reaching out to them on social media (the modern superhero's Bat-Signal), set up meetings and even patrolled with some of them. Finally, I embedded myself with Phoenix Jones' group – the Rain City Superheroes – for several weeks.

There was, though, a major issue for me. I was a police officer, working at Scotland Yard, in London, and I was doing this in my spare time. Patrolling with a bunch of costumed crime-fighters (call them 'vigilantes' at your peril), working outside of the law – taking it into our own hands, at times – while having a day-job as a cop in the UK was, by any standards, a serious conflict of interests. I tried to imagine my bosses' reaction to finding out that one of their officers was moonlighting as a superhero in America. 'British Cop's Secret Life as American Superhero!' was not a headline they would enjoy seeing.

If it ever came to some kind of inquiry or disciplinary proceedings, I wasn't sure where they – or I – would stand, but I was pretty certain that something like this had never come up before. In theory, I was off-duty, on leave, in another country, and what I did in my own time was, to a degree, my own business. But putting on a mask and fighting crime with a bunch of superheroes in America may have been pushing it.

As I continued with other projects, and focused on my career at Scotland Yard, I slowly began to forget about the superheroes of America, and the memory of my time with them became slightly cloudy, almost to the point of me questioning whether it had ever actually happened. The experience was that surreal. Had I really spent time patrolling the dark streets of America with a bunch of superheroes, taking on criminals, living an – *almost* – genuine, real-life comic book existence? Well, yes. I had. I even wrote a book about it – but, worrying about how my superiors would react, I left the electronic document in a folder on my computer, marked 'X'.

It is only now that I've left the police that I have finally agreed to publish this book.

'I'm getting the team back together,' I heard Phoenix Jones say again, breaking my trance. 'What do you say, Mick? Are you in?'

It had been several years since I last saw them – but I was instantly interested to find out what had been happening in the world of the superheroes. My fascination with them was still there. The colourfulness, their downright craziness, the dangers, the stupidity of it all; it still intrigued me. There was only ever going to be one answer.

'I'm in,' I said.

But all this (and more) was still to happen. First we need to go back. Back to a time a few years before that phone call. Back to the day I first heard about real-life superheroes. Back to the time in my life when I myself became a part of the team.

This is the story of how a very sceptical British police officer became the *London Fog* – a real-life American superhero.

Well, sort of.

1

The Evildoers of Winter Park

My first experience with Real-Life Superheroes was not a good one. In fact, it was so hopeless that I nearly gave up on the whole thing before it even began. The "superhero" I met was based in New York, yet seemed to have never heard of the Empire State Building (we had arranged to meet nearby but the superhero got lost repeatedly, and that was after previously cancelling on me because it was raining). I'd been leaving messages on his phone. His recorded message informed me, somewhat optimistically, that he "*DESTROYS EVIL!*"

We eventually spent an evening "patrolling" in a tourist bar, where he encouraged me to take photos of him with "hot women" in the background, as we knocked back pints of beer. After finally talking him into actually hitting the streets, all he did was throw dollar bills at homeless people – literally throwing them; he seemed genuinely scared of getting too close.

He also handed out MRE's – military, *Meals Ready to Eat*.

'The homeless will eat anything,' he informed me. 'They'd eat dog shit if you gave it to them. It tastes gourmet to the homeless.'

I wasn't sure if he meant the MREs or the dog shit.

But the most memorable part of the evening (and this was back at the bar) was when the superhero divulged to me that he had a plan to kidnap the president of Sudan and bring him to justice. Suddenly, and wholly unintentionally, I had found myself at the heart of some international conspiracy. The first step, he told me, was to use his network of spies and contacts in some rebel army to help him find the capital of Sudan. (It seemed he had never heard of Khartoum. I mean, even a basic Google search would have revealed that secret.)

So it's fair to say, it wasn't a good start.

But if I'd given up then, I'd never have discovered the other world – the one where the superheroes really did believe in their missions, and really did try to make the world a better place. Some time after my encounter with the would-be avenger of Sudan, I heard about another superhero who, I was assured, was much more along the lines of what I was searching for. He was – and then some. And I quickly came to realise that what was interesting about Real-Life Superheroes wasn't so much their outfits and what they did or claimed to do, but the people behind the masks – the superheroes themselves. They were some of the most unusual, fascinating and unexpected people I had ever met.

*

As the frightened teenaged boy walked through the eeriest part of the eeriest cemetery in New Orleans, he had to force himself to continue moving forward and finish what he had set out to do. He was searching for something – something he wanted more than anything else: superpowers.

At the solid, graffiti-covered, Greek Revival tomb of the 19th Century Voodoo Queen, Marie Laveau, in the centre of St Louis Cemetery No.1, the terrified boy marked the grave with a customary "X" – a voodoo tradition, to have wishes granted – and placed an offering. The boy was tired of the bullies, tired of the abuse he suffered at the hands of his father, tired of seeing others suffering at the hands of evildoers, so he made his offering and asked the long dead Queen for superpowers so that he could fight evil.

Afterwards, wandering the cemetery in a daze, he found himself lost and took shelter in a dank mausoleum. The large iron door slammed shut, trapping him inside. In the darkness he began hearing voices speaking to him in a mysterious language that he could somehow understand, telling him that he would never be able to leave, telling him that he would be entombed forever.

The terrified boy yelled and screamed for help – but no one came. In desperation, the boy called out to the Voodoo Queen, "Marie Laveau! Marie Laveau! I need the power now!"

'And with that, I managed to kick the door open. I knew then that I had my wish.'

I had been listening to a man I knew only as *Master Legend* (he wouldn't reveal his true identity) as he told me this incredible story. I was on patrol with this Real-Life Superhero in his "Justice Van", in the small, suburban city of Winter Park, Florida, close to Orlando.

Before meeting him, I had had some serious concerns. Master Legend had agreed to meet me late at night in Winter Park, but I had some doubts that he would be there. After first making contact with him online, we had then spoken on the phone and had made arrangements for my visit. But when I called him, he told me that he was in his "Tower" recovering after cracking some ribs. I imagined his "Tower" to be a secret lair somewhere, filled with gadgets and flickering television screens, though it was probably nothing of the sort.

'What happened to your ribs?' I asked.

'I was doing some life-threatening manoeuvres,' he told me. 'Superhero stuff, yer know? And I got hurt.'

Master Legend wouldn't expand any more than that. He told me that he had been in some pain but would still do his best to meet me.

A few days later, as I stood in some dark back street at eleven o'clock at night, watching as a large, beaten-up, beige coloured van slowly approached me, I had to ask myself just what the hell I thought I was doing. This feeling of dread grew as I caught a glimpse of the man driving the van. He was middle-aged, wearing a black and white spandex facemask that came down over his nose and around the sides of his face. He had a tin army helmet on his head, with a mane of golden hair flowing out the back, and a grey coloured all-in-one spandex suit that included silver coloured body armour. Climbing into the cluttered, front passenger seat, I saw that his suit had been completed with silver Kevlar shin and arm guards.

Then, as I pulled on my seatbelt, he handed me a short, rusty metal pipe.

'That's for you, in case we get any trouble,' he told me, in a strange, nasally Southern accent. 'I didn't know if you'd brought any weapons or not?'

'I have a pocket knife,' I told him, though I hadn't intended to use it as a weapon.

'Okay, whatever is good for you,' he said.

It wasn't really good for me at all. The last thing I was planning to do was pull a knife on someone. As for the metal pipe I had just been handed, well, I wasn't really sure what to do with it. What if we were pulled over by the police? More than anything, it was the police asking me awkward questions that concerned me the most. Getting arrested in the company of a superhero was not something

I needed to happen. But what if I was faced with the option of having to use the metal pipe? Would I? I felt both nervous about having it but also slightly relieved, in case there *was* a need to defend myself. In the end, I figured that, if it really came to it, I would just use it and then try to explain myself to the cops afterwards, hoping that they'd understand.

I stuffed the metal pipe down the side of the seat. 'What do *you* have if there's trouble?' I asked.

He reached down and pulled out the biggest metal wrench I have ever seen. He called it "*Mr Wrench*".

Other than the wrench, Master Legend explained that he didn't carry much weaponry anymore.

'I'm a very skilled fighter,' he told me. 'I don't need to carry too many weapons. The stuff I carry these days is to help people, like this utility belt and CPR device. I *did* used to carry a shock baton.'

Master Legend's "shock baton" was an extendable police-type baton crossed with a taser. It sounded kind of nasty; something you could beat someone with while at the same time sending electric volts through their body. I imagined it to be the sort of thing cruel men used on cattle in abattoirs. But Master Legend didn't have it with him, as it wasn't working.

Overuse? I wondered.

'And in the back of the van I have a couple of chainsaws,' he said.

My head started to spin. I had heard stories about Master Legend, about how he had a much more "hands-on" approach to dealing with those he called "evildoers" – but chainsaws? I silently hoped they were used for helping rather than punishing people. The last thing I wanted to hear was the loud, shrill sound of a chainsaw starting up behind me, and the evening's patrol turning into some weird Winter Park Chainsaw Massacre.

'I also have a special cannon called the *Master Blaster* that I made myself. It's like a modified potato gun. I use Right Guard deodorant to propel it.'

The "Master Blaster" wasn't only used as a weapon. Master

Legend had adapted it to fire the ends of ropes over a tree branch or building so he could climb up or lower himself down somewhere. This once happened, he told me, when two kids were in a "snake and alligator infested lake". Their boat had over-turned and Master Legend had lowered himself off a bridge to reach – and save – the kids.

'Those kids were gonna drown,' he told me. 'But I used my climbing skills and roped myself down to them. They were all tangled up in vines but I managed to get them out.'

When not firing ropes, the Master Blaster was capable of more serious damage. Master Legend had little plastic Easter eggs that he had painted silver – his signature colour.

'I can put anything in those eggs – like rocks. If I put a rock in with wadding, like wet newspaper, it will go through someone's head. I don't want to use it like that, but I will use it on a child molester and blow their head off. If I have to go to jail, so be it. As long as I save a child from a child molester.'

'Have you ever been to jail?' I asked.

'Yeah. I had to wear a special coloured band on my wrist, as I was considered one of the worst.'

'Why? What did you do?'

'I beat up a child molester. He eventually went to slammers-ville for his evil acts, though he had a few less teeth thanks to me,' he chuckled.

Master Legend clearly had a very real (and understandable) hatred for child molesters. I quickly realised that they, more than any other criminal group, seemed to be the focus and reasoning for using his superhero persona to fight "evildoers". It left me wondering just what sort of dark past he had suffered himself.

When I questioned the legality of the weapons Master Legend had at his disposal (including the metal pipe I had stuffed down the side of my chair), he told me that believed these items only became weapons when you used them as such. Before that they were simply items that "*could be considered illegal*".

'I could tear a beer can apart and suddenly it's a weapon, even though it was just a beer can a second before', he told me. 'But, like I said, I try not to use any weapons. I like to handle people with *fist-city* instead, though I also carry small packets of cyan pepper powder, which I can fling into peoples faces.'

We had set off into a warren of dark, gloomy residential backstreets. Although he often patrolled downtown Orlando, Master Legend's mission for this evening was to track down some illegal drug activity and to help out some of Winter Park's homeless population.

Winter Park had a fairly low crime rate – but that didn't mean it was all farmers markets and country fairs. It was pretty much a suburb of Orlando and, although many of Winter Park's crimes were of the less violent type, such as burglaries and vehicle offences, it wasn't totally untouched by the more brutal side of life; just a few days before, there had been a robbery in a parking lot.

As we drove slowly up and down near-identical, run-down streets, I took the opportunity to dig a little further into Master Legend's past. I wanted to know about this superhero's life. Had Master Legend ever been hurt doing superhero work?

'I've been stabbed a few times,' he said over the growl of the Justice Van's engine.

He used his teeth to pull off one of his black-and-silver Kevlar padded gloves, and showed me a knife wound below his left thumb.

'What happened?'

'Some guy attacked me with a knife – but I got the knife off the guy and stabbed him in the butt.'

'You stabbed him in the butt?' I asked. 'Didn't you get into trouble?'

'Sure. I went to jail for that one. I've been in jail many times for doing good deeds and helping people. But I always ask for solitary confinement, otherwise I end up fighting those horrible, disgusting people. Jail is full of disgustingness! The worst kind of people. Horrible people.'

Master Legend pulled the Justice Van into a dead-end street. The houses were small wooden bungalows, run-down for the most part, with trash in the unkempt gardens and property boundaries hard to identify. The trees were overgrown and shrouded in eerie veils of long, grey Spanish moss that leant a sinister and ghostly air to the dark neighbourhood. Master Legend was on the lookout for a known drug dealer and, as we searched the streets, he continued to reveal his past to me.

'My daddy was a mean man. He was Ku Klux Klan and he made me and my brother train to be Klan fighters. We were trained by World War Two and Korean War veterans. We'd be driven around in a van and, when they found some black folks, we'd be thrown out the back and made to fight them.' He paused. 'I have nothing against black people, just evil people. Sometimes my daddy and the other men would put me in a large cage with another kid and we would be made to fight like you see with chickens.'

Master Legend had grown up a fighter, whether he had wanted to be one or not – but, in his mind, he was now using those skills against "evil". As awful as his life had been, it was also incredible. A young boy from New Orleans, abused and bullied as a kid, forced to train as a Ku Klux Klan fighter by war veterans, given special powers by a dead Voodoo Queen – how could he be anything *but* a superhero?

Of course, he hadn't started out as Master Legend. Before that he had been "Captain Midnight".

'At school there was this bully. He'd pour milk over the heads of other kids and push his fingers into their food,' Master Legend told me. 'He tried it on me once and I knocked him to the floor. I got into trouble for that and realised that the only way to handle a bully in future would be for no one to know who I was. I always read comic books as a kid and this inspired me to make my first mask. I called myself Captain Midnight. I saw the bully again hitting these kids, so I put on my mask and beat him up. No one knew who I was. I was Captain Midnight for a long time.'

To complete the image of Captain Midnight, he got himself a

shirt and sewed a moon and star onto the front – but he would eventually lose the name after he found that it had already been used for a character in radio and television adventure serials in the 1940s and 50s.

'Where did the name "Master Legend" come from?' I asked.

'I became a motocross rider known as "The Legend". I also did Kung Fu. I used to teach kids how to break boards and bricks with their bare hands. It was the kids who started calling me Master Legend.'

We turned into another street and Master Legend stopped the Justice Van, nodding his head towards a house that was set between thick bushes and clumps of trees. A white man and woman were banging frantically on the door.

'That's a drug dealing place,' Master Legend told me. 'I've been keeping an eye on it for some time. I'm building up evidence to pass on to the police.'

We watched the pair as they stood outside the house. The woman was looking around as the guy thumped his fist on the door. Master Legend turned the headlights off and reversed the Justice Van into the shadow of a high wall. There was no one else around. The streets were deserted.

Eventually, the couple were let inside. They quickly looked around themselves before stepping through the door. They hadn't noticed us watching.

Master Legend told me that he had been spending many of his evening patrols photographing suspected drug activity and noting down car numbers to pass to his police contacts. There were two cops that he regularly passed information to – a deputy with the Orange County Sheriffs, and a sergeant with the Winter Park Police Department. Master Legend regarded the Winter Park sergeant in particular, as his very own "Commissioner Gordon" – the Gotham City police commissioner from the Batman comics.

'So the police know about you and know what you do?'

'Sure. They know who I am. The cops don't bother me.'

As well as reporting drug activity to the local police, Master Legend also held his own opinions about how "*these people*" should be dealt with. And he didn't mince his words.

'For some of these people all they understand is a good beating,' he told me. 'It's certainly all an evildoer will understand. You gotta beat them up.'

'But should a superhero be doing that?' I questioned. 'Beating people up? Doesn't that just make you a vigilante?'

'No. Vigilantes will go looking for trouble. Superheroes stop trouble when they see it. We're *not* vigilantes,' he stressed.

But looking for trouble was exactly what we were doing. Our next stop was to the house of a guy that Master Legend had been after for some time. He was apparently another drug dealer, who had even attacked Master Legend in the past. It was a score that was clearly unsettled in Master Legend's mind.

'This guy I'm still waiting to beat up,' he told me, as we pulled up, stopping directly outside the man's small, tatty bungalow.

A light was on in an enclosed wire porch and, inside, a nasty-looking dog lifted its head and stared at us menacingly. It was probably just a Labradoodle, but as far as I was concerned it was Cujo, the rabid, killer hound from the Stephen King horror novel.

Master Legend ignored Cujodoodle and stared at the house. 'His time will come,' he said, more to himself than to me.

Master Legend clearly had a personal vendetta against the guy. I began to twitch in my chair, concerned that the guy might actually come out. If he did, I had little doubt that we would end up rolling around, fighting in the street. I felt a slight prang of panic as I imagined myself handcuffed in the rear of a police car.

'I don't want to go to prison,' I blurted out loud.

Master Legend gave me a slightly baffled look.

But no one came out to challenge us and, a short time later, we moved on. The visions I had of me standing on the street waving a metal pipe at the jaws of a rabid mutt, whilst Master Legend stomped on some guy's head, had caused a few drops of sweat to cross my brow. The thing is: Master Legend really *did* want to beat the guy up, and seemed bitterly disappointed that the guy failed to appear. Personally, I had no problem with breaking up a fight or preventing a criminal from committing a crime; by stepping into something like that, I was simply a member of the public doing my civic duty. But just hanging around outside a person's home, even the home of a suspected drug dealer, waiting to beat them up, made me feel uncomfortable to say the least.

'I heard you've been shot,' I said, in an attempt to lighten the mood.

'I've been shot twice. I was shot in the knee while helping a woman who was being attacked, and another time in New Orleans when I was with Team Justice, a group of superheroes who used to patrol with me.'

'What happened?' I asked.

'That time in New Orleans was a gang brawl. I was shot in the arm. Good thing my arm was there – it stopped the bullet going into my lung! That first bullet I managed to dig out myself with needle pliers and a bottle of whiskey.'

I was growing to like Master Legend. He would throw in these "pliers and whiskey" type comments all the time and, although I had started out being concerned about his sanity and my safety, I was beginning to look forward to his next astonishing tale of derring-do.

Master Legend had also received four concussions – hence the tin army helmet that was now very much part of his uniform.

'Superheroes don't come from just jumping off the sofa,' he told me. 'It comes from things that have happened to us.'

We drove out of the residential streets and pulled into a small industrial area. Master Legend wanted to patrol on foot, to look for some homeless people he was keeping an eye out for. We stepped out of the Justice Van and for a moment I wondered if I needed to bring the metal pipe. *Had we come here to beat somebody up?* But Master Legend assured me I wouldn't need it.

An old beaten-up pick-up truck was parked close to where we had stopped and on the ground, half under the truck and half out in the street, was a large bundle of something covered in a thin red sheet. Master Legend kicked the bundle with his metal toe-capped boot.

'HEY!' someone shouted from beneath the sheet.

Master Legend leapt back a few feet and dropped into a *fighting stance*, lowering his body and putting his arms out in front of him like he was getting ready to do some karate. 'Who's that?' he demanded. 'Brett? That you?'

'Yeah,' came the voice.

'You doin' okay?'

'Yeah. Doin' okay.'

'What's he doing under the truck?' I asked Master Legend.

'He's homeless. He's just using it for some shelter is all. It belongs to the old lady who lives here.'

It was only then that I noticed a house behind a thick clump of trees and bushes. It was the only house in this small area.

As we pushed our way through the overgrowth, Master Legend pulled a flashlight from his utility belt and illuminated the front of the house, checking that everything was secure and okay. It was.

At the side of the house was a wide alley, lit by a single dim streetlamp, giving a small, concentrated area at the centre of it, a flickering, platinum glow. Together, we stepped into the alley. As we walked, the silence was pierced by whispering voices coming from behind another large truck that had been parked somewhere further along.

As Master Legend moved into the shadow of the building line, I slipped in behind him. *Maybe I should have brought that metal pipe after all*, I thought. If there was a drug deal going on down there, then there was a good chance that the dealer would be armed with something; a knife perhaps, or worse. And there was an even better chance that the superhero I was with would want to kick some butt. My heart rate picked up a little. As we drew closer,

Master Legend jumped towards the truck and stood in his fighting stance.

'Hey! ML! How you doin'?'

Two men and a woman were sitting on the ground behind the truck. They all knew Master Legend and they were all extremely drunk. It was the homeless group that "ML" had been searching for.

'How's it going guys?' Master Legend enquired.

The woman lifted herself up and staggered towards us. She looked as though she was in her late sixties but she may have been younger, the effects of drink and drugs having taken its devastating toll.

'Who's this?' she demanded, struggling to lift one of her arms, so she could point at me.

'This is Mick from England,' Master Legend told her.

'Well, hello Mick from England. I'm Terrie Berry. Shake my hand.'

I looked down. Her hand was covered in filth and stained black from long periods of neglect. Master Legend noticed that I wasn't wearing gloves and immediately came to my rescue.

'Oh, he doesn't touch people Terrie,' he told her.

'Why the fuck not?'

'He has a disease,' Master Legend lied. 'Believe me, you don't want to touch him.'

'Well, I'll have to kick his butt instead then.' And with that she came at me in an absolute frenzy, swinging around her arms and legs in an attempt to hit and kick me. *Kickin' butt* seemed to be a common, Winter Park activity.

I stepped back, out of her range –but she continued to stagger towards me with badly aimed kicks. This was ridiculous.

Master Legend laughed. 'Terrie Berry The Fighting Woman!' he proclaimed.

'This isn't funny!' I said. 'Get her to stop!'

But before Master Legend could intervene, Terrie Berry The

Fighting Woman unexpectedly broke into song, treating us to a slurred rendition of American Pie, followed by just about the entire Queen back catalogue.

'They're not *bad* bums,' Master Legend told me, as we returned to the Justice Van. 'Just your friendly neighbourhood drunks.'

Looking out for the homeless was one of Master Legends chosen duties. He had once been homeless himself, but it was an incident from his childhood that had really stuck with him. As a kid in New Orleans, he once saw a "bum" begging for money. The bum was covered in sores and the young Master Legend had given him a couple of bucks – all the money he had in his pockets.

'My daddy was with me,' Master Legend told me, once we were back in the van. 'He sprayed pepper juice into that bum's eyes, and then he started to slap me around. That bum then came to help *me*. Told my daddy that I could have the money back. "Just please stop hitting the boy!" It's been ingrained in me to help the homeless ever since.'

'How did you become homeless?' I asked.

'A woman. I ended up spending a year in the woods.'

We pulled up outside another small bungalow, sitting on a scruffy plot of land. A fading light bulb was struggling to illuminate the small porch.

'This is where Brimstone lives,' he told me.

'Who's Brimstone?'

'He's another superhero. We sometimes patrol together.'

'Like a sidekick?'

'Not a sidekick; he's a superhero in his own right. But his woman won't let him out.'

'She won't? But he's a superhero!'

'He's been coming out less and less,' Master Legend told me. 'His woman doesn't like him doing superhero work.'

'It guess it must be tough keeping relationships going when you're a superhero,' I offered.

'The problem is, a woman wants to keep you for herself,' he divulged to me. 'But a superhero is for the whole world.'

While we'd been talking, Master Legend had noticed a van following us. There were three men inside and the sliding door on the side of the van was open, as if someone was getting ready to jump out. Master Legend had been watching it in his mirror for some time.

'Not everyone appreciates that there's a superhero in town,' he said. 'Some people are out to get me. They know I'm here to stop their drug dealing and criminal activity.'

We turned a corner and the van did the same.

'This town was ridden – *ridden* – with crack houses and prostitutes,' Master Legend went on. 'It's taken me years but it's almost cleaned up. Not everyone is happy about that though. People think it's Disneyland around here, but it's more like Dizzyland. Those guys in the van could be getting ready to start shooting. *Prepare yourself!*'

Shooting?

I threw Master Legend a serious look of concern, particularly as he had just driven us into a tight, dead-end street. Reaching down, I grasped the metal pipe, holding it in a tight grip, now actually pleased that I had it and not really giving two-shits what the cops may have to say about it. I didn't know what good it would do against a gun – but, like a child with a blanket, it gave me a sense of comfort all the same.

I stared into the wonky wing mirror of the Justice Van and prepared to fight my way out of the corner we were now in. The Justice Van swung to the left and we bounced over rough ground in an attempt to get away.

'My house used to be on this plot before the Highways Agency tore it down,' Master Legend shouted cheerily over the noise, as the van rocked around on the potholed waste-ground.

We both looked back. The van had stopped following us and I released my grip on the pipe, relieved but still a little concerned that the van may have taken a different route to cut us off. One thing Master Legend had made clear to me was that not everyone in Winter Park appreciated his activities. Helping the homeless was one thing; interfering with the criminal underworld was quite another. Cops do it everyday, and everyone, including criminals, expects them to interfere. But a self-styled masked avenger was a different story.

It was getting late and, as Master Legend began to point out more and more drug activity (dealers walking around, buyers, users), I began to wonder if a metal pipe and Mr Wrench were really going to be enough. Sure, he had his chainsaws in the back of the van – but what I wanted to know was, did he have any *real* superpowers?

'Well, I told you about the strength Marie Laveau has given me,' he said. 'Whenever I need the power, it comes. I managed to rip a car door off its hinges once after a lady had driven into a tree and it caught fire. But I also have some psychic powers. I know things. Sometimes they just come to me. I died twice as a baby and was born with a purple veil.'

(A purple veil, I learnt, is associated by some with psychic energies and the supernatural – purple apparently being the colour of enlightenment and spiritual consciousness.)

'I also have the power to heal,' he continued. 'There was this little girl with two holes in her heart. I used my powers to heal her. I took the evil energy away from her, and into myself. When they tested her later, they found that the holes had healed. That girl's mother was my girlfriend at the time. Me healing her daughter terrified her... and she then became terrified of me.'

'What happened to the girl?' I asked.

'She later died from cancer in the bone marrow. She asked me not to heal her again. She told me that she didn't like it here and wanted to die.'

We sat in a sad silence for a while.

'Have you thought about what you're going to call yourself?' Master Legend then asked. 'Your superhero name?'

I hadn't. Having a superhero identity wasn't something that I had planned to do. I was researching superheroes, not becoming one.

In my head, I was identifying with the reporter or cop type characters from the comic books, not the actual super-beings themselves. But I didn't want to appear aloof or give the impression that I considered them to all be nuts, so I thought quickly about a possible superhero identity I could use for moments like this. I considered keeping a British theme, but Marvel Comics had already taken the obvious ones – "Captain Britain" and "Union Jack". Besides, I had no intention of going full-on brooding, mysterious, qualified caped crusader. I decided to keep it more low key. A *sidekick*, that's what I could be. I was hanging out with veteran superheroes and learning the ropes after all. Sitting here with Master Legend, I kind of felt like Batman's apprentice, Robin.

'I was thinking about Sidekick Mick,' I told him.

'Psychic Mick?'

'Sidekick Mick.'

'Wow! You have psychic powers too? That's great!'

My English accent was clearly not a power. I decided to rethink the name.

'But being a superhero isn't just about having powers,' Master Legend told me. 'People just need to care about others. Stay on top of the criminals. Do your part. Do anything! Donate a pair of socks to a homeless guy. Whatever. If everyone did one little thing, we'd be in a better place. But most people won't even do that. It's a selfish world that we live in.'

We drove down some smaller, tighter streets.

'You see that motor home over there?' He pointed out a large decrepit motor home, which had all its curtains closed. 'A crack guy lives there. His motor home is always moving around. He probably gets his crack from that house I showed you earlier, the one where the people were banging on the doors. He's small potatoes though.'

Then a slim girl in her twenties crossed the street ahead of us.

'That's *Crackie Jackie*,' Master Legend told me. 'She's a crack-whore. She gets her drugs from the doctors and then sells them to others, illegally.'

As she stepped into the road, she stopped briefly and stared at us, looking directly at Master legend's spandex covered face. Master Legend gazed back and the two of them held a brief staring contest, before Crackie Jackie quickened her pace and scurried away.

We drove away and parked on some waste ground, where we exited the Justice Van and stood in the darkness, surveying the town and listening for any cries for help.

Master Legend placed his hands on his hips in true superhero fashion. 'The town,' he said. 'The good town of Winter Park.'

'It's certainly been interesting,' I told him.

'Quiet night,' he said. 'People know Master Legend is on these streets. They don't always know where I am – but they know I'm out there. I *know* where the evil is.'

2

Can You Fly? Let Me See You Fly, Man

The urgent voices of the Clearwater Police Department officers crackled loudly out of the police scanner in the car. There were reports of drug activity in a nearby neighbourhood and units were responding. The superhero sitting next to me was wearing a tight fitting all-in-one red spandex outfit with blue underpants over the top, blue patent leather superhero boots and a yellow belt. His biceps were as wide as my thighs. A yellow circle with large red letters – "SH" – was embroidered on his chest. Pulling down the dark visor on his modified helicopter helmet, he switched on the "helmet-cam", started up the bright red 1972 Chevrolet Stingray – *the Super-Mobile* – turned on the headlights and screamed down Route 19 towards Clearwater, Florida.

It was time to go to work. It was time to fight evil.

The Super-Mobile, which sat low to the ground, roared like something from Jurassic Park as we belted past slower moving traffic. The raised curves of the vehicle's hood, which partly obscured my view of the road ahead, left me feeling as though I was riding in a scarlet-coloured Bat-Mobile.

The superhero next to me was "Superhero". It seemed that he didn't need any other name. No fancy, mysterious, dark identities here. He was simply *Superhero*. But then, what else would you call a forty-something man wearing a red spandex outfit with blue underpants and a utility belt?

'*Signal Twenty*,' Superhero shouted over the growl of the Super-Mobile. 'That's what some of the cops in Clearwater call me. Signal Twenty.'

'What does it mean?' I asked.

'It's one of the codes the police department uses. It means a *mentally ill person*.'

I leant forward and stared into his blacked-out visor, my own troubled reflection staring back at me. 'Are you?' I asked.

'Am I what?'

'Signal Twenty?'

'There are superheroes all over this country. Believe me, some are nutcases – but I am under no illusions. We're just trying to do some good. Give people hope.'

Superhero may not have been *Signal Twenty* – but I, however, was a shit.

'I'm a what?'

'You're a shit,' he told me.

'A shit?'

'Yeah. A Super Hero In Training. S.H.I.T. But don't worry about it. We've all gotta start somewhere, right?'

Even Superhero was a S.H.I.T once, although he actually started life as a pro-wrestler back in the late 1990s (and he still looked like a pro-wrestler, with a huge body-builder's physique, and bald head). In the world of American pro-wrestling, it's important for competitors to have a 'gimmick' – an identity other than just some guy climbing into the ring in a pair of shorts.

'I'd always wanted to be a superhero as a kid, so someone suggested I have a superhero gimmick and simply call myself Superhero.'

But, just as his wrestling life was beginning, Superhero seriously injured his knee, and his pro-wrestling career was quickly over. It was a cruel thing to happen to a young man's dream and, still not ready to put those dreams behind him, he kept his superhero identity, driving around his neighbourhood looking for people to help. It was, he said, "a natural progression".

'Master Legend tells me you've got psychic powers,' Superhero said. 'He said you're gonna call yourself Psychic Mick.'

'Sidekick.'

'Yeah, psychic.'

The police scanner came back to life. Police officers had apprehended the drugs dealers. Superhero took his blue super-boot off the gas, taming the Super-Mobile.

'I need to take a piss,' he said, and swung the Super-Mobile off the freeway and into the parking lot of a McDonalds restaurant.

'Does the suit have a zipper?' I asked.

'No. It's one of the problems faced by superheroes that people just don't think about. How do you take a toilet break in a one-piece spandex suit? Even Superman must have needed to take a pee sometimes.'

I followed Superhero into the busy McDonalds. This was going to be interesting. A man with his mouth wide open, about to take a bite from his Big Mac, stopped dead. Children slurping milkshakes stopped sucking on their straws and stared with eyes as wide as Planet Krypton. Staff behind the counter leant over their tills and followed the red-suited man with their eyes as he headed towards the restroom.

'That's Superhero,' I informed everyone. 'He's a... well, a superhero.'

'You don't say?' said the guy with the Big Mac, as he finally chomped down on his burger.

'You hungry?' Superhero asked me, after returning from the restroom. 'Because I could do with a snack.'

It's not everyday that you see a superhero standing at the counter of McDonalds ordering a cheeseburger and, as he paid the counter-staff, a man got up from a table and approached us. He wanted to shake Superhero's hand.

'It's nice to know that there are people like you out there protecting us,' he said.

'Just doing my bit,' Superhero told him. Then he carried his red plastic tray towards a table by the window.

It was all slightly surreal.

Leaving McDonalds proved difficult as people lining up for the drive-thru stepped out of their cars to have their photograph taken with the man-in-red. Then a gaggle of teenaged girls stepped out of their mum's SUV and crowded around, asking questions.

'Are you really a superhero?'

'What super-powers do you have?'

'Are you on Instagram?'

'How do you go to the bathroom in that suit?'

Superhero answered all their questions with diplomacy and patience (though he never revealed the secret of going to the loo in that suit), posing for all their pictures while taking advantage of their fleeting interest to warn them about staying out of trouble and keeping safe on the dangerous Florida streets.

'If I needed help, would you come and save me?' one of the girls asked.

'Of course,' he told her.

At that very moment, with comic book timing, a huge crashing sound came from the direction of McMullen Booth Road, a busy highway at the front of McDonalds.

'What was that?' I asked.

'I'm not sure,' Superhero answered. 'It sounded like a car crash.'

We ran to the front of the restaurant and looked out, towards the road, much to the excitement of the teenaged girls. 'Oh look! He's going to save someone!'

It was dark and, with the glare of headlights, it was hard to see. Even though the sound of the crash had been loud enough to hear above the noise of the traffic, we couldn't see any signs of an accident. Everything seemed normal. It didn't make sense.

'Let's jump into the Super-Mobile and see if we can track down what happened,' Superhero suggested.

The girls were now ecstatic, jumping up and down on the spot, waving to us as we roared out of the parking lot and onto the highway.

I squinted through the glare of lights at the road ahead of us, scanning for what had caused the noise. Superhero was doing the same. Then, just as we were fed onto an exit, we both caught sight of a black saloon that had come to a stop at the side of the road, on a narrow, grass verge. Thick plumes of steam were pumping out of the engine. The front bumper lay shattered across the highway. A shocked, middle-aged woman sat inside the saloon. A couple of other cars had pulled over, the drivers trying to reassure to the woman.

'Damn,' Superhero said. 'We'll have to drive back around. It's too late to get off this exit.'

We continued down the new highway to the next exit, where Superhero was able to turn around and return in the direction of the accident. Two minutes later, we were there – but now we were on the opposite side of road and had to keep going to find a suitable place to cross back over. Up ahead, we could see the red and white flashing lights of an ambulance and fire truck rushing towards the scene.

'Well, we've just gone from helping to obstructing,' Superhero told me.

With the emergency services now in attendance, we would serve little purpose other than, as Superhero had said, obstructing the professionals. I must admit, I felt a little disappointed – and I got the impression that Superhero was feeling the same way. Here was his *superhero* moment, and we missed it. Maybe it was for the best though. I mean, can you imagine? You've just been involved in a car accident, you're in shock, maybe hurt – and then there, striding towards you through the carnage, is a man in red spandex (and let's not forget those blue underpants). Although, if ever there were times in your life when you wanted to see a superhero, that would probably be one of those occasions.

We changed direction and Superhero took us to Drew Street, a long road that stretched east to west across Clearwater. He told me that migrant workers populated parts of the road and he regularly looked out for their safety.

'These guys always carry their cash on them,' he told me. 'They don't have bank accounts, so they're always getting robbed. Many of them may be illegal – but they work real hard and get paid poorly. The last thing they need is to get their money stolen.'

Superhero cruised slowly down the street, looking at everybody moving along parts of this poorly lit corridor. But it was quiet and there was no one in any obvious need of help, or anybody who may have been up to no good, looking for someone to attack.

'It gets like this sometimes,' he told me. 'Just because you tie a blanket around your neck, it doesn't mean that twenty Nazi frogmen are gonna jump out on you. A lot of people who take up this line of work forget that. They think the world is full of super-villains.'

This got me thinking: *super-villains*. If there were Real-Life Superheroes, then surely there must be Real-Life Super-Villains. Besides, what's a superhero without a super-nemesis? I put it to Superhero.

'There aren't any super-villains that I know of,' he told me, though there was a look in his eyes that suggested otherwise.

'None at all?' I pushed.

'Well, maybe one.'

I grinned. I couldn't help it. There's just something about a super-villain that seemed even more fantastic than a superhero; I put it down to that whole world-domination-come-destruction thing they always seem to have going on.

'Who's the super-villain?' I asked excitedly.

'Dr Psychosis,' Superhero said. 'He's kind of my nemesis.'

'What does Dr Psychosis do?'

'He torments me on-line and sends me e-mails.'

It wasn't quite what I had in mind and I got the impression that Superhero was slightly embarrassed by it. But I was still intrigued.

'He says stupid things about me and other heroes. It can actually be quite amusing – but, for a time, I stopped responding to him just to see what he would do.'

'What did he do?'

'He told me to answer him or he'd kill a kitten.'

'Did you answer him?'

'Yes. I told him that God does that every day anyway when people masturbate and asked him to please not kill the kitten. As far as I know, that little cat is still alive.'

As I talked with Superhero about criminals and the dangers of being a superhero, it became clear that the likes of Dr Psychosis, the kitten-killing super-villain, were the least of his problems. Far more worrying were other Real-Life Superheroes. Superhero had already told me that the "occupation" of superhero attracted a few "whack-jobs" and some had taken a serious dislike to Superhero himself. Word had spread that Superhero was actually a government lackey – a spy in their midst. Some even called him a fascist.

'Why do they think that?' I asked.

'Because I'm quite colourful. Look at this outfit – the bright colours. A lot of younger superheroes that are coming through now aren't like that.'

Superhero explained that many of the newer, younger Real-Life Superheroes were attracted to the darker side of hero work. For them it was more about being the *Dark Knight,* rather than the more genteel and old-fashioned Batman of Adam West. Superhero seemed genuinely concerned about this change in approach.

'They want to be all mysterious, hiding in the shadows, doing hero stuff under the wire, dressing in black clothing. I'm much more out there. I've been on TV shows, I do charity work, let kids take my picture. I once pulled a woman out of a burning car. Stuff like that. But I guess I just rub some superheroes up the wrong way. I've been threatened more than once. They think that I'm a government plant, sent to infiltrate the superhero network.'

'Are you?'

'No! And it's something *you* may have a problem with, being a cop. If other heroes know you're a police officer, they may not trust your motivations.'

This was something that I'd already considered. So far, I'd been straight about my profession with all the superheroes I'd contacted. Regardless, they were more than happy to meet me. Superhero wasn't so sure that this would always be the case though, and I wondered if he would be proven right.

Superhero was arguably one of the more famous Real-Life Superheroes. This was partly down to self-promotion, but it was also down to his identity and suit. His outfit was classic comic book and the Super-Mobile was described to me as being a "flagship" for the Real-Life Superheroes. I suspected that there was some envy amongst others in the community and that this, along with his refusal to be more "dark", had led some to turn against him.

Another problem Superhero had was that he didn't wear a mask.

'If I'd known about all the whack-jobs out there, I would never have had an open persona,' he told me. 'I would have had a mask and been more secret. I thought I was just helping people at the side of the road, helping kids and old ladies. I never thought I would be a target – especially to other superheroes.'

The threats against Superhero had gone international, when one superhero from Italy had even tried to pick a fight.

'I just told him to pack his bags and come on over!' Superhero told me.

Not surprisingly, Superhero took his personal safety seriously. We pulled into a large parking lot and he showed me some of the equipment he carried. Some stuff he had left at home; what he took out depended on what he had planned. But his armoury was impressive. As well as a set of body-armour, he also owned a number of super-weapons. These included an Airsoft Mach 2 machine gun (Airsoft guns being frighteningly realistic gas-powered weapons that fire small plastic balls – a bit like paintball without the paint).

'It fires twelve pellets a second,' he said, smiling. 'It's like being hit by a squadron of bumblebees. You won't die but you'll wish you were dead!'

He also had a 9000-volt zapper stun gun, a police style extendable baton, an enormous can of bear mace (*"Which can also be used on alligators"*) and an "Arma 100 Stun-Cannon", which Superhero claimed was officially listed as a tool rather than a weapon. I had no idea what a Stun-Cannon was but it certainly sounded very superhero-ish. Superhero, sensing my interest, pulled out his cannon.

'It used to belong to a cop who patrolled an Indian reservation,' he said, handing the cannon to me. 'He used it on drunk Indians.'

The cannon was a short, wide, thick metal tube with a spring handle and trigger on the end. The barrel was painted bright orange. It hadn't always been orange – but Superhero wanted to make it look less like a gun and more like a toy or tool, so he painted it. He explained that this was because a Clearwater police officer pulled the Super-Mobile over once, and had mistaken the cannon for a firearm. Superhero told me that the cop nearly shot him.

'What does the cannon fire?' I asked.

'Small beanbags that contain thirty-seven millimetre lead shots. The bag is propelled by a big old nitrogen filled cylinder. It'll actually fire anything you put in it. I even fired a peanut butter and jelly sandwich out of it once.'

'Why?'

'Just to see if it could be done. Wanna have a go?'

I did.

After walking away from the Super-Mobile, we approached a large dumpster, where Superhero loaded the cannon with heavy, teabag-sized beanbag ammunition and handed it back to me. He explained that all I had to do was release the trigger and the bag would fire out and hit the dumpster.

I stood just three feet away from the dumpster to ensure I didn't miss it. Then I leant back a little, expecting some recoil as I pulled the trigger. I released the trigger. There was no recoil. I missed the dumpster. This was all fairly embarrassing.

As I'd been leaning back, the end of the cannon had pointed upwards, aiming above the dumpster. We stood in silence for a few seconds and waited for the sound of the heavy, solid, lead-weighted beanbag to hit something. The first "BANG" came moments later as the bag landed on the roof of a nearby parked car. This was followed by a second "BANG" as the bag bounced off the first car and hit a second. Superhero tried to smile through the obvious concern he was feeling.

'It's okay,' he said. 'I don't think you hit anything.'

I agreed and, after retrieving the bag – which had landed about 70 yards away – we left the parking lot and said nothing more about it.

Superhero had one more weapon at his disposal. He kept it hidden in a pouch he wore around his waist. It was a 9mm handgun. A real one.

'I have a concealed weapons licence,' he explained.

'Have you ever used it?'

'No.'

It seemed odd to me – inappropriate, even – that a superhero would be armed with a gun, even if that superhero was being threatened by the likes of Dr Psychosis and the Italian Hulk. Surely it went against everything that a superhero stood for?

'I don't always carry it when I'm *Superhero*. I mostly carry it off duty. But these can be dangerous streets,' he explained. 'This isn't the comic books. This is being a superhero for real – and that may mean having to take on a real life criminal who is armed, desperate and willing to kill you. It's something you'll have to think about if you're going to become a Real-Life Superhero in the UK. What will you use to protect yourself with?'

I explained that the laws in the UK would prevent me from carrying just about anything. Mace and pepper-spray are classed as firearms under British law. If I were to patrol the streets of the UK in superhero mode (which I had absolutely no intention of doing), then my arsenal would be somewhat thin on the ground. Self-defence and hand-to-hand combat techniques would be the only way to go. The only issue there, though, was my slight lack of physical prowess.

The previous day, I had met Superhero at a gym, to lift weights. Physical training, he assured me, was an important part of being a superhero. But whereas he was pumping 100-kilogram dumbbells with ease, I was struggling to lift 25-kilos. Physical strength seemed sensible; but a gun? What if he – *Superhero* – actually shot someone?

'It would cause quiet a stir,' he said. 'I'd go from being a *Superman* type character to being *The Punisher*.'

'It would certainly get a lot of media attention,' I commented.

'Yeah, but the reaction would depend on what news channel you watched. CNN would call me a "Monster in Spandex". Fox would call me the "New Messiah"!'

Driving through Clearwater, we headed south towards the small, pretty, coastal city of St. Petersburg, where Superhero wanted to do a foot patrol. He parked the Super-Mobile by the oceanfront in a pleasant neighbourhood. St. Petersburg is larger than Clearwater, with a handful of skyscrapers, and although he was mainly Clearwater based, Superhero knew St. Petersburg well. There had been a rapist operating in the city previously and Superhero had spent time on its streets, keeping an eye out not just for the rapist but also for any women he considered to be vulnerable, such as bar workers closing up at night.

St. Petersburg, with a population of around a quarter-million, has a higher than average crime rate, and whereas Clearwater (with a population just over a hundred-thousand) had suffered zero murders in the previous month, St. Petersburg had three. Clearwater had three reported rapes; St. Petersburg had twenty. And, with over eighty robberies in a single month, St. Petersburg was outdoing Clearwater by four to one.

Superhero's foot patrol had, predictably, an immediate effect. Women wolf whistled from parked cars; a drunk guy standing outside a bar called out, saying that he wanted to be Superhero's "Lois Lane"; kids ran up to him and asked if he was a real superhero. One thing was for sure: word would soon get around that there was a superhero in town.

Superhero was keen to check some alleys around a local cinema. As we passed the complex, a group of teenagers approached us. One of them marched straight up to Superhero.

'What you is?' he asked, somewhat cryptically, with his reorganization of the English language.

'I'm a superhero.'

'What superpowers do you have?'

'I give people hope.'

'Can you fly? Let me see you fly, man.'

The kid was a little aggressive, but Superhero calmly explained that he didn't fly and we moved on.

'Whenever I think of superheroes in the comic books, they always seem to be hanging around in the shadows,' I mentioned to Superhero. 'But you're really out there, so I guess you get these kinds of reactions all the time.'

'It's like we were talking about earlier,' he said. 'Some of the new, younger heroes want to be like that; they want to hide away and be more mysterious. I'm not so sure they really know what being a

Real-Life Superhero is all about. This isn't a comic book. It's not just about fighting crime. We also help people.'

Charity work was a big part of what Real-Life Superheroes involved themselves in. Superhero was part of Master Legend's *Justice Force* group, and they would regularly get together, not only to patrol and fight crime but to visit kids in hospitals, dish out bottles of water on hot days, help the homeless and other such things. Not all superheroes felt that this was what Real-Life Superheroes should be doing and, although there were other superhero groups around the country doing similar things – such as The Black Monday Society in Salt Lake City and The Alternates in the North West – there were also individuals who wanted nothing to do with this side of the superheroes' vocation.

'It's the ultimate superhero question,' Superhero said. 'Charity work or crime fighting? It's like, Pepsi or Coke. M-16 or AK-47.'

I wasn't entirely convinced with his comparison between charity work and AK47s, but I got the point he was making.

We walked around some nearby alleys. Most we deserted but, whenever we saw people walking through one, and despite what we had just spoken about, Superhero would do that classic superhero thing and step into the shadows, watching; watching to make sure the person was okay – but also watching to check that they weren't up to no good. We saw more than one person home or back to their car safely that evening, without the person even being aware that we were there. It felt satisfying – but also a little bit creepy.

'What do you think the future is for Real-Life Superheroes?' I asked as we strolled back to the Super-Mobile.

'Someone will get killed,' he said without hesitation. 'Either a hero will be killed or a hero will kill somebody.'

It was a dark prediction from such a colourful character.

Soon after leaving Clearwater, I began to notice a lot of excitement and "chatter" on the online superhero forums. A superhero had been involved in a serious incident in Seattle and had been arrested by the police. That superhero was Phoenix Jones.

Phoenix Jones, it turned out, was a bit of a celebrity in Seattle – albeit a rather infamous one. The incident that the superhero community were all buzzing about involved Phoenix Jones pepper-spraying a group of revellers during a late night disturbance. After his arrest, Phoenix Jones attended court in full costume – which included a black and gold, muscle-sculpted body piece and a Batman-style rubber mask. The judge wasn't impressed – and, soon, Phoenix Jones was made to de-mask and show his face. Suddenly, just like that, his secret identity was exposed. Phoenix Jones – a black guy in his 20s, with a tall, flat top Afro – was revealed to be Ben Fodor, a Mixed Martial Arts fighter. The media went wild.

The incident were he had been arrested had happened in downtown Seattle, late at night. The entire thing had been captured on video by Phoenix Jones' team – the Rain City Superheroes – and loaded onto YouTube. Naturally I looked it up. It made for interesting viewing.

In the video, Phoenix Jones is out on the streets patrolling one night with his team of superheroes, when they come across a bunch of men and women fighting. Phoenix Jones charges towards the angry group, as he shouts to his team to "call 911".

Men and women, who all appear to be drunk, are staggering around, falling over and fighting. One man is kicked in the face. Phoenix Jones sprays some of the group with mace, in an effort to stop them fighting, and to prevent anyone else – including himself and members of his team – from being hurt. The mace has an immediate effect, and the group fall back – all except for one lady who attacks Phoenix Jones with her shoes, striking him repeatedly. As Phoenix Jones tries to defend himself against the woman, the men begin to fight again, and this time one of them is run over by a car. Then, some of the men turn on Phoenix Jones and his team. As one man charges at him, Phoenix Jones is forced to use his canister of mace again, spraying the man in the face. Phoenix Jones is then momentarily – and dangerously – cut off from the rest of his team, and the men begin to move towards him. It's a confusing and chaotic scene. A black SUV turns towards the superheroes and the men begin to throw objects at them, forcing the superheroes to retreat to a nearby ferry terminal. Seattle police officers eventually arrive and begin to make arrests – including Phoenix Jones, who is arrested for assault.

After the incident, Phoenix Jones had his day in court, where he was made to de-mask. His true identity now revealed, he decided there was little point in trying to conceal who he was anymore – and, moments later, he dramatically de-masked again, this time outside the courthouse, for the waiting press and television cameras.

'I'm Phoenix Jones,' he tells the reporters. 'I'm also Ben Fodor. I protect this city. I'm a father and a brother. I'm just like everyone else.'

Only he wasn't like everyone else at all. Neither, for that matter, were the group of superheroes I was about to meet. A group who – just like Phoenix Jones – tended to jump headfirst into fights, brandishing pepper-spray and tasers.

I was going to California.

3

Code: Xtreme

The West Coast. San Diego, California. Despite the fact that I'd been in Florida previously, everything here seemed brighter – the sun, the sea, the sky. It was blue and it was yellow and it was hot. You could say that everything felt more extreme. And extreme was exactly why I was here. *Mr Xtreme.*

Mr Xtreme was the leader of the Xtreme Justice League, a group of Real-Life Superheroes who patrolled the southern Californian city of San Diego – a major coastal city of close to one and half million inhabitants. It's a pretty town with a noticeable US Navy presence and a Mexican flavour (the border is just 20 miles away). It has a laid back feel and is full of people walking slowly along its pretty waterfront, eating in vibrant Little Italy or hanging out in its downtown core of independent bars and restaurants in the historic Gaslamp Quarter. Late at night, it remains relatively warm – but the bars become louder and the atmosphere slightly edgier as the streets fill with people determined to party.

It was close to these streets that I stood now. It was midnight and I could hear shouting and music from bars several blocks away. I was standing alone outside the Hall of Justice – the intimidating, sand-coloured building, with large green-glass windows, that dominates West Broadway. The Hall of Justice seemed like an entirely appropriate place to meet a superhero.

By now I should have been used to seeing people like this but, despite my past experiences with Master Legend and Superhero, I was still taken aback by what was walking purposefully towards me across a four-lane road. Mr Xtreme looked like a cross between a Vietnam War veteran and a Teenaged Mutant Ninja Turtle. He was short and wide and wore urban camouflage combat pants, black boots, black gauntlets, a bulky set of black padded body armour with the words "Evil Suppression Unit" on the front, and a long, dark green superhero cape draped down his back. The rear of the cape had the crest of the Xtreme Justice League that included the "scales of justice". On his head he wore an old-fashioned army helmet, which was covered in various tiny superhero stickers. His face was hidden behind a large pair of ski goggles, which were decorated with large monster eyes.

'You must be Mr Xtreme,' I said, extending my hand. He shook it quickly but convincingly.

'And you must be Mick,' he said in a hasty, muffled voice.

Compared to Superhero's tight-fitting spandex suit, Mr Xtreme's outfit looked weighty and cumbersome. 'That gear looks heavy,' I said.

'It is – but I've been patrolling in this stuff for a while and I've started to get acclimatised to it. Plus, I work out a couple of days a week, so that helps. If you put it all in a bag and carried it, including the boots and all the gadgets, it's close to forty pounds.'

'Do you carry weapons?'

'Yes I do. I have a mace pepper gun that shoots out a big stream of pepper-spray. I've also got this pepper blaster, right here. It's supposed to shoot pepper-spray at about ninety miles an hour, to prevent blowback. And I have a stun gun, too. I can showcase them to you if you like?'

'No. Thank you. And all this is legal?'

'In California it is.' Then he pulled out a heavy, foot-long, black flashlight. 'This is a tactical flashlight. It's called a Cobra Stunlight. What's special about this is it has a light, a laser sight, and then this red button; it shoots pepper-spray. I actually used this about a month ago after we got into a situation on Fifth and E.'

'What happened?'

Twirling the Cobra Stunlight around in his hands, he said casually, 'A bunch of people were fighting in the street and a guy came up and sucker-punched one of my team. So I sprayed the guy in the face. He stopped attacking us after that.'

'Will I meet the rest of your team?' I asked; I was interested to see how a team of superheroes operated differently from individuals.

'They'll join us later tonight,' Mr Xtreme told me. 'But let's start walking while we wait, so I can explain to you the concept of how we patrol.'

We walked up West Broadway, towards the noisy Gaslamp Quarter.

'The main purpose with patrol is to act as a visual deterrent,' he told me. 'We want to prevent crime by making ourselves seen. You really can't tell when crime is going to happen; crime doesn't have a schedule. We also try to reassure people and make them feel safe.'

Across the road was a short guy in a red and black outfit, with black ninja boots and combat pants. His face was completely covered by a black motocross facemask and small circular goggles. On his top half he wore a red hoodie, over the top of which was strapped a red motocross armoured chest-plate. He also wore black elbow pads and gauntlets, and on his left arm was a small patch that read "Hope Agent". He walked swiftly and confidently towards us, like he meant business.

'That's my partner, Urban Avenger,' Mr Xtreme told me.

Urban Avenger raised a friendly hand above his head and waved. 'Hello there,' he said warmly.

After introducing ourselves and shaking hands, I asked, 'Why *Urban Avenger*?'

'I patrol an urban environment. Plus, I consider *avenger* to be a positive term; Captain America was an Avenger – someone who rights wrongs.'

'And are you expecting to right wrongs tonight?'

'Well, the weekends can get crazy. You could learn a lot from this patrol.'

'Between midnight and 3am is when it gets nuts,' Mr Xtreme warned.

'If the past six weeks are an indication, we should be pretty busy,' Urban Avenger added.

Fixed to Urban Avenger's left shoulder was a small video camera, which he could switch on when needed.

'It's come in handy a few times,' he said.

'We also use radios if we have two teams out,' Mr Xtreme told me. 'We use "*Code Xtreme*" to call for help. It means it's an emergency situation, somebody's life is in danger and we need immediate backup.'

'We have equipment, we have armour and we have training,' Urban Avenger said. 'If anything goes down, we'll ask you to step aside and let us handle it. We don't want you to get arrested or deported!'

'Talking of being arrested,' I said, 'I saw what happened to Phoenix Jones after he pepper-sprayed those people...'

'I think if you were with Phoenix Jones he might tell you to take people down and put yourself at risk, but not us,' Mr Xtreme told me.

'I'm actually hoping to see him,' I said. 'I'm still trying to get hold of him but I've decided to head to Seattle next.'

'Well, good luck with that!' Urban Avenger answered, and even though I couldn't see his face, I sensed the concern in his voice.

'I confess, the more I hear about Phoenix Jones, the more I worry.'

'You should worry,' he said.

I decided to put Seattle to the back of my mind, at least for now. 'What made you start to do this?' I asked Urban Avenger, keen to know what his own superhero motivations were.

He stood on a street corner, with his hands on his hips, surveying the streets around him. 'It was after I saw that film, *Kickass*,' he told me. 'Have you seen it?'

I had, I told him. It was a film based on a comic about a normal kid who dresses up in a homemade superhero costume, fights crime, and gets his ass kicked repeatedly. From what I understood, Real-Life Superheroes existed before Kickass, but the film had inspired more people to take up the mask. Urban Avenger was an example of that.

'So there's no big, dramatic back-story? You just saw the movie and thought: *that makes sense to me*?'

'Kind of. Don't get me wrong, I've been victimised by crime before and I was bullied as a kid. Then my car was broken into and I called the police but they weren't interested. I felt betrayed. That's when I wondered why there weren't people out there, being vigilant – not *vigilante* – just vigilant.'

At that moment we were interrupted by two short girls in short skirts, slurping down *Big Gulps* from the nearby 7-Eleven. 'I love your costume!' one of them told Urban Avenger, casting him a lingering look as she sucked on her straw.

'Oh, thank you,' he replied, casually.

She walked slowly away, looking back towards him a few times as her friend hung off her arm, giggling.

'Does that sort of thing happen often?' I asked Urban Avenger.

'Kind of,' he said. 'I've had girls come up and grope me and kiss my mask before. I don't really think anything of it. Maybe they have some weird mask fetish. But if you're asking if I've ever gotten laid because of this suit, no.'

'And do you carry any weaponry?' I asked.

'I carry a stun gun, pepper-spray, a Maglite, handcuffs and marbles.'

'Marbles?'

'Yeah. I throw them on the floor and trip people.' He paused. 'But mostly, I'll just reach for my stun gun.'

'And the cops don't have a problem with that?'

'Not really. The cops usually don't mind what we do.'

'The police department wants us to be "eyes and ears",' Mr Xtreme said. 'Observe and report but don't intervene. But if somebody's life is on the line right there and then, we have to do more than just *observe and report*. By the time we get done observing and reporting, somebody could be dead. People are getting stomped out here without the cops even showing up. It's fucking ridiculous and that's part of the reason why this movement – the XJL – exists.' Mr Xtreme was starting to sound angry. 'People's apathy, indifference and fucking laziness – like it's not their problem,' he said, shaking his head.

'I guess people don't want to get hurt,' I offered.

'Fine, but at the very least pick up the phone and call 911. We're talking about human beings. That could be *you* needing help.'

The Gaslamp Quarter was rowdy and chaotic, but most people were in a friendly mood. We were repeatedly stopped so people could have their picture taken with the superheroes and I inevitably became the camera guy. To avoid more attention, we turned down Market Street, a wide road that ran west to east, lined with youth hostels, cafes, restaurants, modern and colonial-style buildings. It was a place people came back to after partying it up in the surrounding streets and it was slightly quieter than the bars areas.

Two girls, leaning over a hotel balcony, jokingly called for the heroes to rescue them. 'Save us! Save us!' they giggled.

Walking deeper along Market, we turned into 16th Street, east of the Gaslamp Quarter. Mr Xtreme wanted to show me a side to San Diego, away from the busy Gaslamp Quarter. It was an area he referred to as "San Diego's Skid Row", a bleak and desolate set of streets crammed with boarded up buildings. Below the dim, yellow glow of the streetlamps, I saw groups of homeless people, curled up in damp sleeping bags and cardboard boxes. The lucky ones had tents.

The sheer number of homeless people in a single area shocked me.

'There are homeless all over the city,' Mr Xtreme told me. 'But this is the biggest concentration in the whole county.'

As we walked amongst the torn and dirty canvas dwellings, c I noticed a van driving towards us. It was the first vehicle I had seen since we had entered this area. It was a U-Haul rental van and it drove slowly past us. Turning to look, I noticed it stopping. Then it started to reverse backwards. *What's he doing?* I thought to myself. Just before he came alongside us, the driver honked the horn, briefly swerved and came to a stop. The driver stepped out. A white man in his forties, wearing mostly black and grey clothing, he had an unkempt look, with overgrown, greasy hair and a couple of day's growth on his craggy face.

'Greetings,' he said.

'And you are?' Mr Xtreme asked.

'Let me introduce myself, I'm Johnny Wolf,' he said. He had a low, deep voice that managed to sound both slow and hyperactive at the same time.

'Johnny Wolf?'

'Johnny Wolf.'

'Okay...' Urban Avenger said, sounding unsure.

'*Wolf*,' the guy said, emphasising this part of his name for some reason.

'Okay. Hi.'

'Rock and roll society,' Johnny Wolf said, bizarrely. Was that some kind of a greeting? None of us seemed sure and there was an uncomfortable silence before he added, 'I'm a superhero too.'

'Okay...' Urban Avenger said again, still sounding unconvinced.

'Kind of like a Bruce Wayne, Batman character.'

More awkward silence.

'So what are you guys doing?' Johnny Wolf asked. 'I've seen you guys cruising around here before.'

'We're just on patrol, showing him the ropes,' Urban Avenger told him, pointing his thumb at me. 'How about yourself? What are you doing?'

'I'm working on getting a secure and remote broadcast station and studio in a couple of different places around town.'

'Okay.'

'I need a way to get a hold of you to make my resources available. And vice-versa.'

'Okay...'

'Let me give you a card,' Mr Xtreme said, breaking Urban Avenger's repetitive line of "okays". 'You can get hold of us that way.'

'You say you're a superhero too?' I asked.

'I guess you could say that.'

'Are you on patrol now?'

'I'm actually going home to crash. I've been moving equipment for the last few days. I've been inheriting buildings.'

'Inheriting?' Urban Avenger asked.

'Yeah. A heritage hotel and a hookah lounge. We have the *Grand Army of the Republic*. I'm with the Republic. The Imperial Guard, I guess you could say.' He put a cigarette to his lip, cupping the end with his hands as he lit it, looking like a character from some noir spy movie. 'This is my fucking outfit, you know what I mean?' he said, laughing.

But I didn't know what he meant and I didn't see what he was laughing at. Grand Army of the Republic? Imperial Guard? Wasn't that something from Star Wars? To be perfectly honest, he seemed like a complete nut job, and there was an atmosphere that had travelled several stops past uncomfortable. I felt extremely uneasy as we continued to listen to Johnny Wolf's ramblings. We were standing on a deathly quiet street, in a remote and poor part of town, talking with a complete stranger with a U-Haul van who seemed to me to be either high on drugs or else completely insane. Possibly both. For a moment, I wondered if the sliding door on the side of the van was going to open and we would be rushed by Johnny Wolf's *Grand Army*, or if he was going to pull a gun, force us into it, drive us away, rape us, kill us and bury us in the woods. Suffice to say, I was keen to get away from him. Instead, we continued to stand there as he rambled on about his army, inheritance and hookah lounges.

'Okay...' I heard Urban Avenger say, as I snapped out of the waking nightmare I was having.

'We are fucking militia, musicians, fashion militia,' Johnny Wolf continued. 'We use guitars and fashion instead of guns and bombs.'

I had no idea what he was talking about.

Urban Avenger said, 'Okay.'

'There's a lot of them out on the street that have nowhere to go – but there's a lot of them that want to fight that fight, dude. They're sick of what's going on around here.'

'Right.'

'I'm talking mass media domination. I'm talking about, if I choose to, I can send a signal to NBC. That's what I want to do.'

'Like a pirate radio kind of thing?'

'If I choose to. I'd like to do it legally, and I will. We already do. But I want to have that flexibility "*to interrupt this broadcast*" and have the technology to stop them from shutting my broadcast down. I have a regiment of staff and my demands are simply to end the police state.'

As we listened to Johnny Wolf's manifesto, I suddenly

remembered that I was recording everything he was saying. Realising that this may not go down too well (he seemed unhinged enough already), I attempted to hide the small recorder I was carrying and to cover the bright red "on" light with my finger.

But it was too late.

'Are you recording?' he asked, piercing my guilt with his wild eyes.

'Yeah. I'm interviewing these guys and learning about superheroes.'

'Yeah? Well, you should let somebody know sometimes...'

'What's that?' I asked, puffing up my chest, unhappy with his challenge.

He lowered his voice menacingly. 'That you're recording.'

I was suddenly furious. I had been having a perfectly nice night, walking around with a pair of superheroes in a neighbourhood of drug dealers, when he – "Johnny Fuckin' Wolf" – had decided to stop his U-Haul van, state that he was Batman and tell us that he was creating a Star Wars army to smash the police state. We didn't ask him to stop and, frankly, he was starting to piss me off.

Perhaps sensing my rage – or more likely because he was an actual lunatic – his demeanour suddenly changed and he said, 'I'm cool that you're recording me. I have no fucking problem with that dude.'

And with that, he stepped back into his van and drove away.

'That was different,' I muttered.

'Yeah,' Urban Avenger agreed. 'Hopefully he means what he's saying.'

What?

'Yeah, well, let's see what happens,' Mr Xtreme replied.

Really? I thought he was a total fucking loon talking absolute nonsense. Surely they had realised that too? But it seemed not.

'I never hold my breath unless I see it signed, sealed and delivered,' Mr Xtreme added.

'If he's inheriting buildings and he's telling the truth, that might mean something for us in the future,' Urban Avenger said.

'We do need a downtown headquarters. That would be great.'

'Yeah, somewhere we could have an office and training facility.'

'If we had a downtown headquarters, we could patrol every single day.'

'Or at least have a rotating staff so that we don't all have to patrol six or seven nights a week,' Urban Avenger said, before turning to me and adding, 'It could be like the police, where everyone has a shift.'

'Almost like your own little precinct,' I said.

'Yeah, but that's a few years down the line. I don't know if we'll ever get as big as an established police force.'

'Oh, I don't know...' Mr Xtreme said, his mind drifting off to some future that was never going to happen. But then you have to have dreams, I guess – even if that dream is to have your own superhero police force. Or a Grand Army of the Republic, for that matter.

Leaving the area, we began to make our way back towards the increasingly raucous Gaslamp Quarter. Mr Xtreme had received a message that the rest of his team had arrived for the night's patrol and, when we got there, they were waiting for us. There were four of them and each one was distinct from the others. Urban Avenger pointed each one out as we approached. There was *Devine Force*, a young, thin man in black, with a purple coloured scarecrow hood pulled over the top of a black facemask that had two misshapen eyeholes cut out of it. He didn't look particularly tough and he had a slightly awkward, gangly way of walking, but even so, he looked like a scarecrow from a child's nightmare. Next was *Rouroni,* who was also tall and slim and looked like a character from *Big Trouble in Little China*. He wore all black clothing with a black scarf tied around his face, and a large, Asian-style, conical straw hat, which he pulled below his eyes every time I looked at him.

Then there was *Radnor*, who was wearing mostly black, with a thin, brown leather jacket, a tweed flat cap – and, to hide his identity, a white Phantom of the Opera type facemask (although it looked more like a mask that had been broken after being stepped on rather than something artistically moulded to fit his face). He looked like nothing other than a short, slightly overweight Eastern European gangster with a penchant for Andrew Lloyd Webber musicals.

Finally there was *Grimm*. Grimm seemed totally different from the rest. There was something unnerving about him. He was the tallest in the group. He wore black ninja boots, a pair of blue combat pants, black leather motorcycle gloves and a terrifying blue skull mask-come-helmet with blacked out eyes and long black shreds of material dangling down from the skull's teeth, which made it look like he'd just been eating a Rastafarian and was now slurping up the dreadlocks. Whereas Radnor, Rouroni and Devine Force looked like a bunch of kids who had taken their role-playing fantasies a bit far, Grimm looked like a total badass; like he meant business. If I were a troublemaker, Grimm would be the one I would least want to fight.

As we were now such a large group, Mr Xtreme decided to split us into two. He would team-up with Rouroni, Radnor and Devine Force, leaving me with Urban Avenger and Grimm. I was happy with the split; Urban Avenger and Grimm seemed like the most capable heroes in the group, even if I did find Grimm slightly scary. He towered over me and seemed utterly uninterested in who I was. I decided to try and break the ice.

'So, Grimm, not a very happy name is it?'

Grimm stopped dead in his tracks. I could feel him glaring at me through his blue skull mask, with total distain. He was Grimm and I was a maggot. He took a long, slow breath and folded his arms.

'A while ago someone pissed me off,' he said.

Was that a warning?

'They keyed my car,' he continued. 'So I carved "GRR" into their front door. Like, "grrrrr", you know? A snarl. My first initial is "M", so I wrote dash [/] M after the GRR. That's how I ended up with the name Grimm.'

'I see.'

He turned and walked away.

'Who keyed your car?' I asked, chasing after him.

'An ex-girlfriend's, ex-boyfriend.'

Before I had a chance to ask anything else, a young white guy wearing a black top and black baseball cap sauntered up to us with his hands in his pockets. 'I've got to know, what are you guys doing?' he asked.

'We're on patrol,' Urban Avenger told him.

'Patrol?'

'Yeah, we're superheroes,' Grimm told him flatly.

The guy started at Grimm in silence for moment. Grimm stared back.

'*Superheroes*?' the guy asked. Then he blew dramatically out of his mouth and started to laugh in Grimm's face.

Perhaps fearing what I was fearing, Urban Avenger quickly said, 'Have a good night, sir.' And we walked away.

The neighbourhood had become busier, louder. There were more photos with drunks and lots of explaining of who they were. As we walked along 6th Avenue, we could hear a loud argument. We picked up our pace and, at the rear of the House of Blues, four Middle Eastern men were shouting at one another. One of the group started to get pushy, ramming his palms violently into the chests of the other men. Urban Avenger and Grimm stopped at the top of the street, fifteen feet away and watched. The men noticed them and the argument quietened down immediately. Two of the men walked away and one waved at us reassuringly. Whatever the argument was about, it had stopped as soon as the superheroes appeared.

As we continued along the street, Urban Avenger's phone rang. He stopped walking and stepped aside to take the call. It was hard to hear what he was saying over the general downtown noise but I did hear him say the words "gun" and "shot". He finished the call and stepped back towards us.

'What happened?' I asked.

'There's been a shooting.'

'Where?' I asked.

'Fifth and Market.' Then Urban Avenger lowered his voice. 'Where that guy laughed at Grimm.'

'Oh.'

'I don't know what happened, but somebody pulled out a gun and somebody got shot. The police are looking for two Latino males. It was literally ten minutes after we left. Mr Xtreme and the others were walking towards it and, when they got to the intersection, the whole street was roped off with police tape. Pretty wild.'

I could hear police sirens in the distance, getting louder, closer.

'I don't know whether it's good or bad luck that we weren't there,' I said.

'Yeah, it really depends on how you think about it, right?'

With a gunman in the area, and not knowing what the shooting had been about, Mr Xtreme decided to reunite the two teams. We met up again outside a nearby cinema. Rouroni, Radnor and Devine Force were buzzing with nervous excitement about the shooting. Along with Mr Xtreme, they had been just a block or two away from where it had happened.

It was now past 1 o'clock in the morning, but it felt busier than ever as people started to stream onto the streets, from the clubs and bars. Myself, Grimm and Urban Avenger walked on one side of the streets, as the others walked on the opposite side, still in safe view of each other.

As we walked along 5th Avenue, I noticed a large group of black men spilling out of a club. They looked like a bunch of hip-hop gangsters in baggy clothing, hoodies and hats, and they were looking around as if trying to find somebody. Then they started to march in our direction. I looked at where they were looking and noticed a Hispanic guy wearing a waistcoat and tie – he looked like a waiter – rushing away, down the road.

The black men started shouting at the guy, repeatedly calling him a "motherfucker". Then the group came to a collective, silent stop as they noticed Grimm and Urban Avenger (but not so much me) standing in front of them. They gave us a *what-the-fuck?* look – but it was a long enough delay to allow the Hispanic man to get further away. Then one of the black men shoulder-barged me out of his way, knocking me sideways. I fell back against a wall, expecting the rest of his friends to storm past – but instead they called out to their shoulder barging buddy, who was still intent on catching the Hispanic man.

'Come the fuck back here, nigger!' one of his friends called out.

The shoulder-barging man stopped. 'Yeah, you'd better walk away, motherfucker!' he shouted at the Hispanic man.

As he returned to his group, he glared at me angrily and, for a moment, I fantasised about reaching for Urban Avenger's stun gun. Then the group started to shout abuse at other people in the street. They were out for trouble.

Urban Avenger and Grimm, their view partially obscured by their masks, had missed all of this. They were looking around, wondering who was shouting – but, as they couldn't see what was happening, they continued patrolling, leaving me alone as I continued to keep my eye on the group. When I turned around, Urban Avenger and Grimm had gone. I now stood alone on the street corner.

I noticed the black men looking over, and a friend of the shoulder-barger walked back towards me.

Shit. I needed pepper-spray or a stun gun. Or both. Perhaps even some marbles.

'What magic powers do you have?' he asked.

'What?'

'You're a superhero, right? What magic powers do you have?'

'I don't have magic powers.'

'You can't make magic happen?'

'No.'

He smirked at me before returning to his friends, laughing. This group were bad news and other people out on the street seemed to realise it as well, avoiding the men as they went past.

I looked around for Urban Avenger and Grimm, hunting for the *wake* in the crowd that was always left when the superheroes walked along the streets, as people stopped to get out of their way and stare. Then I noticed Devine Force standing amongst a crowd. He had been watching the men as well and called over the other superheroes. The group of men, seeing that they were being watched, began to calm down. Eventually they walked away and left the area.

We remained on the crowded street and a man walked up to us. 'Hey, I think you should take a look at that girl over there,' he said, pointing to a drunk woman with short black hair and an even shorter black dress.

She was staggering around, tripping over her own high heels and appeared to be in some distress. We went over.

'Are you okay?' Urban Avenger asked her.

'No, I'm lost,' she told him. Mascara stained tears ran down her face, in long, dark streaks. 'Can you tell me how to get to the Gaslamp Motel?'

Urban Avenger quickly pulled out his iPhone and tapped at the screen, looking for the location of her hotel as the girl stumbled left and right, attempting to keep him in focus. Urban Avenger found the information but decided that she should be escorted to her hotel, as she was obviously incapable of getting there on her own. Then the woman wrapped her arms around Urban Avenger's neck and moved her face towards his, as if she were trying to kiss him. She reached out and grabbed hold of Grimm as well, like a spider catching helpless flies.

'I wanna see your face,' she told Urban Avenger, grabbing his mask and attempting to lift it. Urban Avenger leant back, away from her spidery fingers.

Grimm, fighting against the drunk woman's octopus arms, looked over at the other heroes, who were gathered around a tourist, for a photo.

'Rouroni!' Grimm shouted. 'Get over here!'

Rouroni looked up and quickly obeyed Grimm.

'Take this lady back to her hotel,' Grimm ordered.

As we stood on 6th and F Street, watching as Rouroni struggled with the drunk woman, two men nearby started to get into a row.

The first guy shouted, 'Fuck you! Fuck you!' and shoved the second guy in the chest, pushing him back a foot or two. The second guy was one of the men from the black group, who we thought had left the area.

Draped off Rouroni's arm, the drunk woman, who clearly had no idea what was going on, decided it would be a good argument to join. Pointing drunkenly at the men, she cried out with a distinct slur, 'Fuck you, motherfuckers! Fuck you!'

Rouroni looked horrified and attempted to swing the girl around, away from the men. But they were already gearing up to fight with each other and paid no attention to her. The black guy, who had been pushed backwards, suddenly lunged forward with his left arm extended as if to grab the first guy, and raised his right fist in the air. The first man took an instinctive step backwards and raised both of his fists.

Radnor, Devine Force, Grimm and Urban Avenger, rushed towards them. There was a melee of pushing, swearing and grabbing – and I noticed Urban Avenger reaching down for his pepper-spray, grasping the handle of the canister in his fist as he pushed one of the men back, away from himself. But then the friends of the first guy jumped in and dragged their friend away from the fracas. The black group did the same with the second man. The heroes stood in a tight defensive circle, facing outwards at the two parties, who were now backing away from each other and from the superheroes.

'Fuck you, motherfuckers!' the drunk girl shouted one last time.

Rouroni led her away.

Two men approached the superheroes, thanking them for stepping in and stopping the fight.

'Oh, no problem,' Urban Avenger said cheerily.

Once again, it seemed that the Xtreme Justice League had actually done some good. I remembered their earlier comments about people getting stomped during fights, but the only thing that had occurred here – thanks to their intervention – was a bit of pushing and shoving. I had seen no cops in the area for some time and had little doubt that the fight would have developed into something far worse had the superheroes not been here to stop it.

We returned to watching Rouroni and the drunk woman. She hung off him like a determined, desperate lover.

'He can't take her on his own,' Grimm said, realising the hopelessness of Rouroni's situation with the woman, who was outmanoeuvring him at every step.

We all agreed and walked over to assist Rouroni in escorting the woman to her hotel, where we were met by a security guard. He recognised the woman and allowed her in. A group of party girls nearby gave the heroes a round of applause and a loud cheer. They had watched the whole thing.

The team took one last look around the streets, which were beginning to quieten down, and then we slowly made our way back to the Hall of Justice, calling it a night.

It was the last time I would see Rouroni. A few months later, he was killed in a car accident, along with three other people. He was 20 years old.

It's easy for people to make fun of these Real-Life Superheroes, treating them like a bunch of loonies who don't actually do anything of real consequence, but after spending time with the Xtreme Justice League, I realised that this would be a lie. Give them a chance and you will see that they can make a difference and even do something heroic, whether that's walking a vulnerable drunk back to her hotel or stopping two men from beating the crap out of one another. My opinions about the Real-Life Superheroes had been low, but I was starting to change my mind. There's nothing funny about jumping into a dangerous fight. They were putting themselves out there and they meant it. People could – and do – get hurt.

With these thoughts in mind, I began to think once more about Phoenix Jones, who I was hoping to meet next – and who was, according to other superheroes, in a completely different league. I wasn't sure whether that was a good thing or not. I thought perhaps not. I had seen stories online that claimed Phoenix Jones had been stabbed and shot previously, and this concerned me all the more. I had a bad feeling deep in my gut, and Superhero's words of warnings that someone would end up getting killed didn't help.

Neither did an email Superhero sent me just before I left for Seattle. It read: *Beware of that Douchebag.*

4

An Emerald in the Rough

Being located in the Pacific Northwest, Seattle can still seem like a frontier town, despite its metropolitan downtown core of tall, modern skyscrapers and apartment blocks. A city on the edge of America, Seattle – known as the "Emerald City" due to its proximity to the wet, evergreen forests – was the setting for the TV hit sitcom Fraser, but is also the birthplace of Boeing, Microsoft, Starbucks and grunge. It may be "out there" geographically – not to mention at times, philosophically – but it has still managed to influence and lead in many areas of everyday life.

But Seattle is also a city with problems. For a start, it feels as though its police department is under siege, as if everyone is out to get them – the mayor, the public, the media. Everything they do, it seems, is scrutinised and questioned.

A smart, young deputy I knew from the King County Sheriffs Department, whose policing area bordered the city, told me that it sometimes felt as though the Seattle police couldn't do anything right.

'Seattle takes all the heat from the media,' he told me. 'They take the heat for us. In King County we don't get treated too badly by the media – but Seattle gets hammered. For some reason, people like to go after Seattle PD.'

And go after Seattle PD they did. In 2011 they were the subject of a Department of Justice investigation into the force's practices, and its officers. There had been a number of high-profile incidents where Seattle police officers were seen (and in some cases, recorded) to carry out actions that the public and the media deemed unwarranted – everything from verbal and physical assaults, to shootings. A Department of Justice report stated that the "SPD engages in a pattern and practice of using unnecessary or excessive force". Some of their actions were found to be in violation of the United States Constitution. And, although the Department of Justice report found that there was no actual pattern or practice of discriminatory policing, it was quick to point out that there were still concerns. The writers of the report had spoken to community groups who felt that the police were against them, and there were cases where police officers had been captured on video using force "against people of color".

All of this could, of course, undermine the people's faith in their police, and to a degree, it certainly had. The Seattle police were lacking in trust and respect from the public they had sworn to serve. And, no matter how hard the Seattle police had decided to fight back – seeking to regain citizens' trust and respect, with reforms that included addressing biased policing and training officers in the use of force – the truth was that the battle was far from over. Seattle was still a centre for protestors, anarchists and the "Black Bloc" – a name taken from a tactic used by many protestors that simply involves dressing in black clothing, including a mask or scarf worn across the face, and then appearing as one large, usually violent, group. The Black Bloc were often the last thing people wanted to see; to many, they were a group that would hijack others causes, simply to start trouble, damage property and attack the police.

For Seattle – and for that matter, the United States – the Bloc came into its own on 30th November 1999 during the now infamous WTO (World Trade Organisation) Protests – also known as the "Battle of Seattle". Tens of thousands of anti-globalisation protesters had descended upon downtown Seattle, and the police had resorted to firing stun grenades, tear gas and rubber bullets. The Black Bloc went on a rampage, smashing windows and attacking stores. A state of emergency was declared, a curfew was put in place – and battalions of the National Guard were called in to assist the outnumbered and overwhelmed police officers. Hundreds were arrested, though many were later awarded financial damages after a jury found that the protestors' constitutional rights had been violated. The chief of Seattle's police department would later resign.

Even though the Battle of Seattle had happened some years ago, in a liberal city like Seattle, this approach towards demonstrating against authority and the police continues; the Bloc and other anarchist groups are still active.

On my first evening in Seattle, I took a walk to Capitol Hill – a trendy, student filled neighbourhood just east of downtown. Almost immediately, I found myself swallowed up in crowds of chanting protestors. Being Seattle, this didn't surprise me much.

'F. U. S. P. FUCK YOU SEATTLE POLICE!'
'F. U. S. P. FUCK YOU SEATTLE POLICE!'

A blue-grey coloured Seattle police department cruiser drove across the intersection of Broadway and Pine, heading towards the hundred or so chanting protestors gathered outside the Seattle Central Community College building. The red bricks of the college were dark with dampness and the sodden tarmac road squelched under the tyres of the police car. Rain can often "stop play" at demonstrations, but in the Pacific Northwest rain is as common as heat in a desert. People are used to it to the point of barely noticing it.

The students and other protestors lurched towards the squad car, shouting obscenities at the officers sitting inside, waving their placards in the air and punching their fists towards the dark, low, moody sky. I read some of the placards and banners: "Queer Liberation is Class Struggle", "Smash Racism", "We Say No More" and "Stonewall Was A Police Riot" – the letter "A" being in a black circle and made to look like the Anarchy symbol.

Many of the protestors were dressed in black with scarves, hoodies and bandanas covering their faces – the *Black Bloc*. Their presence on this cool, damp evening was unsettling.

The demo had come about after an incident a few days before, where a man, apparently out celebrating the annual Pride Festival, had been pepper-sprayed by a police officer. The incident had been captured on an amateur video. The Seattle police officer involved had responded with force after the reveller had apparently attacked him. It was claimed that the man had kicked the officer, who then used his pepper-spray to incapacitate the man, before moving in to arrest him. But the officer's version of events was disputed and others claimed that the police officer had overreacted and that the man had never kicked him. The video of the cop pepper-spraying the man had been posted on the Internet and had become a reason for the protest.

The mob began to move. The Seattle Police Department's East Precinct was just few blocks away, and the target for the protestors. They continued to chant and lift their banners and flags into the air. The Seattle police officers who had been standing nearby on street corners and against the building lines, stood with their arms folded and watched as the protest moved down East Pine Street. We were only a mile or so from downtown but there were no tourists here. The road dipped down before rising again at the intersection of 11th Avenue, just one block west of the East Precinct. The protestors were a couple of hundred feet away from the intersection, where there were lines of riot cops standing behind metal barriers. Behind these cops were mounted officers on heavy-set horses and, behind them, marked police cars with emergency lights flashing red and blue. The dampness enhanced the brightness of the police lights and saturated the colours, making them more intense, more forceful. I moved with the mob towards the police lines. As a police officer, I had worked many demonstrations and fought in a number of riots, so it felt especially weird to be on the opposite side of things.

As we drew closer, I took more notice of the first line of officers standing behind the barriers. All were dressed in black uniforms – black trousers and black shirts as opposed to the usual light grey-blue shirts usually worn by Seattle police officers. Each was also wearing a black riot helmet, with the visor pulled defensively down in front of their faces, and black gasmask bags attached to their legs. To make their point, each officer held a three-foot long, brown wooden baton, clenched purposefully in their fists. The metal barriers had yellow police crime scene tape woven through the bars: *POLICE LINE DO NOT CROSS*. You would be asking for trouble if you did, that was clear.

As we reached the front of the barriers, two clowns (and I mean that literally) stepped quickly though the rest of the protestors, to the very front. Both wore circus clown makeup on their faces – white paint with big red mouths and large, diamond eyes. Both wore foam noses and one had an old-fashioned "Keystone Kop" style police helmet on his head. The "Keystone Clown" had the name "General Malaise" painted onto the rear of his long, black cotton jacket. The second clown's short, green, army-style jacket had the words "Clandestine Insurgent Rebel Clown Army". They began to make silly noises at the cops and danced around each other like over-excited children, trying to taunt the cops with their daft routine. The cops stood completely still, staring straight ahead and showing no interest in them whatsoever.

One of the black-clad, masked protestors from within the crowd began calling out, 'How do you spell homophobe?'

The crowd responded, 'S. P. D!', meaning the Seattle Police Department.

This chant took over all others for a short time, being noisily repeated over and over.

A student, with a black bandana covering the bottom half of his face, marched towards the stoic officers. Seemingly agitated that the cops weren't responding to the taunts, he walked up and down the line, sticking his middle fingers up at the officers and shouting, 'FUCK YOU! FUCK YOU! FUCK YOU!'

Some of the crowd stopped their homophobe chant to listen, before deciding that the previous mantra was a better choice.

'How do you spell homophobe?'

'S. P. D!'

The level of hatred and abuse directed towards the officers was intense. I am not naïve; I have seen many protests and riots, in London and abroad, but the absolute venom with which the words were spat out suggested that this was more than just some frustrated demonstrators wanting to make their point. No, this felt different. Some of these protestors were almost delirious in their hatred. The message of the demonstration seemed to be secondary – or even irrelevant – compared to the opportunity to swear at and abuse the officers, who were standing their ground, unmoved.

I wondered if any of the demonstrators would try to get past the barriers. The protestors outnumbered the officers on the street by five to one – but the crowd began to march slowly back towards the college, perhaps content that they had made their point, as well as accepting that they would not reach the precinct without a serious response from the cops.

As we walked up East Pine, back towards the Broadway intersection, a dozen cycle cops, again dressed all in black, seemed to come out of nowhere. They rode in pairs, slowly behind the group.

The Keystone Clown – *Captain Malaise* – reached the intersection and pulled out a whistle, holding up his hand and mockingly waving the cycle cops through. The protestors marched through some of the surrounding streets but everything came to a stop again outside the college. The cycle cops waited in silence as the demonstrators began a new chant.

'WHOSE STREETS?'

'OUR STREETS!'

'WHOSE STREETS?'

'OUR STREETS!'

A female student ran up to the cycle cops, stopping next to a sergeant at the front of their line. She pulled up her tatty, grey coloured vest, exposing her small, bare breasts. 'We can do what we want! These are our streets!' she screamed at him.

The cop stared at her for a moment before looking away, uninterested.

As everyone stood at the intersection, waiting for something to happen, I noticed three more masked protestors suddenly appearing on the corner of Pine and Broadway. As the trio stood in a tight group under a traffic light, I took in their clothing – or rather their *outfits*. Although they were wearing mostly dark and black clothing, it wasn't in the style of the Black Bloc. These guys looked different – *very* different.

One wore a black and grey outfit with a full facemask and Spiderman-style mesh eyes. Another of the group wore a black and white leather mask with pointy ears, similar to Batman. The third was wearing mostly grey and had his face covered by a black, Lone Ranger-style eye-mask. He was carrying a large, black, ballistic shield – the type used by police SWAT teams, only this one was in the shape of a bat. They were superheroes. These were the people I had been looking for.

And at that moment everything changed – for the protestors, for the police, for the superheroes and for me.

I hadn't been alone in noticing the costumed group standing on the street corner; the protestors and the police had also seen them. The cops stayed where they were, leaning against the building line with their arms folded or resting against their bikes. The protestors reacted differently, however. Their attention immediately switched from the cops to the masked, mystery men.

The crowd instinctively surged forward, rushing manically across the intersection, forcing the few cars that had decided to drive through the demonstration to stop violently. The superheroes looked up at the sudden charge of people, and drew closer together, all trying to get behind the "bat-shield". Within seconds, they were surrounded by up to fifty protestors – and I seriously feared that they would be beaten to the ground. The cops, however, stayed in position and made no attempt to intervene.

The Black Bloc and the other protestors began pointing at the costumed men, poking them in the chest with their fingers or reaching through the throng in an attempt to grab hold of them. Some reached for the superheroes' masks, attempting to remove them.

The crowd then started shouting obscenities at the superheroes, just as they had done to the cops earlier. To repeated shouts of, "FUCK YOU!" and "GET OUTTA HERE!", the superheroes, sticking together in a tight group, tried to retreat towards the police line, only to find themselves cut off by the crowd, who forced them away from the officers, isolating them. More abuse and threats were directed at the superheroes, with many of the demonstrators filming the attack on their mobile phones and shoving cameras into the superheroes' faces, causing them to squint and turn away from the barrage of flashes.

'You're worse than the cops!' a masked protestor shouted at them. 'Fuck you, you freaks!'

The superheroes stared at the demonstrators, saying nothing, doing nothing. Finally, a handful of officers forced their way through the crowd, reaching the costumed men and attempted to lead them away from the mob. Everywhere I looked, there were people wearing black and people in masks. It was hard to differentiate between the protestors, the Black Bloc, the police and the superheroes.

'What kinds of superheroes hide behind cops?' someone in the crowd shouted.

People laughed.

The cops ushered the superheroes away and they made their way up Broadway, still pursued by a handful of Black Bloc members and the clowns.

Whatever their reasons, turning up at the demo had been a humiliating mistake for the superheroes, and had threatened to give some of the demonstrators the excuse they needed to turn the protest violent.

I overheard one of the cycle cops mentioning to his colleagues that the superheroes were part of "Phoenix Jones' crew".

Looking at the group, I could see that Phoenix Jones wasn't amongst them, and being caught up in the melee of the demonstration, I didn't have an opportunity to approach the superheroes; though that was probably a good thing, as I could have ended up being set upon by the protestors, or pepper-sprayed by the defensive superheroes.

I still hadn't managed to contact Phoenix Jones, however, so maybe I should have chased after the superheroes after all. Instead, I returned to my hotel and continued trying to communicate with Phoenix Jones online. He hadn't proven to be as easy to contact as some of the other heroes I had met. But I eventually got the contact details of a photographer who claimed to know Phoenix Jones and who acted as his occasional spokesperson. The photographer's details had been passed to me very reluctantly by Superhero, in Florida, who still had serious reservations about me meeting with Phoenix Jones. After a number of emails – mostly questioning my motives – the photographer agreed to set up a meeting between Phoenix Jones and myself.

After a few days silence, I finally received an email explaining where and when to meet. The location was a coffee shop in the University District, just north of downtown Seattle. The time was 11 pm – late I thought, but then I guess superheroes work mostly at night, and sleep during the day; a bit like vampires.

The lateness of the hour, being in a part of town I didn't know, and the fact I was meeting a complete stranger who believed he was a superhero, should have set alarm-bells ding-donging around my head – but by now I was starting to get used to these strange setups. I had previously got into a van with a guy armed with chainsaws, after all. At least in a coffee shop there would be other people around. Even so, I confess to a few nervous thoughts, and everything I had heard about Phoenix Jones made it all the more daunting.

5

Bulletproof Americano

'Yes, I'm on the list of people who is probably going to be killed.'

I stared at the superhero sitting opposite me in the late night coffee shop in a rain-soaked neighbourhood of Seattle, as he casually told me that he expected to die.

The hero was Phoenix Jones and he made the comment after I had brought up what Superhero had told me in Florida, about a superhero killing someone, or a superhero being killed.

'But I'll keep doing this until I'm killed or they find someone better to replace me,' he added.

Phoenix Jones was the leader of a larger, Seattle-based superhero group, known as the Rain City Superhero Movement (*RCSM*). I had been warned that they often focused their patrols on the bar areas of the city around closing time, since it was then that "a lot of fights break out". I was also warned that there was a lot of drug trafficking as well as other violent crime that the superheroes targeted. It was stressed to me that they were very well organized, and that "more than any other superhero group working today, they had been instrumental with stopping crime and protecting people".

Everything about Phoenix Jones felt different from the other heroes I had met. He seemed altogether more serious. He looked me straight in the eyes and everything that came out of his mouth was said with total confidence and conviction.

The coffee shop where we had arranged to meet was filled with Insomnia-suffering students staring into the glowing screens of their laptops. Phoenix Jones had arrived half an hour late. I had been expecting to meet him for a chat over a coffee, perhaps conduct a short interview and give him the chance to get the measure of me, with the ultimate goal of convincing him to allow me to patrol with him one night in the future. Most of all, I was expecting him to turn up in a pair of sweatpants and a hoodie. But, when he eventually arrived, the entire coffee shop came to a cliché, Western-movie saloon standstill – not dissimilar to the reaction Superhero had created in McDonalds. People froze mid-sip into their flat whites. Fingers hovered over send buttons. Lower jaws fell off faces and bloodshot eyeballs plopped into steaming cups of camomile tea. He had come dressed as *Phoenix Jones*. He walked into the place wearing black leather gloves with steel-plated arm guards, black combat trousers, black tactical boots, a muscle-moulded, black rubber bodysuit with golden flashes on the breast and shoulders and a black rubber cowl – a full head and face mask – complete with large gold flashes painted around the eyes. He looked like Batman without the ears and cape.

It was the same outfit I had seen him wearing in the video where he'd been arrested. Perhaps this should have been expected; it's just that I wasn't expecting it. Even so, seeing him in his outfit – which he would describe to me as smelling like "rubber and justice" – was an impressive sight.

With him was a young, slim, white woman. She wore mostly black – black fingerless gloves, black combats, black leather biker jacket, black kneepads and a black hood pulled up over her head. Apart from her glassy brown eyes, her face was covered with a purple scarf. She looked like a street fighter.

'You must be Phoenix Jones,' I said to the man, somewhat redundantly.

'Yes, and this is Purple Reign,' he told me in a deep but young voice, pointing to the woman.

Purple Reign was Phoenix Jones' partner. I asked how they had met, thinking perhaps it had been on some dark rooftop, late at night, like Batman and Catwoman. But it was far more mundane than that; a mutual friend had got them together. Over a coffee, Phoenix Jones ('Call me Phoenix') delighted in telling me about their first date. I had wondered if Purple Reign ('Call me Purple') had known about Phoenix's alter ego before they met. She hadn't.

'I'd only just become a superhero,' Phoenix told me. 'On our first date, I'd actually been stabbed the night before and I had to glue the wound shut in order to make our date. During the evening, it just started bleeding everywhere.'

Phoenix laughed as he thought back to this happy, romantic memory. Purple took a sip of her drink and smiled lovingly at her partner.

'What happened?' I asked.

'Two homeless people were fighting and I came in to break it up. I pushed one away and, as I did, I felt a sharp pain in my side. I turned around but I didn't see anything, so I took him down and called the cops. When the cops came, they said, "Hey, you're bleeding!" But I couldn't go to the medics or anything because I didn't want to revel my identity. I realised I could superglue the wound, so that's what I did. I just super-glued it shut. I had a date with Purple the next day and I didn't want to ruin it, so I went and, as we were sitting there, talking and laughing, it burst open.'

I asked Purple what she had thought about Phoenix's nocturnal activities when she eventually found out about them.

'I don't think what he does, when he's dressed up as Phoenix Jones, is much different to how he is in his regular day-to-day life. He's always had the mentality of standing up for others and stopping crime,' she told me.

'But dressed up as a superhero?'

Purple went to remove her facemask to make it easier to talk to me.

'Wait a minute,' Phoenix whispered, holding up his right hand.

He looked around the coffee shop at the other patrons. We had taken a table in a dark corner and Purple had her back to the rest of the shop.

'You should be okay,' he told her. 'Yeah, you're okay.'

She pulled her mask down to reveal her slim face.

'I guess I was a little bit nervous because I didn't want anything to happen to him, and I don't want him to get hurt. He has a child and I have a child, so we're parents, we've got kids to look after. But the way that he does this, the way that *we* do this – going out with the protective gear, with the team, with the video camera, the way it's organised, I feel it's safer doing it dressed up than it is in our day-to-day lives.'

'But even with all your equipment, you've still been hurt, haven't you?' I asked.

'Sure,' Phoenix Jones said. 'I've been shot and stabbed several times.'

'You get shot and you continue to do this?'

Phoenix smiled and took a sip of his drink. He was looking down at the table and nodding his head.

'I've came close to giving up, I'll admit. A friend of mine – he works in a comic shop that I go to – knew what I was doing and he gave me an old World War Two bulletproof vest that he had. Two days later, I'm on patrol in an alleyway in Tacoma. I'm just standing there and all of a sudden: BOOM! I'm on my back and I can't breathe and the world is swirling. I catch my breath and I roll under a dumpster and I'm kind of like, crying-slash-breathing and trying to get my wits about me... and I realise that I've been shot! It broke my ribs. It looked like someone had just taken a bat to my stomach. I managed to get out of there and I called 911, but then realised that I couldn't stick around; I don't want to be the superhero who gets shot in an alleyway – my ego won't let me do that. So I hop in the car and I drove away and I thought, *Okay, that's it. I'm fucking done*. Like, done patrolling. Just done.'

Purple grabbed Phoenix's arm with both of her hands and leant closer towards him. Phoenix took another sip from his drink.

'What made you continue?' I asked.

'I found better bulletproof armour. Then I went to the gym, got myself back in shape and I was ready for the streets again. Since then, it's slowly evolved – and every time I get injured, I find a way to make sure it doesn't happen again. But it's one of those things where, no matter what kind of armour you get, no matter what kind of protection you get, when you're fighting criminals, you're naked. You have to be smarter than them, you have to know where in the city you are, that you have a girl at home with a tracking device watching you and a lawyer to bail you out and a crew of guys to back you up. That's the only way you will succeed in this. And everyone else who doesn't do it to this level, who doesn't put in this much time, they're going to fail. This – *fighting crime* – has literally ruined my life. But you have to be willing to go to that extent.'

I looked at Purple Reign who had been listening intently to Phoenix.

'Has it ruined *your* life?' I asked her.

'Well, we have no social life. We don't really have friends to hang out with. We don't do social events.'

Phoenix disagreed a little with Purple. 'Well, I have two friends,' he said.

'If I wasn't a part of all this, our relationship wouldn't work,' Purple continued. 'This is something that we can do together.'

'And that makes it okay,' Phoenix added. 'I mean, I leave in the middle of the night and at all hours. I'm extremely restless when it comes to crime activity. Plus, I don't let her carry a purse in public because I'm worried it's a target.'

'I don't wear heels anymore and I don't carry a purse,' Purple confirmed.

'She's not allowed to wear heels because she's not effective if we have to chase somebody,' Phoenix told me.

His choice of words – "I don't let her", "She's not allowed" – bothered me, but maybe that was just the way he spoke. We had only just met, after all, and I really didn't know anything about this super-couple. But still, it left me feeling a little uncomfortable.

'I wear a bulletproof vest for ninety percent of my life,' Phoenix Jones continued. 'Being a superhero has literally changed the way that I live.'

'Then why do you do it?'

'It has to be done. No one's doing anything and it has to be done. The criminal element in one part of my city is out of control and peoples' response to it is, "Well, it's just the way it is."'

'We're sending a message to the community and to the world,' Purple added. 'And I think we're making a difference with all the work we're doing.'

'What made *you* become a superhero?' I asked Purple Reign.

Phoenix Jones leant back in his chair staring at me. Then he turned to look at Purple Reign, who had fallen silent and was now looking down at the table.

Had I said something wrong?

'I'm a domestic violence survivor,' she said, softly.

Phoenix Jones shifted uncomfortably in his seat.

'Being Purple Reign has helped me deal with my past. It's also helped me with other survivors,' she said.

'I see,' I told her.

'But others are getting inspired by the work we do, and are getting involved,' she said, moving the subject away from her past.

I decided not to probe any further. Not yet, anyway.

'I have a whole team of guys,' Phoenix told me. 'We've got guys who are fully trained, who are either ex-military or ex-fighters. We're all extremely good at what we do. You'll meet them. People like Cabbie, Midnight Jack, Evo. Good guys, all of them. One of the guys on the team is an active police officer – but he has to be real careful. He can't get caught doing this, because it's against the rules.'

'Wait. Did you say one of the Rain City Superheroes is a *police officer*?'

'Yeah. You'll meet him tonight.'

'Is he a Seattle cop?'

'No, he's from one of the smaller forces outside the city.'

'A *cop*?' I asked again, just to be sure.

'Yeah, a cop. Why? Is that weird?'

I found it shocking that a police officer would choose to actually do this. I also had to question *why* they would do this. Why, if you spent your time working a job that involved patrolling the streets, looking for criminals and getting paid for it – not to mention doing it in the knowledge that the law, the courts and society were behind you – would you then choose to don a superhero outfit at night, doing pretty much the same thing but without any of the benefits or protection? Being a cop during the day and a masked, anonymous superhero at night seemed to me to be a serious conflict of interests, and I wondered if the cop had simply gone *rogue*.

'Is he not concerned that he'll be found out, even arrested?' I asked.

'He's extremely concerned!' Phoenix told me. 'But he says that, as a cop, he has all these situations where he can't do the right thing, where he can't help people because of all these dumb laws, and he's just tired of it.'

This concerned me all the more. How exactly did being a

superhero allow the cop to deal with criminals in a way that he couldn't as a police officer? Police officers' shouldn't be *anonymous*. By wearing a mask and giving yourself a pseudonym, you remove an important level of protection afforded to the public – be they criminal or otherwise.

'You're a cop,' Phoenix Jones said, almost accusingly.

This was true, of course, and I must have sounded like a total hypocrite. But, as far as I was concerned, I was there in the capacity of a writer, not a police officer. And that was truly how I felt. I was an observer, someone with an interest in this extremely curious sub-culture. I wasn't a superhero and I wasn't an undercover cop. I was researching a book; that was all. (If I had known then, what I know now, I would probably have kept my mouth shut.)

'How much time do you think a cop spends doing paperwork rather than fighting crime?' Phoenix asked. 'And then how much time do you think we spend actively looking for crime as *opposed* to doing paperwork?'

'But cops are answerable to the public and the city.'

'We're answerable to the same city.'

'Not really,' I said. 'You're not city employees.'

'But if I break the law, I'm responsible.'

'But walking around tonight, doing this, you're not answerable to anybody. In the eyes of the law, you're a member of the public.'

'I personally hold myself to a very high standard of accountability. I respect people. I think that's something you lose when you get the power that the police have; you start losing respect for people.'

'I can assure you, you have that wrong,' I told him.

'Listen, maybe the cops are different in England, but when a person with idealistic ideas becomes a police officer, they get smashed pretty quickly and then, after they get smashed, they find themselves in a weird-ass mask, walking around the streets with *me*,' Phoenix said. 'At least that's the case with this guy.'

'Who's the cop?' I asked.

'That's not for me to say. The last thing he wants is for his bosses to find out that he's a superhero. He'd be out of a job and he could lose his pension.'

'Will you ask him if he'd speak with me?'

'Sure, I'll ask, but don't expect much response.'

I didn't. I knew that the police officer on the team had everything to lose if his identity was revealed. So, although I wasn't expecting to find out which one of them was the cop, as time went on and I got to know the superheroes better, I would start to have my suspicions.

'What about you?' Phoenix Jones asked. 'When did you become a superhero?'

'Sorry?'

'You're a superhero too, right?'

No! I screamed internally.

'I hear you've been doing missions with other heroes around the country.'

'I wouldn't call them "missions", but yeah, I've met a few different heroes.'

I told them about the superhero I'd met in New York and my evening of drinking, photos with "hot women", and throwing money at homeless people. (I skipped over our plan to kidnap the President of Sudan.)

'There are a number of superheroes in New York,' Purple Reign told me. 'We're friends with one online, called *Tothian*.'

'He doesn't actually patrol, though,' Phoenix Jones told me. 'I think he's more of an *online* hero.'

'But he has a genuine superpower,' Purple added.

'He does? What is it?' I asked, genuinely intrigued.

'Getting kicked in the balls,' she told me.

This was perhaps one of the last things I expected to hear Purple say.

'You don't know about that?' Phoenix asked, laughing.

'No. Weirdly, I haven't heard about it.'

Phoenix pulled out his phone and brought up an online video. It was titled, rather graphically but descriptively correct, as: "Amazonia kicking Tothian in the balls". In the video, a female superhero – *Amazonia* – kicks New York superhero *Tothian* in the balls, three times.

The video had received 129,997 more hits than Tothian's balls.

'Is he wearing a box?' I asked.

'No, man, he takes the ball-shot like a champ!' Phoenix whooped in glee.

'Who else?' Purple Reign asked.

'Master Legend, in Orlando,' I told her.

'Master Legend?' Phoenix Jones asked, excitedly.

'Yeah. Do you know him?'

Phoenix Jones smiled and nodded his head. 'When I was twelve years old, I was at a baseball game in Florida. Master Legend was there and I spoke with him. He actually told me that I could be one of the most famous Real-Life Superheroes ever.'

'Well, he does claim to have psychic powers,' I said.

'Anyone else?' Purple Reign asked.

'I've also met Superhero, in Clearwater.'

Phoenix Jones' face instantly changed from a beaming smile to loathing.

'Do you know him, too?' I asked.

'I think he's a tool bag,' Phoenix Jones said.

'Really?' I said. 'I think he's a good guy.' And I meant it.

'Nope, he's not.'

Purple spoke up. 'I think the problem is, these people might be nice in person, but online they're bullies and they spew nothing but hate about Phoenix and me.'

I questioned if the alleged hate directed at Phoenix from other superheroes was due to the way he was doing things. *Phoenix Jones'* philosophy may not have been the philosophy of all Real-Life Superheroes. The incident where he had been arrested, for example, may have made other superheroes feel tarnished; just like the police, where one bad cop can turn public opinion against all the good ones. I wasn't suggesting that Phoenix was a "bad apple" – but it was easy to see why other superheroes would be wary of his antics. In truth, though, I thought there was more to it than that. I guessed that envy played a part and some people simply didn't like all the attention he was getting.

'I don't think they understand how we do things out here,' Purple said. 'They say a lot of nasty things. They jump to conclusions and talk shit instead of coming directly to us and asking questions.'

Phoenix Jones had fallen silent during this part of our conversation and I wondered if I had overstepped my mark, questioning him about his tactics. After all, we had only just met. But then he spoke up, changing the subject.

'So, do you have a superhero name?' he asked.

'Well, Superhero in Florida told me that I'm a S.H.I.T.'

'You don't have a superhero name? A superhero identity?'

'Not yet.' (*Not ever*, I thought to myself.)

'You need to think about getting one,' Purple Reign told me. 'We can't call you "Shit". Not even "Super-Shit".'

Still unsure about a name, but quietly confident that I didn't want to be called "Super-Shit", I continued with my questions.

'And what is it you do within the team?' I asked Purple Reign, still uncertain of her role.

'I look at where's best to patrol,' she told me. 'The Seattle police department have all their police reports, all their incidents and all their crimes posted online and available for all to see. I go through them and look at where it's best to focus our patrols.'

'But you patrol too, right?'

'Sometimes, but not always. I'm one of the few females involved in this type of work. I do patrol and I've got years of martial arts and kung fu training, so physically I'm prepared – but we have kids, so sometimes I'll be at home looking after them while he does his thing.'

'But if she stays home, she's still assisting us,' Phoenix said. 'We'll be in radio contact and she'll monitor the police channels and crime maps to see what's happening while we're out patrolling. I know what my bread and butter crime is. I'm not going to prevent a carjacking unless I just happen to be in the right place at the right time – although that has happened more than once. But, given the correct data, I can stop random street assaults. I can stop street violence – people with knives and guns. Bar fights too. I can stop those because she regionalises it for us.'

Purple Reign pulled out a map of the city, along with some Seattle Police Department crime maps. She explained how the city was split into different police precincts and beat areas – just like any other large city would be. By scrutinising the maps and data, Purple Reign could establish what areas were seeing the highest volume of crime and at what times, as well as the types of victims and assailants. Purple would study the maps and reports and then plan the team's patrol, down to the exact areas, the exact streets and time of day.

'We're going to be patrolling in police sector M, tonight,' Purple told me. 'There have been twenty-two assaults in the past month in that sector. It's been as high as sixty-five assaults before. It beats everywhere else in the city. The stats don't lie.'

'This is far more sophisticated than I'd been expecting,' I said.

'Exactly,' Phoenix answered. 'But nobody else is doing it.'

'I think my mind is a really powerful tool,' Purple Reign told me. 'I feel that's what I bring to the team.'

I was impressed. What they were doing was far more organised than anything I'd seen with any of the other superheroes I had met. The information that Purple Reign was collating – and analysing – was available online for all to see, but this took real effort and organisation. Police departments paid full-time researchers to carry out this type of work, but here was a superhero doing exactly that. I wondered what it was that motivated them to go to this level.

'When did you first think to yourself: *You know what I'm gonna do? I'm going to put on an outfit and patrol the streets as a superhero?*' I asked Phoenix Jones.

'There're two kinds of superheroes,' Phoenix Jones said. 'There are the guys who wake up one day and think: *You know what would be cool? Dressing up like a superhero and fighting crime.* Those are the guys that are going to fail. Then there are people like me, for whom it was a step-by-step change. I only did what was necessary at the time to survive.'

For Phoenix Jones, *surviving* started off in high school, where he was bullied "a lot". But then he started to train and grow, physically.

'When I got big, it was my turn to bully people,' he said.

'But that's not what you did,' Purple quickly added. 'You stuck up for others.'

'Well, yeah. What I mean is, the bullies were no longer the big guys. I had my first black belt by the time I was fourteen. I got my second one at sixteen and became a professional mixed martial arts fighter. I beat up a lot of bullies. I even got suspended from high school once for stopping a fight and beating up the bully. So, from an early age, I'd figured what my stand was going to be. Then, when I was seventeen, I started a business where I would drive my brothers' drunk friends downtown, drop them off and pick 'em up. I'd sleep in the car, do homework, play games, or whatever. Well, while I was doing that, I would see these bar fights, so it was kind of fun for me to just run out, beat up both of the guys that were fighting and then hop back into the car. That evolved into where I would walk around and I'd hear people say, "Hey, that's the guy who breaks up bar fights". But it got extremely sketchy, because I'd be in Walmart and some dude would come and sock me in the face, because I'd beat him up the previous weekend. So I realized, *Okay, I can't do this, my partner and I have a kid coming.* So I let it go.

'Well, one day I'm at a water park and someone breaks into my car. They used a rock wrapped in a ski mask to smash the window. I put the rock and mask in the glove compartment and forgot about them. Then, one night, I was outside some nightclub and someone was hit with a stick and cut badly across the face; it was gushing blood. So I run back to my car to get my cell phone to call for an ambulance, I open the glove compartment and I see the mask. Then I start thinking: *It's just like breaking up bar fights but no one's going to see me this time.* So I put the mask on, put on a blues brothers' hat that I had in the back of my car from a Halloween thing and I go after this dude. I chased him down the street and tackled him and held him for the police. It was then that I gave the cops the name *Phoenix Jones*. I already knew what my alias name was going to be – I'm a comic book guy and I'd always known. The next day I read in the newspaper: "*Masked superhero tackles street crime.*" I smiled and I was like: *That's it!* I only had 15 dollars to my name at the time, but I went to a Walmart and I bought some blue long johns. I threw 'em on, along with my mixed martial arts cup and some fight gloves. Then I threw some shorts on over the long johns, put on a ski mask and then I'd hide out in my car and wait for crime to happen. I'd just beat the crap out of people.'

Purple Reign laughed.

'One time I ended up getting stabbed,' Phoenix continued. 'The cop shows up and says, "No way! We've heard rumours about you but we didn't think you were real!" He's like, "We've got to get a photo!" So we get a photo and then the media got a hold of it. A couple of days later, the cover of the Seattle Times has a big picture of me in my blue suit, arms folded standing next to a cop and it says: "Superhero and cops fight crime". After that, I thought to myself, *Okay, so that's me, I'm the superhero. I'm going to fight crime.* And that's what I did.'

I was keen to seek out Phoenix Jones' views about the incident where he had been arrested. The meeting was going well and he seemed more than happy to talk to me. In fact, his and Purple Reign's openness surprised me. The build up to meeting them had made me believe that the meeting would be superficial at best, but Phoenix Jones and Purple Reign were talking to me like we were old friends.

'I was so excited when the police arrived,' Phoenix told me when

I asked about the incident. 'There were sixteen calls made to the police and they were all from my crew. The guys from the other group didn't call once.'

'So why did the cops arrest you?' I asked.

'I flagged the cop down, and when he gets out of the car I see it's this officer who I have history with. He hates me. Doesn't like what I do.'

The officer threatened to arrest all of the heroes and "clean things up". But after the other group alleged that Phoenix had pepper-sprayed them when all they had been doing was dancing, the officer placed Phoenix Jones in a set of handcuffs and took him away.

'It's important to point out that the officer didn't interview any of our team or cameraman,' Purple told me.

Phoenix was then taken to jail, and he explained to me how things went from bad to worse.

'They booked me into the jail. I'm still in my super-suit. I'm handcuffed and I'm sitting there and I look across the room – and a dude I arrested for gun possession earlier in the night, along with a guy from a bar fight, are both sitting right across from me, but they're not handcuffed because they've already been processed. But I am handcuffed, so I'm thinking: *Oh shit*. And I'm still trying to keep my identity secret, right? So I reach over and I bite off my nametag that the jail put on me and I swallowed it. I put my hands in the toilet and I rub my arm – because they write your name on your arm in marker pen. At that point, the guys are saying, "You're not so tough without your fucking mask." And they're getting all uppity with me. So I realized that, if I'm going to be crazy, now is the moment to really sell that I'm crazy. So I stand up and go, "Come on! You want it? Let's go!" I didn't think it would really happen – but both of them charge me in this jail cell. So I sidestepped them and slammed one of their faces in the wall, then slammed the other side of his face into the glass, which made like a "blood angel" on the window. He fell down and then the other dude comes at me, and I booted him in the face and dropped him.

Then the police in riot gear come running in, so I dropped on the ground and I spent the rest of my time in solitary confinement – six or seven hours. The police asked me if I wanted to press charges, and I did. So I pressed charges against those two people, but I'm also suing the police for endangering me by putting me in there in my super-suit.'

Phoenix Jones then went court, where all charges relating to his arrest were dropped.

'I walked right out,' he told me.

Right out of court and right into that media-frenzy. A frenzy that had plastered his face across TV screens and newspaper pages around the world and had ultimately led me here, to Seattle.

'So there you go,' Phoenix Jones said. 'You still want to patrol with us?'

I felt my head nodding. It seemed I did, despite everything in me saying: *No way! You guys are freaking nuts!* Even when thinking about Master Legend and his Chainsaws of Justice, or Superhero with his handgun, everything about Phoenix Jones felt different to everything else I had so far experienced. There was no more playing around. This felt line being on the front line.

'You're going to need to put this on tonight,' Phoenix Jones said.

He threw a black, bank-robber style balaclava and a bulletproof vest onto the coffee table. It landed with a heavy *thud* that made me jump and spill some of my latte.

I decided immediately that I didn't want to wear them. I was convinced that the Seattle police would shoot me dead within minutes. I mean, why would you walk around the streets in the middle of the night wearing a balaclava and a bulletproof vest, unless you were planning to rob a late night store?

Phoenix Jones stared at me through his black and gold latex mask. He explained that he carried a large can of pepper-spray (dyed orange for easy identification of people he's sprayed) and a Phazzer – like a taser, only with interchangeable cartridges, such as pepper balls and rubber bullets. 'At this point in my superhero career, I've been shot once and stabbed twice,' he told me. 'I've had a broken nose, a couple of broken ribs and a baseball bat to the head. I carry the pepper-spray and Phazzer for a reason. Wear the gear if you're going to patrol with us.'

We came to a compromise; I would wear the vest under my jacket and roll the balaclava up into a beanie-style hat on my head.

'Okay, let's do it,' he said. 'Let's stop some crime. Ready?'

6

Meanwhile, Across Town...

We were driving down the I-5 expressway, the Space Needle – Seattle's most iconic and famous site – brightly illuminated to our right; the tall, white structure, shining out above the city like a tripod from War of the Worlds.

I could hear the wetness, as the tyres of our old white car splashed along the road. It had been teeming down with rain as we had been chatting in the coffee shop. It was still coming down but was now more of a fine, cold drizzle. I pulled the balaclava onto the top of my head for warmth.

The car was being driven by Boomer, a friend of Phoenix Jones, and a member of the Rain City Superhero Movement, who had picked us up at the coffee shop. Boomer was wearing a black jacket with yellow flashes across the chest and arms (giving him a similar look to Phoenix Jones), black combat trousers, and a belt rig holding various black, military type pouches. On his face he wore a crash-test dummy neoprene mask. He looked quiet portly – not fit and muscular as Phoenix Jones appeared to be.

As Boomer drove us closer towards downtown Seattle, we saw the flashing lights of emergency vehicles at an intersection, up ahead.

'We've got a situation here on the corner,' Phoenix said. 'Keep your eyes peeled.'

'There're a number of cop cars, ambulances, fire crews and EMS,' Boomer said excitedly, leaning forward to get a better look at the scene. 'Holy jeez, they have the whole intersection blocked off!'

'Someone died. That's a murder scene,' Phoenix said. 'When you place *caution tape* like that and park cop cars in that way, that's a murder – or at least a possible murder.'

This seemed like pure speculation to me. It could have been anything, but I kept quiet and stared out of the window like everyone else as Boomer slowed the car down, rolling past the scene.

'Is it up on your thing yet?' Phoenix asked, turning to Purple.

'No. It won't come up on screen until the situation is closed.'

Purple Reign had been tapping away at her iPhone, trying to establish what was occurring. She was looking at the Seattle police online incidents system. It gave Purple every incident that the police were dealing with in the city.

'We're at M3 right now, right?' Phoenix asked Purple.

'We are,' she told him, still tapping at her screen.

'M3 or "Mary 3" – that's the beat code in this area for the local police precinct,' she said, turning to me.

'The thing is, I know that there are only sixteen cops that patrol this area,' Phoenix said. 'They have sixteen patrol cars and there were five or six at that incident alone. So that means that there are only ten patrol cars left. That's not good. That's over one third of the police for the entire night, in one area.'

'In an area with the highest crime trends in the city,' Purple added.

'Erm... Cabbie called,' Boomer said, interrupting Phoenix and Purple's flow.

'Yep?' Phoenix said, in a *so what* tone.

'He said that a homeless guy got robbed. He's chasing down the suspect.'

Boomer spoke in a soft, unsure voice. Because of that, it took a second to take in what he was actually saying. Cabbie was another of Phoenix's Rain City crew. The words Boomer used – saying that Cabbie was "chasing down a suspect" – were urgent but his tone was not. We all squinted at Boomer and Phoenix Jones leant forward to try and establish exactly what he had meant.

'Chasing a suspect? Right now?'

'Yeah.'

Phoenix still didn't seem sure. 'Where?'

'He said he was on First and Pike.'

'Okay, let's roll!' Phoenix ordered.

'Well, that's where he was when he called in. Ratchet is there now.'

Phoenix flopped back in the seat. 'Ratchet is on First and Pike?'

'Yes. Ratchet is looking for Cabbie.'

'Okay, mask up, suit up,' Phoenix told us. 'Let's get ready.'

As Boomer put his foot on the accelerator, Purple pulled her scarf up, to cover the bottom part of her face. The engine quickly grew louder and we hurried towards the downtown area.

'Did Cabbie manage to get out a description of the robber?' Phoenix asked, as he tightened a strap on his rubber suit.

'No,' Boomer told him. 'But I can call him back and try and get him on the phone.'

'Yeah, call him back for me.'

Phoenix continued to clip various bits of his outfit together, strapping his black gauntlets over his arms and hands.

'Give me the camera, bro. I'm gonna lock it in,' Phoenix said.

Boomer handed Phoenix a small GoPro video camera, which Phoenix locked into a plastic case on his chest, so that the camera would record everything that Phoenix was looking at.

Boomer's car was small and cramped and we were all banging our heads on the inside roof, nudging each other with our elbows and knees as we attempted to dress and get ready.

'Cabbie's not rolling solo, right?' Phoenix asked.

'He is,' Boomer told him, in his soft, quiet voice.

It wasn't the answer that Phoenix was looking for. 'He's going solo? Fuck!' He turned to me. 'Every time I've ever been hurt, I've been patrolling solo.'

'We've got rules for the guys,' Purple told me. 'And going solo is a no-no. It just isn't safe.'

Boomer picked up a small black walkie-talkie. 'Cabbie, where is your location? Come in Cabbie.'

Silence.

'Cabbie, come in,' he tried again. 'Have you found the guy? Do you have the robbery suspect?'

There was no reply. Then, just as Boomer was dropping his hand down, away from his mouth, a crackly voice punctured the worried silence in the car. It was Cabbie – but he was hard to hear above the static of the walkie-talkie.

'Can you say that again?' Boomer asked. 'Where are you?'

'I'm in Pike Place Market at Post Alley.'

Purple frantically tapped at her iPhone. 'Got it,' she said, looking at the map on her screen.

Phoenix leant forward to speak into Boomer's radio. 'Do you have the suspect or a description?'

'I don't have him,' Cabbie called back. 'He had a mini backpack thing. Dark clothes.' Everything else that Cabbie said after that was unintelligible.

We had reached downtown Seattle, and Boomer drove quickly over humps and dips as we headed towards the market area where

Cabbie had chased the robbery suspect. There was barely a soul around. A couple of taxis passed us, going in the opposite direction.

'Stop here! Stop here!' Purple told Boomer. 'Post Ally is right over there. Take a right.'

The large, pink neon lights of the Pike Place Farmers Market sign reflected in pools of rainwater, as Boomer's car rumbled over the cobblestones outside the closed market. Pike Place Market was about as touristy as it gets in Seattle. It was the Pacific Northwest's answer to London's Covent Garden or San Francisco's Fisherman's Wharf. Overlooking the waters of Puget Sound, during the day it was heavy with European accents, buskers and market stalls – but, at night, it was a different place altogether. It was deserted, windswept, and creepy.

'Let's park here,' Phoenix ordered.

Boomer got back onto his walkie-talkie. 'Cabbie, we're right above Post Alley. We'll be with you in a minute.'

'I'm heading towards the north end of the market,' Cabbie answered.

Phoenix looked around and back through the rear windscreen. 'That's where we are. We're at the north end.'

Boomer came to an abrupt stop and we all jumped out of the car, running back towards the main road, frantically looking for Cabbie. Then, in the faded yellow glow of a streetlight, we saw a tall figure, moseying towards us. It was Cabbie. He was safe and appeared to be unhurt.

As he drew closer, I was able to take in his elaborate outfit. Cabbie (short for "El Caballero") was wearing an all-over facemask, with openings for the eyes and mouth. It looked like the type worn by Mexican Lucha Libre wrestlers. The mask was mostly red with a purple strip running along the top that reminded me of a cockerel's comb, and purple flashes down the sides and around the eyes. Everything else about the way Cabbie was dressed seemed relatively normal, albeit in a 1970s police detective kind of way. He wore a wide-collared pale-blue shirt with a thin set of black body armour strapped over the top of it, a tight fitting (and again, wide collared) black leather jacket, black leather gloves and a pair of tight, slightly too short, tracksuit bottoms. The mask aside, you could almost imagine him driving around the Bronx in a shabby undercover police car.

The robbery suspect was long gone, lost during a foot chase through the back alleys around the market. Phoenix asked him what had happened and Cabbie explained that he had seen a homeless guy having his bag stolen by the other man, who he had chased after. After losing the robber, Cabbie had returned to the market to look for the homeless guy, but he too had disappeared. The only hope now was that Cabbie would spot one, or both of them, during the patrol.

Soon, we were joined by Ratchet, who had been searching for Cabbie. He walked towards us from within the market area. He was noticeably different from the comic book look of Phoenix Jones and Cabbie. Ratchet – so named because he was a bit of a mechanic – was fairly short, but he looked like something from a horror movie or computer game set in some future war. Dressed mostly in black, with a bit of the ninja look that Urban Avenger had gone for, Ratchet had strapped a taser to his leg, a radio to his chest – and he wore black padded plastic, riot-cop type armour on his body. But it was his facemask that really set him apart from the others. It was a black and red skull mask worn over the top of a black balaclava. Grimm had done something similar in San Diego, but the fact that Ratchet had gone almost fully for a black look made him look decidedly sinister. There was nothing nice or fun or comic book superhero about him.

I was immediately reminded of what Superhero had told me. He had mentioned how some of the newer, younger superheroes were going for this darker look. He hadn't liked it and now I could see why. If I saw Ratchet coming towards me, the last thing I would be thinking was that he was coming to my aid. Having a criminal shit their pants at the sight of you could be a positive thing, I guessed, but it probably wasn't the reaction a superhero wanted from the general public.

Cabbie's robber had disappeared but tonight's team were all here, so Phoenix Jones briefed them before the patrol began. Safety was paramount and Phoenix was keen to stress the importance of sticking together, or at least not going off on your own. He specifically looked at Cabbie when he said this. He was also concerned about the possibility of having to deal with an armed suspect.

Phoenix Jones was holding his ballistic shield, the same "bat-shield" I had seen at the demo in Capitol Hill. 'If shots are fired, we stack up behind my ballistic shield, like this,' Phoenix told his team, and demonstrated what he meant, by holding the shield up in front of his body and pulling the other superheroes behind him, so they were stacked-up, in a tight, crouching line, one behind the other.

After the briefing, Phoenix Jones split the team up into two. Two teams could cover more of the downtown neighbourhood we were in and, as it was already getting late, he was keen to have as much of a presence as possible.

'You're with me,' he said, turning in my direction.

I hadn't planned to actually walk with Phoenix Jones or any of the heroes. My plan had been to walk behind them, observing from a distance. I explained this to Phoenix but he didn't like the idea.

'You'll be safer with me,' he said. 'There could be people out there with knives or guns. If you're exposed and alone, you could end up getting hurt or even killed, and I really don't want that on my conscience. If you're going to patrol with us, you need to stick close to me.'

One of the reasons I wanted to distance myself from the superheroes was the Seattle police. Coming into conflict with local officers was something I deeply wanted to avoid. I was, after all, a foreigner. A tourist. Trying to explain to the local police exactly why I was with a bunch of masked vigilantes, getting involved in bar fights or interfering with drug dealers, was not a conversation I wanted to have, not to mention having to explain the balaclava and bulletproof vest. I didn't want to end up in a police cell but, most of all, I didn't want to get deported. It was a fear I'd had with all the other superheroes, but with Phoenix Jones and his team, those fears were amplified.

It seemed, however, that I had no choice, and soon I was teamed with Phoenix Jones and Ratchet. The second team – Cabbie, Boomer and Purple – headed off in a different direction but would remain in contact via the walkie-talkies.

As soon as we started walking, Phoenix noticed a young black guy on the opposite side of the street. Nodding towards the man, he told me to look at his belt. Stuffed into it was a foot-long wooden axe handle, which was wrapped at one end with silver tape.

'He'll use that to mug people with,' Phoenix told me. 'But it's not illegal so we can't do anything about it.'

'How do you know he's using it as a weapon?'

'It's an axe handle stuffed into his waistband. Why else would he have it? What they do is, they put the axe piece in their back pocket and the axe handle in their belt, then they pop them together and they've got an axe. Or they'll leave the actual axe head somewhere nearby.'

We watched as the man walked away. He turned around occasionally to look at us but moved swiftly all the same. Once Phoenix Jones was satisfied that the man was leaving the area, we strolled down 1st Avenue towards a small crowd gathered around a doorway between a late night convenience store and a nightclub.

'Careful,' Phoenix said, as we walked slowly towards them. 'That doesn't look good.'

With the way people were bunched together in a huddle, I wondered if perhaps there was a fight or a drug deal going on. Phoenix Jones was having the same thoughts, and we walked towards the crowd cautiously. No one seemed to notice us as we closed in. I peered through the tight knot of people and saw a man in his twenties, crashed out in the doorway. The way he lay slumped and semi-conscious on the ground suggested that he'd had more than just a few drinks too many. Left alone, this man could be in serious trouble.

'This is what this club is known for,' Ratchet told me. 'Drugs and people getting fucked up.'

Someone noticed us standing there and drunkenly shouted out, 'Protect and serve!'

Others now turned to face us and Phoenix Jones quickly capitalised on the attention to move closer to the collapsed man. 'How you guys doing tonight?' Phoenix asked the crowd, while simultaneously muscling his way through them, followed closely by Ratchet.

A man – a friend of the drunk – was bent down, trying to rouse him by shaking his shoulders.

'Can I look at him real quick?' Ratchet asked.

The friend, who was extremely drunk himself, stared at Ratchet and said aggressively, 'Nah! Nah!'

His reaction seemed fair to me; after all, we had appeared out of nowhere and Ratchet was dressed in his rather alarming black outfit and skull facemask. I wouldn't have let him near one of my friends either.

'This guy's a medic,' Phoenix quickly said, in an attempt to calm the man's fears. 'This is what he does. We just want to check him out, is that alright?'

The guy slipped out of the way and allowed Ratchet to take his place.

'Drop your mask down,' Phoenix said softly to Ratchet.

'Yeah, you're scaring my friend,' the guy added.

Ratchet looked over at Phoenix and indicated towards the GoPro camera on his chest.

'Just face the other way, so we won't see you,' Phoenix told him.

Ratchet lowered his mask, shined a small flashlight at the drunk, and held his wrist to take his pulse.

'You doing okay?' Ratchet asked. 'Do you know what day it is?'

The guy was incoherent, just mumbling and dribbling.

'Okay, we're going to call an ambulance. We'll wait with you.'

Phoenix was already dialling 911. The drunk's friend didn't object. A few minutes later, a fire department ambulance arrived, its bright emergency lights washing the entire street in red and white flashes. Two crewmembers stepped out of the vehicle, pulling on rubber gloves. Phoenix walked straight up to them to explain what was going on. They were both tall, muscular men, wanting to get to the guy on the ground, and they took little interest in Phoenix Jones. Ratchet gave them a brief summary of what had happened and then stepped aside.

After checking the guy's blood pressure and his pulse, they attempted to help him to his feet. No sooner had the guy stood back up, he suddenly slumped back down, almost whacking his head on the wall behind him. He had fallen completely unconscious and the ambulance crew quickly placed him in the recovery position, then called on their radio, saying that they needed a "straight ride", which I suspected meant a stretcher or gurney.

'That's what I told them when I called it in!' Phoenix said. He raised his voice, so the ambulance guys would hear. 'This is what we do, man. We don't just dress up like superheroes. When I say we need a straight ride, get a fucking straight ride!'

A few minutes later, another ambulance arrived, this time an American Medical Response Unit. They pulled a gurney out from the rear of their vehicle and quickly loaded the drunk onto it.

'Phoenix tells me you're a trained medic,' I said to Ratchet as we watched them load the guy into the ambulance.

'Yeah, right now I'm taking an EMT class – Emergency Medical Technician. I'll actually be done in a week and then I'll be EMT certified.'

'Which will be a ridiculously awesome benefit for us,' Phoenix said.

'Are you doing it for the team?' I asked Ratchet.

'No. Myself. I work in lawn care, spraying lawns with fertilizer, and I hate it. I'm looking at getting a job as ambulance crew with those guys – the American Medical Response. Being AMR could kill some of the nights that I patrol with the RCSM, but I'll find a way to work around it.'

'You'd still do the superhero work?'

'Sure.'

'Be careful from a legal standpoint, once you get that certificate,' Phoenix warned him. 'I'd feel really shitty if you're out with us and you lost your licence.'

'Dude, I've got that figured out already. The only thing that I'd do for a civilian is give them a Band-Aid, unless they're shot, stabbed or cardiac arrest. I'll also be carrying a bag-valve mask, not that damn piece of crap that Boomer carries. I'm not putting my lips on anyone.'

By now, the rest of the Rain City Superheroes had re-joined us. They had heard about the drunk over the radio after Phoenix had called it in. We were going to separate again but, as we continued, heading towards the bar neighbourhood of Belltown, Phoenix noticed half a dozen black men standing across the street.

'I know those guys,' he told me. 'They're drug dealers.'

I looked over at the men. They were all dressed in dark clothes. They hadn't noticed us and were walking in the direction of the shopping district.

'Guys, let's go this way,' Phoenix told his team, and we all turned, heading in the same direction as the drug dealers.

We caught up with them at 4th and Pike. The wide crossroad was lined with stores and coffee shops, but everything was closed at this late hour. The entire area was deserted, apart from the group of men who were now standing around on one of the corners. A slow, icy wind crept along the street. It felt like being in a seaside town in winter. The men looked over as we approached and, although I couldn't understand what they were saying, I could hear them shouting and talking loudly among themselves.

'Stay close,' Phoenix told me. 'These guys are unpredictable.'

'You've dealt with them before?' I asked.

'Yeah. I busted one of them one time, so they don't like me too much. But they're just petty drug dealers. No knives or guns or anything like that.'

Phoenix walked calmly to the street corner opposite the men, as the rest of his crew stood in a tight group behind him. Before Phoenix had even opened his mouth, one of the men turned to him and shouted, 'I'm going to kick your ass, bro. I'll knock you out!'

I heard the superheroes shuffling around me, leather outfits creaking, hands dropping to pepper-spray canisters.

'You're going to knock *who* out?' Phoenix asked, challenging the guy.

'We ain't doing nothing, yo,' the man shouted at Phoenix. 'You didn't see me pass no drugs, bitches.'

The man was tall and stocky, wearing a long, dark, woollen coat. Standing around him, under a streetlight, were another four, similar looking men. The rest of the group were talking among themselves, looking over every so often but happy to let this one man do the talking. The Rain City Superheroes seemed equally happy to let Phoenix Jones be their champion.

'You didn't see shit, yo!' the man continued.

'That's right, I didn't see anything,' Phoenix agreed. 'I didn't see you pass anything. I never said you did. In fact it's you who said it. Not me.'

The man was getting increasingly agitated as Phoenix sparred with him and I could sense that the rest of his gang were becoming annoyed with our presence. I was unsure how this was all going to end and it seemed that Phoenix's plan was simply to hang around on this corner and frustrate the men's activities. If we had been cops, this strategy may have worked – but we weren't cops, and therefore the men didn't feel the need to move. But at the same time, we were interfering in their activities and they clearly weren't happy about it.

Now another of the men got involved. 'You ain't no cop. You ain't no *po*-lice. You didn't see me smoke no crack.'

Phoenix folded his arms and shook his head. 'Hey! Yo! You're ranting but you're not listening. I told you I didn't see anything. If I did, do you really think you'd all still be standing there?'

I cringed.

The first guy took a step off his corner and moved into the road, towards us. 'You don't want to mess with me, or...'

'Or what?' Phoenix asked. 'What's going to happen?' And now it was he who took a step forward, onto the road.

There was a moment of silence, with just the sound of the cold wind, and an unseen car travelling along a wet road a block away.

'Ain't nothing going to happen,' the man eventually said.

'Exactly,' Phoenix said. 'Nothing's going to happen. So please walk away.'

But this infuriated the guy. 'What? *You* please walk away!'

'We did,' Phoenix said. 'We're on our corner but you then came all the way over here.'

'Man, you walked a block down the street just to fuck with me!'

'Actually, we were just walking in this general direction.'

'Bullshit! You came a block down the street to fuck with me, yo!'

Purple, no doubt seeing that this was going nowhere other than toward a testosterone-fuelled stalemate, suggested to Phoenix that we move away. 'We've got no crime here,' she told Phoenix. 'Come on, let's leave.'

But Phoenix wasn't finished. As the rest of us turned to walk back towards the market and 1st Avenue, Phoenix marched across the street towards the group of men. He kept going until his face was as close to the first guys as he could get – literally nose-to-nose. The guy starred back at Phoenix dumbfounded, unsure of what was going to happen next.

'Have a good day!' Phoenix said sarcastically.

The guy looked incredulous and began to splutter, eventually shouting, 'FUCK YOU!'

Phoenix walked back towards us without turning around and had a faint, satisfied smile on his face.

'FUCK YOU MOTHERFUCKERS!' the guy shouted again. 'FUCK YOU!'

We walked towards the market.

Although the men had backed down, I was still uneasy. This was a whole new ballgame for me and it was incidents like this, and the risk of being arrested, that made me seriously question what I was doing patrolling with Real-Life Superheroes, and Phoenix Jones in particular. But there was no going back now. Things were just getting started.

7

Seven Superheroes and a S.H.I.T

A couple of days had gone by without any word from Phoenix Jones. I had been hanging out in various coffee shops and bookstores, passing the time and using the free Wi-Fi to delve deeper into the work of Real-Life Superheroes. Then I came across a video that had been posted online by a guy calling himself "Rex Velvet". At first I thought he was another superhero, as the video had come up during a search about Phoenix Jones – but it became very clear, very quickly, that Rex Velvet was no superhero; the complete opposite, in fact. He was a super-villain.

A *super-villain*! This was simply too good to be true. I pressed play on the video, and sat back, clasping my headphones to my ears.

The screen changed from the noise and static of "snow" to a black and white test card showing the silhouetted image of a man wearing a bowler hat, an eye patch and a handlebar moustache. The letters "SVA" and the words "Super Villains Alliance service announcement" appeared on the screen, which then cut to a real image of the man – bowler hat, eye patch, moustache – in a warehouse, swinging around a samurai sword. *Rex Velvet*.

In a calm, sinister, posh English-sounding accent, Rex Velvet said, "My dear city, I can recall a time when I could leave this lair and conduct my duties proudly and without distraction. But now *he's* out there along with his silly gang of misfit Power Rangers disturbing the peace!"

Rex Velvet complained about what he perceived as changes to the city's law enforcement, bemoaning the fact that Seattle had become "protected not by our once respected police force but by a tormented, delusional freak in a mask!"

"How did this happen," he asked, "when I see our boys in blue replaced by a hobo snitch in a mask, gallivanting around with a slew of nerds in tights? The Rain City Superhero Movement must disintegrate. For far too long we've watched as our nation buys into its childish charade, and it's run its course." Then, addressing Phoenix Jones directly, he said, "It's time to get real, Jones. The community would be better off without you! You're doing more harm than good and I'm willing to bet that a sensible, sane majority would agree with me."

In the video, he went on to call Phoenix Jones "a nuisance", "a problem child", "a snitch" and "a fake", and stated that Phoenix Jones "must be stopped once and for all." Rex Velvet then called himself "the people's villain", before warning that he would not give up until the city was rid of Phoenix Jones.

At this point, he threw a sharp, pointed Space Needle bottle opener towards a wooden post with the image of Phoenix Jones's face upon it. The point of the Space Needle stabbed the centre of Phoenix Jones's head.

"Phoenix Jones, you have met your match," Rex Velvet said menacingly.

Then the words "Let's rid our city of these silly, vigilante nerds!" appeared on the screen as the video came to its end.

I sat back, astonished but impressed. The video was amazing and looked professionally produced. But who was Rex Velvet? I wondered if he was part of the anarchist movement or the Black Bloc – who had, I later found out, a real loathing for Phoenix Jones and his team.

I considered asking Phoenix Jones about him the next time we met but decided to leave it until I got to know him better, unsure of how he would react to me watching these sermons preached by an archenemy.

As I was re-watching the video, I glanced down at my phone.

There were three missed calls and a voice message. All were from Phoenix Jones. The Rain City Superheroes were meeting tonight for a training session and I was invited to join them.

I watched the Rex Velvet video one more time before I left.

The setting couldn't have felt more ominous. I had been told to be at Gas Works Park at 10.30 pm, in the mostly residential neighbourhood of Wallingford, on the north side of Lake Union.

Though it was only a few miles from downtown, the taxi driver didn't know the location. He pulled over in a dark, residential side street and we both closely examined my totally inadequate, guidebook map. Wallingford was shown as little more than a grey splodge. As the taxi meter continued to count up at increments of thirty cents every few seconds, I caught a glimpse of the large lake through a break in the streets and told him that the park was somewhere nearby. He drove down more deserted, dark streets until we came out at an industrial area that was lined on one side by warehouses and on the other by tall, dense fir trees. Then, lit up in the taxi headlights, I saw a wooden sign for Gas Works Park and told the driver to pull over. He was happy to do so, and seemed as uncomfortable as I was, driving around this area at night. I threw him some money and jumped out of the cab. The driver literally drove away as I was shutting the door.

The sign had been slightly misleading. The area I had jumped out in was actually a marina, so I continued down the shadowy street, until I finally found a path leading through some trees and into the park itself, where I could hear shouting and loud music. There, under a covered area, a group of twenty to thirty youths were jumping around, smoking, drinking and juggling with fire. These were not the superheroes I had come to meet. I considered turning back but instead walked further into the park. Suddenly, everything opened up. In front of me was the large, Y-shaped, Lake Union. Across the lake were the illuminated skyscrapers of downtown Seattle, with the science fiction looking Space Needle towering above the city. An orange glow, created by the city lights, was penetrating the low, dark clouds that were drifting across city. It was a stunning sight.

The park had its own towers. Gas Works Park wasn't just a name. The park was home to an old gas works, now out of use, but left as a huge industrial relic. The towers and pipes rose above me on all sides, and in the darkness it gave the area a post-apocalyptic feel – these abandoned rusting metal gas works, standing like a modern Stonehenge, amongst the trees.

To the left of me was more of the gas works – the pipes, boilers and huge iron wheels of a former pump-house building. It was here that I could hear more voices and shouts – different from before. There was a ring of men and they were screaming at two others in the centre of their circle, who were attacking each other with heavy kicks and punches.

What the hell was going on? A robbery?

One of the men turned to look at me. He had light red hair and a small, wispy beard and moustache. He was in his mid-twenties, and although he was slim, I could see that he was fit and muscular. He wore mostly black clothing and had his arms folded.

He stared at me a little longer before saying, out loud, 'Okay, somebody's getting their ass kicked tonight. Let's get this show on the road!'

The rest of the group turned around and looked at me. Then the redheaded guy started to walk towards me.

Shit. Master Legend's metal pipe would have come in handy at the moment, I thought. Better still, his chainsaws. I got ready to sucker punch the guy (actually, that's a lie; I was getting ready to run) but, before I did, he held out his hand and said, 'You must be the English guy, right?'

'Mick,' I told him, warily.

'Hi, I'm Jack. Midnight Jack.'

'You with Phoenix Jones?'

'Yeah, I'm part of the Rain City Superheroes. PJ isn't here though, so he asked me to look out for you.'

'Mick!' A short, overweight guy walked towards me. 'It's me, Boomer.'

'Oh! I didn't recognise you without your mask.'

Midnight Jack and Boomer brought me into the circle. The fight, which was just a training exercise, had come to a stop and both of the men were bent over, breathing hard.

Boomer introduced me to "Evo". He was the tallest one in the group and, as with Midnight Jack, he wore all black clothing. Evo was broad and muscular. He stood straight and had an air of authority about him. Welcoming me to the group, sounding serious but friendly, he told me that he would be leading tonight's training.

'Evo spent time in the military,' Boomer told me.

'That's where my name comes from,' Evo said. 'It's short for Evocatus, which is a Latin term for a soldier who has served his time and been honourably discharged. A lot of the stuff we'll do tonight are things I used to do in the army – fighting, kicks, punches, hand to hand defence techniques, that sort of stuff. Are you up for joining in?'

'Of course he is,' Jack answered, slapping me on the back. 'Mick came here especially to have his ass kicked.'

'Ignore him, Mick,' came a voice from behind us. 'If anybody gets their ass kicked tonight it'll be Jack, as usual.'

I turned around but didn't see anyone. Then I looked towards the ceiling and saw a young guy, eight feet up in the air, walking along some narrow metal frames that formed part of the building we were in. His arms were held out for balance and he skipped across the metal frame like a trained gymnast.

'That's Griff Grey,' Midnight Jack told me. 'Wait until you see his jacket!'

'What do you mean?' I asked.

'His super-suit! He has this weird-looking wool and leather jacket thing he wears. It's fucking hysterical, man.'

Griff Grey didn't respond and instead continued with his balancing act.

The others in the group were Ratchet, who I had met during

the first patrol, USID, a short, thin man who looked to be the eldest in the group, with a slightly life-beaten face and a bald head, and Night Sabre, the shortest member of the team, who looked as though he spent a lot of time pushing weights down the gym.

Evo handed a large black pad to USID and asked him to hold it in front of his body. Then Evo demonstrated some of the kicks and punches he wanted us all to try. It was the sort of thing I did at training sessions with the police. Evo launched at the pad with hard, solid strikes, creating a satisfying "CRACK!"

'Aim higher,' Jack called out to Evo. 'You're missing his face!'

Evo took the pad from USID and stood in front of us as we each took our turn attempting to emulate what we had seen. Griff Grey kicked like a pro and, despite being almost half the size of Evo, still managed to knock him back a few feet with a powerful roundhouse. Evo was highly impressed, as was I.

'You see that?' Evo said. 'Grey may only be 130 pounds but he's doing the kick right. You do the math. It's all to do with strength and technique.'

I noticed that Boomer was struggling to keep up with the constant kicking and punching, and he took a break, walking away from the group and leaning against some of the old plant equipment, to catch his breath.

Griff Grey was now doing high kicks at the pad. He was clearly the most agile of the group.

'Remember to bring your legs back after the kick,' Evo instructed. 'We don't want to do pirouettes.'

'You're telling us that this is *Fight Club*, not *Broadway*,' Jack said.

'Exactly.'

After several more variations of kicks and punches, we took a break. USID was standing away on his own, lighting a cigarette. Whereas the rest of the group had been highly vocal and animated, USID had remained cool and quiet throughout the training. He wasn't antisocial, just relaxed, maybe slightly introverted. I walked over to join him.

'So what does USID mean?' I asked.

'It's an acronym of Undercover Suspect Identification Division. I do all the undercover work, so they call me USID. When they're running around in their masks and capes, I'll be walking around dressed just like anyone else. It gives the team an extra set of eyes. I may see things that they wouldn't. Most people pay no attention to me when I'm walking around.'

'You don't want to wear a costume?'

Taking a long drag on his cigarette, he slowly blew the smoke down at the damp ground before speaking. 'It's not that I don't want to, it's just that my body is breaking down way too fast for someone my age. I'm thirty-seven and there are days where it will take me literally twenty minutes to get out of bed. It's probably better that I stay anonymous when we patrol.'

Evo was calling people back to restart the training, but USID decided to light another cigarette. Midnight Jack then moseyed over and joined us. Evo had begun strapping Griff Grey's fists with long pieces of faded white cotton. Night Sabre was doing the same with his own fists.

'Are they going to fight?' I asked.

'Yeah,' Jack said. 'Grey verses Night Sabre. This could be interesting.'

'A boxing match?'

'Sort of. Kind of like a no-rules boxing match, although there's an agreement that we don't drag our knees into each other's crotch repeatedly. Other than that, it's all fair game.'

'How long is the fight?'

'It's a five minute spar. The reason it's five minutes is because that's the average response time for the Seattle police to arrive on scene. So, essentially, what we're doing is defending ourselves for five minutes until the police arrive.'

'Five minutes of non-stop fighting seems like a long time.'

'Yeah, people who don't really know what they're doing get pretty exhausted pretty quickly. Have you seen the video of PJ fighting the drunk?'

I told him I hadn't and he pulled out his iPhone to show me the video, which had been posted online. In it, three drunk men start to shout insults at Phoenix Jones and his team on the street. After a few minutes, a Seattle cop car arrives, with its red emergency lights flashing. A K-9 unit quickly follows behind. Phoenix Jones, tiring of the insults, challenges one of the men – the biggest and stockiest of the trio – to "mutual combat". Mutual combat, I was told, was some strange law in Washington State where two people are legally allowed to fight if they both agree to it.

The drunk accepts Phoenix Jones' challenge and, as the cops literally stand to the side and watch, PJ and the stocky drunk square up to one another. One of the drunk's friends laughs excitedly, convinced that the rubber-masked superhero is about to get his ass whipped. But Phoenix Jones starts to bounce around on his feet like the professional mixed martial artist he is. Within moments, Phoenix Jones lays a kick to the guy's left leg, causing him to drop to one knee – but he gets back up and continues to face his opponent. At no point does the man lay a single punch or kick on Phoenix Jones and, as he backs into a shop doorway, Jones punches him once and the man crumbles to the ground, apparently knocked out. At no point do the police intervene.

'That's the law,' Midnight Jack told me. 'If both parties agree to fight, they can fight. It's only when one of them doesn't want to fight or when they say that they've had enough, that the cops will step in.'

The incident caused a small media storm and resulted in yet more unwanted criticism of the Seattle police, who explained that the officers were simply following the law.

'I take it you don't fight much,' I said, turning to USID.

'Not so much,' he told me. 'Not with the pain I get.'

'Are you able to work?'

'I work with disabled kids and I'm a trained masseur. The thing is, in Europe massage is considered health care. Over here, due to so much prostitution, if I set up a business at my home, I can't stop the cops from searching my premises to make sure I'm not a prostitute!'

'USID is the sort of masseur where you come in with two-hundred dollars and you get a "special" massage!' Jack said, laughing. 'He walks in with a cigarette in his mouth and his deep husky voice, asking, "Hey boy, you want the *special*?"'

'Jack, fuck off before I kick your balls into ovaries,' USID said.

Jack, who was clearly the team joker, walked away laughing, and we re-joined the rest of the group. The fight between Griff Grey and Night Sabre was about to start.

Night Sabre tested the distance between them by punching his gloved fist towards Griff Grey – but very quickly it became obvious that there was no contest. Night Sabre, older, heavier and slower, struggled to keep up with Grey's pace. Griff Grey was jumping around and landing hard kicks and fast punches into Night Sabre. Every time Night Sabre – who tired quickly – got too close, Grey would lunge at him and, before you knew it, he would wrestle Night Sabre to the ground. It was impossible for Night Sabre to do anything other than use that time to catch his breath. Then, like a cat playing with a mouse, Grey would release Night Sabre, only to continue beating the crap out of him. I had to hand it to Night Sabre though – despite the fact he was losing badly and clearly struggling to breathe and stay on his feet, he kept going for the entire five minutes. By the end of the fight, Night Sabre was utterly exhausted. Griff Grey celebrated his win by swinging gymnastically on some metal frames.

The evening's training had come to an end. Ratchet and Night Sabre decided to call it a night but Evo, Boomer, Midnight Jack, Griff Grey and USID were meeting Phoenix Jones downtown for that night's patrol.

'You coming, Mick?' Boomer asked.

'Sure.'

'PJ told me that you're a cop,' Boomer said, as we walked away from the park.

'Yes. Is that an issue?' I asked. The question was a genuine enquiry rather than a challenge.

'Not at all. I think everybody will be pleased to have another cop on the team.'

'You don't think they'll be suspicious about my motivations?'

Before Boomer had a chance to reply, Midnight Jack stepped into the conversation. 'Who's a cop?' he asked. 'You?'

'Yes,' I told him. 'But being here has nothing to do with me being a cop.'

Midnight Jack stared at me, nodding his head. 'Cool,' he said.

At that point, I knew nothing about Midnight Jack. Had I known at that point about his past, I may have been more concerned. But that was all to come.

'Did you bring body-armour with you?' Boomer asked.

'No,' I told him.

Even though I had brought my own vest to Seattle, I had left it in my hotel room. I'd felt uneasy the previous night, wearing the set that Phoenix Jones had made me put on. I was here to shadow the superheroes, not to be one. And, besides, I didn't want to tempt fate.

But Boomer seemed concerned. 'Do you want some pepper-spray?' he asked.

'No. Definitely not.'

'Well, that's your choice – but you need to consider these things...'

8

Don't Touch the Americans

We had been standing in the rain on a side street close to Pike Place Market for about ten minutes, but Phoenix Jones was running late.

'I don't want to be subordinate, but should we just go and patrol and let PJ catch us up?' Boomer asked the group.

'No,' Midnight Jack said, firmly.

'Okay, I'll call him,' Boomer said. 'I'll call him but you talk to him. I don't want him to nag me.'

Just then I noticed a man striding towards us; heavy droplets of rain were sliding down his black and gold suit. *Phoenix Jones.*

'How's it going?' I asked.

'Just fighting crime and I'm medium famous,' he proclaimed. 'I can't walk through this city without people either thanking me or telling me that they hate me.'

The small group of superheroes gathered around Phoenix Jones, awaiting his instructions.

'Tonight we're going to look for bar fights and violence,' he announced.

Then he, Midnight Jack, Griff Grey, Evo and Boomer, began to kit up, taking various pieces of outfits, weaponry and body armour from the trunks of the cars and strapping them on. I stood on the sidewalk with USID, watching, as a cool breeze travelled along the narrow road, and rain dripped from my hair, into my eyes. Evo lifted out a heavy, black leather jacket, which had thick, serious-looking padding fitted across the shoulders, chest and arms.

'Is that a biker jacket?' I asked.

'Yeah, with police riot pads moulded onto it,' Evo told me.

'It's heavy duty padding with an extremely hard plastic shell,' Midnight Jack added.

'Do you have your blackjack on you?' Evo asked, turning to look at Midnight Jack. 'Wait, what am I saying? Of course you do!'

'Of course I do!' Midnight Jack confirmed, his smile showing through his mask. He whipped out a flat, black object from his pocket, maybe 10 inches long – the *blackjack*.

'Okay, hit me with it,' Evo told him.

'In the face?'

'No, you idiot! Hit the armour.'

Midnight Jack took a couple of steps backwards and then ran towards Evo, lifting the blackjack behind his head before striking Evo's chest. It made a loud, quick, sharp cracking sound but appeared to have no effect on Evo whatsoever.

I took a closer look at the blackjack. It was basically a large, black leather strap with a lump of lead stitched into one end. It was just about as nasty a weapon as you could carry, like something an old-school gangster or thug would have used to bludgeon people to death.

'What the hell are you doing with this?' I asked. I was shocked at how vicious it looked.

'Protection,' Midnight Jack told me. 'Listen, I've actually hit people with this shit, bro, and it works.'

'I believe you! The thing is, you're going to kill somebody with this.'

'That's why I tell him not to bring it out!' Phoenix Jones said. 'Although, at least he's a bit more reasonable now with his weaponry; he used to be totally unreasonable.'

As if to confirm Phoenix Jones' point, Midnight Jack said, 'Do you remember that fighting knife I used to have? And those batons? I had two batons, a fighting knife, a blackjack, pepper-spray, and a stun gun – all this shit I didn't need, and I was like: *Why does my belt weigh a million pounds?* That shit was ridiculous. But now it goes like this...' He held his hands out defensively, in front of his body. 'Negotiations–' He pointed to his pepper-spray canister, '–

aggressive negotiations –' Finally, he lifted up his blackjack, '– negotiations have failed.'

'Dude, you're not bringing that blackjack out with you tonight,' said Phoenix Jones.

'Why the fuck not?'

'That blackjack is a no-no. I don't want to see it tonight.'

Midnight Jack huffed but it was clear by Phoenix Jones' tone that he was being absolutely serious. The question of the blackjack was not open to discussion. *Negotiations had failed.* Jack grudgingly tossed the blackjack into the trunk of the car.

It was already past midnight but, as far as Phoenix Jones was concerned, the later it was the more likely we were to run into crime and trouble. Purple Reign had been going over the crime maps and statistics for the downtown area and they confirmed that post-midnight was the premium time to patrol.

Starting our patrol, we walked along Pine Street, towards Westlake Station. Four transit cops, from the Kings County Sheriffs Department, were standing on the street outside. One of the officers had images of comic book superheroes tattooed over his arms. PJ recognised another of the officers and we walked over for a chat. PJ and the deputy bumped fists in a friendly, familiar manner – and, after a few pleasantries, I asked the officer what his thoughts were about the superheroes.

'These guys? They're an extra set of eyes out here to call things in or break stuff up. That's how I look at it. We can't be everywhere. But I still scratch my head and wonder why the hell would people do this.' He paused. 'But I guess it's no different to us fools who joined the military out of high school.'

'I wish the Seattle Police were as friendly with me as the Transit Police,' Phoenix said as we walked away.

'Aren't they?' I asked.

No,' he said, shaking his head. 'They called me a "menace".'

We headed north, along 1st Avenue, and then began to weave though the side streets.

'Do you know the difference between places like Baltimore and Seattle?' Phoenix asked. 'In Baltimore, you can just stay away from the shitty areas. But in Seattle you can get mugged anywhere; you can get mugged on First Avenue. This place is full of drugs and the mentally ill.'

Seattle cops I knew had told me something similar, once. They had mentioned how, more than many other places, Seattle seemed to have more people on the streets suffering from mental illness. They had attributed it to a lack of social care and the closing of the hospitals and institutions that had previously cared for the vulnerable.

Phoenix Jones had his own take: 'I saw something on TV that showed the top thirteen serial killers in the country were all from Washington State. Apparently it's because vitamin D doesn't get through our clouds.'

'Do you think that's right?' I asked.

'Yes and no. I think it's because Seattle is a very liberal place. We don't identify things for what they are. We try to smooth things over. I don't think people are crazier here than anywhere else, I just think they get noticed for it elsewhere. Whereas here we tell them that they're not crazy, even if they are.'

We entered the side streets, which were dark and shadowy, and stopped by the sheltered doorway of a closed business. Huddled in the near pitch-black alcove were a middle-aged black man and woman. Boomer shone a flashlight at them. The pair had heavily tracked and taut skin, as well as gaunt faces. They were clearly addicts.

The woman was hunched over, holding onto some burnt foil, which contained a few crumbled rocks of crack cocaine. Turning away from the light, she attempted to hide the rocks.

'Don't be doing your drugs here,' Phoenix told them firmly. 'We don't want drugs in this town.'

The couple mumbled something incoherent and shuffled away, into the late-night drizzle that had begun to fall, still hunched over their precious crack.

Boomer shone his flashlight into the doorway, checking that no drugs or paraphernalia had been left behind.

'Shall we mace the floor?' Midnight Jack asked. 'It would stop anyone from taking their drugs here.'

Phoenix gave this idea some thought but then said, 'No, we'd better not.'

We walked away from the door and stood in the street, looking for trouble, but it was deathly quiet. A cold wind whipped along the dark avenue and soggy, yellow leaves slapped against our legs and body.

'Let's hit Belltown,' Phoenix said. 'It'll be busier.'

Belltown was a short distance north of the touristy Pike Place Market. It was also where many of the city's late night bars were located.

'Belltown can be touristy during the daytime,' Phoenix told me. 'But it's a different beast at night.'

'In what way?'

'At night it's just a bad place to be.'

Belltown, named after one of Seattle's first residents and founders, William Nathaniel Bell, was well known for its schools and university campuses, art galleries, restaurants and trendy bars. It was hard to imagine it being "a bad place to be" but Phoenix was adamant. He had been at the receiving end of alcohol-fuelled punches when trying to break up fights in the area, and his team were very aware that their outfits – along with their pledge to intervene – could attract abuse and violence. This didn't deter them though. Despite the violence they had experienced, they continued to go into the areas where they felt they were most needed. I still had to wonder, though, if their presence wasn't simply escalating already volatile situations. As we entered the boisterous streets of Belltown, I figured I was about to find out.

The contrast to the peaceful, empty streets around the market was extreme. Suddenly we were enveloped in a storm of shouting, screaming, flashing lights, sirens and crowds of people tumbling from doorways. There was raucous activity everywhere, most of it poached in alcohol. The arrival of the superheroes was like a firework going off in the middle of a party. People started to leap around in excitement. Some could barely believe what they were seeing. For most people, though, the arrival of the superheroes presented nothing more than a fun photo opportunity. Groups of partygoers continually approached us, requesting to have their photo taken with Phoenix, Evo, Boomer and the others. Some didn't bother to ask and simply draped their limp arms around the superheroes' shoulders and instructed their drunken friends on how to operate their camera phone.

'So, am I safe right now?' a man slurred in Phoenix's face, as his friends pressed the screen on his phone, to take a picture.

'Well, put it this way,' Phoenix told him. 'Only one of us is in danger of being arrested tonight and it's probably me.'

A group of Hispanic men approached us and stared at Phoenix with a look of loathing. 'You're nothing more than a cop in a mask,' one of them spat, before shaking his head and walking away.

Midnight Jack, who had been trying to avoid the camera-wielding drunks and was standing by the kerb, called over. 'Hey Phoenix, there could be a fight over here.'

We looked over, Phoenix pushing his way through a gaggle of drunken women. On the opposite side of the road, three men were shouting and pushing each other in the chest. One of them, a young white man in a torn, white, Oxford shirt was being held back by one of the other men.

Phoenix called out to the rest of his team. 'Guys, on me! On me!'

Avoiding the slow moving traffic, which was itself trying to avoid the swell of screaming drunks staggering about the road, we darted to the opposite side of the street. The trio had moved into a parking lot just off 1st Avenue. We headed towards them and the superheroes spread out, creating a small semi-circle, as they approached the men. Phoenix and Jack both had their hands low, close to their waists, ready to pull a weapon. Seconds later, two

Seattle Police Department cars roared into the parking lot, drenching the surrounding brick buildings in electric flashes of red and blue emergency lights. They were almost immediately joined by a couple of cycle officers who had raced to the location through a back-alley. An officer from one of the cars jumped out and sprinted after one of the fighting men, who had run off and leapt over a wire gate.

'Okay guys, let's leave it to the police department,' Phoenix said. 'There's nothing for us to do here.'

Returning to 1st Avenue, we stood with our arms folded defensively, watching people milling around. We took a closer interest in a few of the more heated arguments that spontaneously erupted every now and again, although nothing developed into anything more serious than a few drunken insults and brave men telling their friends to "hold me back". No one, it seemed, really wanted to actually fight.

'Can I buy you a drink?' a man asked Phoenix as we stood outside one of the bars.

'I don't drink,' Phoenix told the man. 'But I'll take a Red Bull if you're offering?'

As the rest of the team remained outside, keeping an eye on the street, I walked into the bar with Phoenix. The place looked like a Wild West saloon after a fight, with small wooden tables and chairs strewn about, and spilt alcohol pooling on the stone floor. The bar had mostly cleared out, other than a small group of men chatting to staff.

'Drinking on the job?' one of the group asked, jokingly.

This same man then challenged Phoenix to an arm-wrestling contest.

Phoenix shrugged his shoulders and said, 'Okay.'

I looked at the guy who had challenged him. He was tall, and smartly dressed in a lilac coloured shirt that was still neatly tucked into his designer jeans. He looked like he was just starting his night rather than ending it. I wasn't convinced that the man had what it would take to beat Phoenix, and judging by way Phoenix had said, "okay" to the challenge, Phoenix clearly had no doubts that he could take the guy. This was going to be a quick contest.

Phoenix knocked back his Red Bull as a table was quickly cleared of empty glasses and bottles, the spilt beer wiped with a damp cloth. Two wooden chairs were brought over for them to sit on. They locked hands and Phoenix immediately pushed the guy's arm onto the table. The guy's friends barely had time to take a photo with their phones. The scene had all the makings of a new advertising campaign for Red Bull. Then Phoenix stood up to leave, without saying another word.

'You're welcome any time,' the barman said as we were walking out. 'You ever need a drink when you're patrolling, just pop in, the Red Bulls are on me.'

'I've been getting a lot of that lately,' Phoenix told me, outside the bar. 'People keep giving me stuff for free – food and drinks, especially.'

'That's how it used to be for cops,' I told him.

'Perhaps when the cops walked the beat, it was – but when do you ever see that these days? This is why people respond to me,' Phoenix said. 'I'm like a beat cop from back in the day. I talk to people. And because I talk to people, they give me information and tell me stuff. That's how it used to be with the cops, but now people come to me and the other superheroes. They don't want to talk to the police anymore.'

Moments later, we came across a pair of Seattle police officers who had detained and handcuffed a man outside one of the bars. A crowd of people had stopped along with us, to watch.

'Fuck the police,' a man standing beside us said out loud. 'I fuckin' hate the cops.'

'Why?' I asked him.

'They fuckin' hate us man, so we hate them back. Fuck them!' he said, and walked away with a group of friends, laughing and joking about their night out.

We left the main bar area of Belltown and walked into the backstreets, which were mostly deserted. As we walked up 7th Avenue towards Virginia Street, Griff Grey spotted a leg poking out from a doorway of a small, modern apartment building. Walking towards it, we found a middle-aged man crashed out. He was dark skinned and looked Native American, wearing a crumpled, red lumberjack shirt, his jeans soiled with all manner of stains. He was lying face down with one arm thrown out above his head and the second looking crushed under his leaden body. Next to him was a near-empty bottle of spirit, around his waist and legs a dark pool of urine.

'This is not just a drunk, sleeping,' Jack told the rest of the group. 'This looks like he was out walking and just fell down. This dude could be in real trouble.'

'Is he awake?' Phoenix asked.

Boomer bent down and took a closer look at the man. 'He's out of it. I can smell vomit, too.'

Phoenix crouched down by the guy. 'Sir, are you okay?'

The guy started to moan and gurgle, so at least he was alive. But the gurgling sounds he was making caused the team more concern – particularly Boomer and Jack, who seemed to know more about this type of condition than the others.

'You see the vomit by his face?' Jack asked me. I could see it. It was smeared around his mouth and clumped in his hair. 'He's pissed himself as well. Whenever you see someone passed out like that, it's likely alcohol poisoning.'

'This guy needs an ambulance,' I said.

'Oh yeah. We can't just leave him here. If we do, he could throw up again, choke on his own vomit and die.'

Phoenix asked Griff Grey to film him on the GoPro camera as he spoke a commentary towards it. 'We're gonna call 911 at this time and get a medical professional to check him out. He is non-responsive and we have not touched him or moved any of his possessions,' Phoenix said.

Boomer dialled 911 and asked for an ambulance, and Phoenix recorded that as well. After the call had been placed, I asked Phoenix about the recordings.

'Evidence,' he said. 'I need to show that we haven't touched him and that we've thought about what we're doing and why we're doing it.'

'Have you always done that?'

'Not always, but I do it more now than I used to.'

'Is that because of the time you were arrested?'

'Yes and no,' he told me. 'After that arrest, I became more open to civil suits because my name was known. Before, if someone wanted to civilly sue me – that is, sue *Phoenix Jones* – no one would show up. But now that my real name is known, they can sue *Ben Fodor*. Since I was de-masked, I've been civilly sued twenty-seven times. I've never lost one case though.'

'EMS is on its way,' Boomer called out.

I noticed that USID had moved away from the rest of the superheroes. He was sitting on a wall across the street, rolling up a cigarette, with the hood of his top pulled over his head. Figuring there was a chance the police may show up as well as an ambulance, and not wanting to be associated with the superheroes, I decided to join him.

'Do you always stand away from the others when something's going on?' I asked.

'Right now, there's no video or images on the Internet to link me to the RCSM. I'd prefer to keep it that way,' he said. 'Besides, you've seen for yourself the reaction the others can get when we're out.'

It seemed like a good idea to have someone like USID on the team; someone who could check things out, without the superheroes having to rush in and potentially escalating something, but I had thought that dressing up as a superhero and creating an alter ego was all part of the attraction to becoming a member of the Rain City Superheroes. The fact that USID didn't go down that route made me wonder why he did this at all. During the training session at Gas Works Park, he had told me about issues he was having with his back and his health but still, there is no glory or acknowledgment in being undercover. I was becoming increasingly intrigued by USID. Perhaps it was his semi-anonymous role within Phoenix Jones' band of superheroes or his relaxed, slightly disconnected approach to the patrols. He had already told me some things about his life but I suspected that there was far more. The dressing up bit – being a *superhero* – clearly wasn't important to him. Neither was the celebrity side of being in the RCSM. So why exactly did he do this?

USID cleared his throat. 'I went to school with Boomer – middle school and high school,' he told me.

'So Boomer got you involved in this?'

'He contacted me towards the end of last summer and asked if I wanted to join the team and be the *eyes*. Everyone knows PJ and almost everyone knows Jack, by name. They see them coming from two blocks away,' he told me. 'No one knows me.'

'But still, *why* do you it?'

'Because, if you have the ability to do something, you should,' he said. 'I told you that I worked with disabled kids, right? Well, I've also got nearly twenty years service in the military. I've already told PJ that I'm never going to mask up as long as I'm in the army, because it's my career that I'm putting on the line. But once I've got my twenty years in and I retire, I may mask up or I may not. I may stay as the scout. I do have a balaclava, though, just in case I need to cover up.' USID took a long drag on his cigarette. 'I do it mainly because he's been injured,' he said, pointing at Boomer, who was still crouched down, checking the drunk. 'I do it mainly to keep an eye on him.'

So that was the reason USID was doing this – friendship and loyalty. He was looking out for his old school buddy.

But there was another, more mundane and personal reason that USID had taken on this role. 'It gets me out of the house,' he told me. 'I was unemployed for two years. Now I'm in the National

Guard, so I only do the army stuff one weekend a month. For two years I sat in my house doing absolutely nothing, bored out of my fricking mind. This at least gets me out. I now walk three or four miles a day.'

As we chatted, I noticed Evo walking off with Boomer. Boomer looked upset, even with his mask on. His shoulders were slumped and he was looking at the ground as they walked slowly away, up Virginia. I walked over to Phoenix, Jack and Grey.

'Is everything okay with Boomer?'

'Yeah. He'll be fine,' Phoenix told me.

'Fourth of July problem?' Jack asked Phoenix.

'Yeah. Stay here,' Phoenix told Jack. 'I'm gonna walk with Mick a little.'

Phoenix led me away from the others.

'This is personal team stuff,' Phoenix told me, seriously. 'We all have triggers that can set us off. For instance, Evo was in the war in the Middle East, so he has a problem with the Fourth of July – all the big flashing lights and stuff. So that's what we call it when one of the superheroes has an issue now – a *Fourth of July problem*. Jack has issues, Boomer has issues, I have issues – we all have something that triggers us.'

'So what's the problem with Boomer?'

'Listen, you're still new here. Maybe when the team gets to know you better, they'll open up. Just not yet, okay?'

A few moments later, an ambulance showed up. Phoenix approached the operators and briefly spoke with them, pointing out the guy in the doorway. Both crewmembers from the ambulance seemed to know exactly who the superheroes were and appeared unimpressed. One of the ambulance crew pulled a trolley from the rear of the big, boxy vehicle and began to set it up as the other checked the drunk.

'Good, they're going to take him to a hospital,' Phoenix said. 'Our work here is done. Let's leave them to it.'

We started making our way back towards Pike Place Market,

where most of the team had left their cars. It was now the early hours and the patrol was coming to a close.

As we walked along 1st Avenue towards Pine, a black man came sprinting out of an alley and ran across an open parking lot. Clutching a dark coloured holdall close to his chest, he kept looking behind himself as he ran.

'That doesn't look right,' I said.

'No, it doesn't,' Jack agreed.

The speed the man was running at, and the way he kept looking back from where he had come, convinced me that he was in a panic to get away from something. The way he held onto the bag led me to think that he was a thief, and I remembered the first night I had been with the team, when Cabbie had been chasing the guy in Pike Place Market.

We all started to pick up our pace. Then we heard some shouting coming from the alley from which the man had just appeared. That did it. Something was wrong and I started to race after him. The others did the same. Any previous concerns I had about being arrested by the Seattle police suddenly vanished. There was shouting, and there was a suspicious man running away holding a bag – that was enough for me. *Once a cop, always a cop,* I guess.

The man ran across 1st Avenue and dived into Pike Place. Ahead of him, just under the large, pink neon market signs, was a dark stairwell leading down to the waterfront. I didn't want to lose sight of him, so I picked up my pace, rushing towards him as he started to run down the stairs. As I reached the top of the stairwell, I could see him on the floor below. I bounded down the steps in one giant leap, almost landing on top of him.

'Stop there!' I shouted. 'Stay where you are!'

The man froze and stared at me with wide, frightened eyes.

'What are you doing?' I asked.

The man didn't answer but looked up as the rest of the team joined me.

'Why are you running?' I demanded.

'I... I... I just need to take a piss,' he said.

'Bollocks,' I said.

'Did he just say *bollocks*?' I heard Jack asking behind me.

Phoenix sent Evo and Grey to the alley to see if they could find a reason for the man to run the way he had, or to locate the person who had been shouting.

'What's in the bag?' Phoenix asked him.

'Just my stuff. Look – you can look!'

The man opened the bag and started pulling out various items of clothing.

'But why were you running like that, man?' Phoenix asked. 'You weren't running down here for a piss.'

'Some guys in the alley were trying to take my stuff from me,' he finally said. 'I thought you might have been with them.'

'Someone tried to rob you?'

'Yeah. I was just trying to get away.'

Evo and Grey returned. 'There are some people hanging around – the usual types,' Evo told Phoenix. 'It all seems calm there now.'

'Do you want us to call the police for you?' Phoenix asked the man.

'No. I just want to get on my way.'

The guy picked up his possessions and hurried down the stairs to the waterfront. None of us were particularly happy with his story, but there was nothing more to be done, so we returned upstairs to street level to debrief the night's events. It was this incident that Phoenix wanted to focus on though.

'When we approached the runner, it was all pretty good,' he said. 'But there were a couple of tactical errors. When we came down the stairs, Mick was leading the charge. I appreciate your enthusiasm, Mick, but it wasn't the best thing for you to be leading.'

'I couldn't help myself,' I told him.

'I know. I saw you. You literally got all *cop-serious* when you ran after him. You charged off like Sir Galahad, which was kind of awesome to see – but do you know the first thing you did when you got to him?'

'What?'

'You touched him. You do realise that, don't you?'

'Probably.'

'No, *definitely*. You walked up to him and you grabbed his arm,' Phoenix told me, sounding annoyed.

'I didn't want him to get away.'

'We don't touch people. As far as we know, he hadn't done anything wrong. So the minute you put your hands on that guy, I shit myself. If that dude wanted to get hostile, we were all going to jail for assault.'

'I wasn't,' Jack said. 'I was going to say that I was with a different superhero team. Fuck you guys!'

The others laughed – but Phoenix was serious. He wasn't at all happy that I had grabbed hold of the man, even though it was something I had done by pure instinct, something of which I'd barely even been aware.

'We don't put paws on people,' Boomer told me.

'Okay, note to self,' I said. 'Don't touch the Americans.'

9

Purple Reign

Phoenix and Purple had invited me to their apartment for dinner. Being invited to their home felt special, as though they now trusted me. Our relationshiop had progressed to the point where it was beginnng to feel that we were becoming friends. But as we sat down to steak and asparagus, I almost immediately ruined eveything.

Although I had felt somewhat guilty about it, I had been watching Rex Velvet videos repeatedly. Another one had recently appeared online. Produced to the same high standard as previous videos, this time Rex Velvet had taken to calling the superheroes "super zeroes" and "dorks". A menacing soundtrack played in the background, along with images of rioting in Seattle, and in the video Rex Velvet had stated that the "world is not impressed" by Phoenix Jones' "playground movement" or his "ability to aim or fire a silly can of mace". The video showed images of posters pinned to posts throughout the city, flapping in the wind: *Superheroes not Welcome*, they read.

"This city really is sick of you. Sick of your antics, sick of your games, sick of being embarrassed," Rex Velvet intoned. "The people are taking action against the Rain City Super Zero Movement..."

So, as I had been getting on so well with Phoenix and Purple, I decided it was a good time to ask them about Rex Velvet.

'I've heard about some guy,' I said. 'He's kind of an anti-hero. Rex Velvet?'

Phoenix and Purple fell silent and the atmosphere quickly turned icy. I immediately regretted bringing him up, but continued to casually chomp down on my steak (which was delicious, by the way). They stared at me for a moment, with a look that questioned how I had heard about Rex Velvet – but this then changed to one of resignation, as if it was only a matter of time before I brought him up.

'He's like a video productions guy,' Purple told me. 'He's trying to steal some thunder and make some money. Then he came out with a vodka brand or something like that.'

This was true. Rex Velvet had released a vodka brand, and it seemed his attacks of the superheroes was one way of promoting it.

'You're not a fan then?'

'No,' Phoenix said. 'I don't like that kind of tomfoolery. If you're going to market yourself, market good deeds, don't market being an asshole. The world has enough assholes.'

We spoke a bit more about Rex Velvet, but it was clear that Phoenix and Purple didn't want to discuss him. It wasn't because of any dark, uncomfortable reason, but simply because they didn't want to give Rex Velvet any extra publicity. As far as they were concerned, Rex Velvet was using them – and trying to make fools of them – simply as a way to sell his vodka.

Though I hadn't seen Purple out on patrol for some time, she had continued to keep herself busy as an active member of the Rain City Superheroes by checking the Seattle police crime maps, working out where best to patrol and looking for trends in criminality. She had also been working hard with her own projects, particularly the domestic violence work with which she was involved. In fact, she had some good news to share. I was aware that part of Purple's motivations, with regards to her superhero alter ego, was to do with her fight against domestic violence and the protection of abused women. This purpose and hard work had now been recognised. She had received an award by the University of Washington for her domestic violence work and fund raising (which had resulted in thousands of dollars worth of donations for domestic violence charities). She showed me the framed certificate and "Women of

Courage" satin sash with which she had been presented. The sash was, rather appropriately, coloured purple.

I was pleased that Purple had been recognised in this way. I was fascinated by what Phoenix and the other superheroes were doing, with their late-night street patrols and crime fighting, but there had always been something more – something deeper – with Purple Reign. She had found a way of using the superhero movement to push forward a message that was not only extremely important, but also very personal. I didn't quite know how personal – but I was soon to find out.

However, there was also some friction between the superhero couple tonight. I had noticed some images of Purple that had appeared online. In them she was not wearing her mask, and her face was now fully exposed. For Purple Reign, there was no more hiding behind a scarf. Phoenix wasn't at all happy about it.

'There's no reason to take your mask off in public,' Phoenix told her. Then, turning to me, he said, 'No matter what she tells me, there's just no reason. It's illogical.'

'Whereas I think it goes against my cause completely if I do wear it,' Purple countered. 'I feel like I'm helping more women by taking my mask off. Wearing a mask – having my mouth covered up – goes against everything my campaign stands for.'

I had to agree with her. It seemed hypocritical to be telling women to speak out when, at the same time, you were covering up and hiding who you were. Perhaps unwisely, I told Phoenix that I was in agreement with Purple and wondered if he could see her point.

'No, I don't,' he said. 'I can understand why Purple doesn't want her mouth covered up – after all, my mouth isn't covered – but then get a different mask. The rest of her face should be covered.'

'It's just the symbol of the mask in general,' Purple continued.

'That's not negotiable. You're wrong,' Phoenix told her. 'But you can do whatever you want. Listen, when it comes to outfit choices, I don't even talk to you about it. I don't tell you what to wear.' He turned to me again. 'She doesn't understand how an outfit works. You brand the idea of the outfit. When I show up, people say, "That's Phoenix Jones", because of my outfit. Sometimes people don't even believe it's the real me. They'll argue, "No, Phoenix Jones is way taller", or "Phoenix Jones is way buffer", or "I saw Phoenix Jones kill ten people". It's because the outfit is bigger than the person underneath. That's the point. But Purple changes her outfit all the time.'

'I'm a girl,' she said. 'Girls do that.'

'It's dumb,' Phoenix said, but then quickly added, 'But the work she does is really cool. I stand by that. She stands by me doing the crazy stuff I do on the streets, so I'll stand by her taking her mask off if she wants to. I just personally know it's a bad choice. There's right and there's wrong. It's wrong.'

'It seems to me you have to think about what's more important to you – the crime fighting or the domestic violence work,' I told Purple. 'But I agree, you can't fight for domestic violence victims and stay covered up yourself.'

'Exactly,' Purple answered.

Phoenix got up from the table and walked into the lounge. I wondered if I had overstepped the mark. I was a guest in their home, after all.

'Are you walking out because you're pissed off with me?' I asked him.

Phoenix walked back into the room, holding a small pot of salt. 'If I'm mad, I'll tell you. I can just see that two people are agreeing on a bad decision, that's all that's happening here right now.'

I wanted to speak to Purple about her own experiences. I had known, from our first meeting at the coffee shop in the University District, that she had been a survivor of domestic violence herself, but I had never felt comfortable enough to probe her about it. I had gotten to know Phoenix and Purple well enough for some of that discomfort to disappear, so I asked Purple if she would be happy to talk to me about her past. It was, after all, partly the reason she had become *Purple Reign*.

'Not in front of me,' Phoenix said. 'I hate this story. I hate hearing it. It makes me mad. If you want to tell him, fine – but I'll be in the other room.'

As Phoneix left the room again, Purple poured me a glass of wine, and soon she was preparing to tell me about her history.

'I was married previously but got divorced when my son was just a baby,' she started, quietly. 'Then when my son was about two years old, I met this guy. We were only together for a year or so but it escalated quickly and got to a bad place.'

'What do you mean, *bad place?*' I asked.

Purple shuffled in her seat and pulled her knees up to her chest, wrapping them with her arms. She looked like a little girl who had something terrible to share but didn't know whether she should. I knew I was pushing her into talking about her past, but that was partly why I was here tonight. Then, after a moment, she looked up and the expression on her face changed. The anxiety started to fall away and Purple Reign, the tough, determined superhero, appeared. Her knees, however, remained where they were.

'I have a woman's intuition and I trust my instincts,' she said. 'Generally I'm right-on about stuff when I meet people. Well, when I first met this guy, I got a certain vibe. Not a good one, though. I did not like him. There was something a little bit creepy there and he turned me off the wrong way. He'd ask me out and I'd turn him down. I didn't want anything to do with him. But he pursued me over the course of a couple of months and then he got his friends to talk to me and tell me what a nice guy he was. Then I ended up hearing about his whole life story – his mum had died of cancer, his dad abused him and beat up his brother – all these really sad stories, which touched me. I'm a sensitive person and it made me start to feel sorry for him. I ended up being around him more and more. Then there was one mutual friend of ours in particular who would email with me – she was a friend of his who had moved to New York, so I never actually met her in person, but I open up easier with women in general. Men always make me a little bit nervous. Anyway, we emailed all the time and she was always telling me what a great guy he was, and that he was just misunderstood. So finally I was like, "Okay, I will go on a date with him." And then from there we started dating.

'Almost immediately he had some problems with his roommates, so I'm like, "Just come live with me." And as soon as he moved in, it became like every other typical DV [Domestic Violence] situation. It started with the controlling – he wanted to know where I went, who I went there with, what time I came home. And he was always putting me down. I want to say I'm generally a confident person and that I feel pretty good about myself – but I became super, super insecure. I was afraid to leave him because he told me how worthless I was and how no one else would want me. He was so manipulative that I just started believing everything he said. He would get so angry, spitting red in the face. But he didn't touch me for the longest time – it was all emotional and psychological. Then I ended up turning his computer on and his Facebook account was still open. It was logged onto that girl's account – our mutual friend in New York.'

I looked at Purple, not quite understanding what she was telling me.

'*He* was that girl,' she said. 'It was him, pretending from the very beginning. He'd been manipulating me. Who even knows if his stories were true? I tried confronting him about it but he denied it. He accused me of being the one who was lying and tried to turn everything around on me. I ended up going out with a couple of friends and told him I'd be home by 10 o'clock. But, when 10 o'clock came around, I still didn't want to go home. I stayed out later and the whole time he's calling me and freaking out, saying that he's going to come after me. Finally, at the end of the night, I came home and snuck into my room and locked the door because he was sleeping on the couch. Then he came to the room, pounding on the door. I told him to go away or I'd call the police. I'd never threatened to call the police before and part of that was because he was a convicted felon – another thing I didn't know at the beginning. He'd been arrested for theft – embezzling money – something really big. He told me that he would kill me if I went to the police, and I believed him. But I held my ground, even though I was so scared. I got on the phone to call the police, but then he busted the door down – and he was a big guy, a football player type of guy. He came in and I tried to sneak behind him but he took my phone and threw it and... like... the whole attack happened.'

Purple's voice had become stalled. Each new word was being released more slowly from her lips as she recalled what had happened. In the lounge, Phoenix had turned the volume up on the TV.

'He tried to kill me,' she said quietly. 'He strangled me, beat my head down, you know... it...' She took a breath and continued. 'It reached the point where I thought I wouldn't survive. I thought my life was over and I gave up fighting. I'd tried to fight back but he was so big and overpowering that there was nothing I could have done. It was only when I gave up fighting that he finally stopped hurting me. He just left me there. Just got up and walked away. I think he went outside and smoked a cigarette. But I was so afraid, I didn't leave, I didn't call the police – and, besides, my phone was busted anyway because he'd thrown it against the wall. I crawled into my bed and cried all night long. I didn't tell anybody about it. But my friends saw the strangle marks on my neck, the busted lip and the bruises. They said, "We know what's going on." They told me I had to leave and said I couldn't bring my son up around that – *what if he does this to him?* That's when I finally realised that I couldn't do this anymore. I had friends come over as mediators and they made him leave. He moved out and then I went to court and got a restraining order. We broke my lease and I moved here, where it's safe. And I've been here ever since. I saw him at court and he tried lying, telling the judge that I liked getting beat up. Saying the craziest things and, of course, that freaked me out. My anxiety got worse but the judge totally granted me what I asked for.'

I felt terrible. I had come over and asked Purple to tell me about these awful events from her past. She was upset. Phoenix was upset. I was upset. But Purple assured me that she was happy to talk about these things. From it she had managed to find a new life and purpose.

Soon after moving away from her ex, she met Phoenix and found that there was a way to channel her hurt, by becoming Purple Reign. From there she moved into assisting other victims of domestic violence, becoming more involved in helping women. And here she was now, winning awards and being – perhaps literally – a lifeline to others facing similar situations to the one she herself had endured.

'Bruises take weeks to heal,' she told me. 'But emotional damage can take years. It's easier to talk about now. It's not something that I can stay quiet about. So my goal is to help other women. Most women don't know that there is help and resources out there for them.

'When people ask me about it, I used to get really nervous – I still do get uncomfortable – but, if what I have to say can help somebody else realise that what they're going through is definitely not healthy and normal, that's a good thing; because I thought everybody was in relationships like that. I thought my parents were the one perfect couple. But all the relationships that I was in growing up, the guys were not that nice, they were mean, they put me down, sometimes they were physically rough – and I thought that was just how it is. But when I started talking to friends, they told me that it wasn't normal, that's not how a relationship should be. Phoenix is the first person I've ever been with who hasn't touched me. Never yelled at me. Never called me a name. Never put me down. It's a perfectly normal, healthy relationship, whereas I thought everything I had experienced before was normal.'

Purple trained to become an advocate and, after she met

Phoenix, she started to wonder what it would be like to take on a costumed activists approach as a way of bringing more attention to the domestic violence cause.

'I was supporting Phoenix fighting crime out on the streets, and I thought about my own cause – domestic violence. So I combined them. That's when Purple Reign really came into her own. But the crime fighting and the advocacy work started out separately. They were each going strong and then I brought them together.'

On the streets, the dangers were clear, but I wondered about the domestic violence side of Purple's activism. Getting involved with angry spouses and partners carried its own risks. I asked her about the negative side of her cause.

'The negative? Well, I've helped a lot of women, but there was only one time where this woman's husband contacted me. He was really angry. He made some threats against me. I don't have a place of business or an office, so no one knows how to find me here. The most they can do is send me an angry email, unless they get my phone number from their wife. But I talk to them about such things as deleting their browser history, not giving out my number, and we'll make a safety plan and get them out of their houses without their husbands or boyfriends knowing who helped them.

'But this one time it slipped through and this guy sent me all sorts of angry messages. "Mind your own business. Don't stick your nose in, this is family issues between husband and wife", that kind of thing. It was actually more threatening towards the wife, trying to make me feel like I needed to stay out of it or else he was going to hurt her more. But actually, making threats like that is only going to get me more involved. Plus, now we have written notes and emails to show the police to prove that he's hurting her. So that actually helped our case.'

Purple was less forthcoming with the positives and her own achievements – not because she hadn't had any, but because her view was that it was the women themselves who had achieved something, by being brave enough to take those steps in the first place; Purple had simply been there to help them along. She had, of course, been more than just a sounding board, but Purple seemed almost as uncomfortable about taking credit as she was talking about her own, dark past.

'It's hard to say what I've achieved. I've got some women who email every day, checking in with me and letting me know where they're at with the progress of leaving their relationship, building their safety plan and building up their resources. Other times it's helping them get funds or getting connected. There are so many different levels, so I can't really talk about what I've accomplished. Some will tell me that I've saved their lives or tell me that they left their man because they'd heard my story. So I know that I've helped people – but I feel more uncomfortable talking about that because I don't feel like I've... I don't know... that's not something I can take credit for. That's them, finally getting the courage to stand up and walk away. Maybe I helped inspire them to do that or gave them the resources to do that but... I don't know... that's just part of my duty.'

'Do you think the character "Purple Reign", is helping?'

'All this work is done as Purple. It's easier for me to do it as Purple than it is to do it as myself. I think I feel braver as Purple and I think people respect me a little bit more, or listen to me more. Part of it is the costume, the attention that it brings and the awareness that it raises. The costume gives me confidence. It definitely makes a difference. Doing this as myself, I don't think I would have been as successful. I wouldn't have been able to get so many businesses to come together and donate funds for the shelters or donate items and supplies. Before Purple, it was just me as an advocate – someone on the phone. People call in, you help them, you give them advice. But as Purple Reign, I feel like I've been able to build something – a place women know they can come to. The anonymity helps. I'm a character, a persona; I'm not the police and I'm not a friend or a family member. I think, as a victim, you feel safer going to an anonymous person and calling anonymous hotlines. But, at the same time, I still have a face, and a personal story for them to feel connected to. Before Purple, I was used to people not paying attention to my cause and what I was doing. People were more drawn to Phoenix and the whole big superhero thing. But now I also have an audience. I'm no longer that victim. I'm Purple Reign.'

10

Hero to Zero

A few nights later, Phoenix picked me up from my hotel, downtown. Midnight Jack was already sitting in the front passenger seat, so I jumped in the back.

Jack had begun to accompany Phoenix more and more, feeling a sense of loyalty towards him that had extended to a kind of responsibility.

'If I'm not around to save him, he tends to get hurt.'

'That's true,' Phoenix agreed. 'Jack's saved my ass more than once.'

Neither of them was wearing their superhero outfits. When I asked why, Phoenix told me that tonight we were going to be doing a stakeout.

'An actual stakeout?' I asked. 'For what?'

'People breaking into cars,' he told me.

'I'd rather do a regular patrol but he's the boss,' Jack said, waving a thumb at Phoenix.

I asked Midnight Jack how he felt about Phoenix being the leader of the Rain City Superheroes; even though Phoenix was in the car, I figured it wouldn't sway Midnight Jack from saying exactly what he thought.

'Well, he hasn't fucked me over too bad, yet,' Jack answered. Phoenix and I laughed, but Jack was being semi-serious. He continued, 'If anyone else were to lead this shit – let's say, El Caballero – I would probably quit.'

Phoenix then became quiet, wanting to hear what Jack had to say.

'Why would you quit?' I asked.

'Because you have to do things in a certain way. What we do is a combination of a few things. Being a superhero is a little bit of theatrics, a little bit of police procedure and a little bit of tactical, black-ops, commando style shit. You've got to get all three of those things together in the right way, because if you don't, it falls apart. Cabbie would want to run this like it's a fucking democracy. But you can't do it like that; you can't spend fifteen minutes letting everyone have their say, while people are out there getting hurt. Phoenix will tell everyone: *This is your job, that's your job and this is your damn job*. That's how it is and that's how you gotta do it.'

Phoenix seemed pleased with Midnight Jack's opinion and I noticed him lean back into his driver's seat, feeling more relaxed.

But Jack wasn't finished. 'His communication skills suck, however.'

'Thanks,' Phoenix said, leaning back up.

'He's also late everywhere he fucking goes. But I'll take that over some of the other options that are presented to me.'

We were driving down the I-5, towards the city. I mentioned that I had heard that Phoenix had fired superheroes in the past. The reasons ranged from disagreeing with him about the way he ran the team, to choices of weaponry.

Midnight Jack nodded his head, enthusiastically. He was particularly keen to bring up a previous Rain City superhero called "Mantis".

'Man, you were telling me how this guy was gonna be so awesome,' Jack said to Phoenix. 'You told me that he was super-capable. Wrong!'

'Okay, it's true. That was one of the biggest mistakes I've made in my super-career,' Phoenix agreed. 'He was a good martial artist though.'

'No he was not! He was a pussy, bro! He's the biggest pussy I ever met in my entire life. He once ran into a regular fistfight and said, "I don't know what to do! I'm terrified!"'

Phoenix nodded his head. 'Yeah, that's true.'

Mantis's choice of super-weapons also left a lot to be desired, it seemed.

'Forks,' Phoenix told me. 'He tried throwing forks at people.'

I stared at Phoenix for a moment. 'Forks? Like, dinner forks?'

'Yeah. They were sharpened forks, but regardless, it was still forks. He also tried throwing spoons. The spoons were really funny.'

Midnight Jack was laughing as I tried to imagine a guy in a green mantis costume chucking sharpened table cutlery at people. Jack told me that Mantis also smoked "immense amounts of marijuana" before each patrol.

'Mantis did some dumb stuff,' Phoenix agreed. 'We eventually fired him because his drug habit got out of control and he pawned a bunch of our bulletproof vests and equipment to go pay for drugs. Then, on top of that, he once told me that he'd ripped out someone's heart. I was like, *seriously?* But then he told me, "Okay, I was just kidding. I've never done that. But I do have the skills!"'

But Mantis, with his Temple of Doom fist and sharpened forks, was nothing in comparison to another superhero Phoenix had once had on his team. Midnight Jack was practically fitting at the mention of the next guy as Phoenix started to tell me the sorry tale.

'So we had this guy show up called *Platypus*, who's telling me all about his skills. He's like, "I've got my fists, I've got my hands, I've got my knees and I've got my secret weapon." Obviously we're like, "What's your secret weapon?" He says, "I've got these special balloons, man. These *toxic* balloons!"'

'Balloons?' I asked. 'Like, party balloons?'

'Yeah. And we're looking at him and say, "Well, what's in the balloons?" He says, "I'd prefer not to say, man. It's a secret. It's my secret duck recipe." We're like, "No, man. Listen, we need to know. Seriously, what's in the balloons?" He says, "All right. I'm gonna tell you. It's dehydrated urine."'

Once again, I stared at Phoenix. Midnight Jack was cracking up.

'Now, at that time, I also had a guy on my team called *Mist*. Mist didn't play around. He was a six-foot-six, two-hundred-and-eighty pound, former pro-wrestling black dude. Mist takes one look at Platypus and goes, "You sick motherfucker. We should kill this motherfucker." And all of a sudden, this duck-billed guy rips his facemask off and goes, "Come on man. Do you know how hard it was to pee into all those balloons?" Needless to say, he didn't make the team.'

These former superheroes sounded nuts. Balloons filled with dehydrated urine? Sharpened forks? But then, what made Phoenix Jones, Midnight Jack and the rest of them any different, with their pepper-sprays and blackjacks?

'But you still have to be a bit crazy to do this, right?' I said. 'To dress up in a superhero costume, give yourself a superhero name and patrol the streets?'

'Yeah,' Midnight Jack said.

Phoenix laughed gently. 'It's hard for me to lie to you and tell you that some of my guys weren't insane.'

'We're doing a crazy thing in a not very crazy way,' Midnight Jack added.

'My crew are the most sane crew of all the superheroes that you'll find,' Phoenix said.

'There are people who will actually think they have superpowers,' Jack added. 'I once had someone on the Internet, who called himself *The Superboy*. He told me I was a coward for wearing a bulletproof vest. He claimed he had superpowers and bullets would bounce off him. This guy's insane and he's going to die, thinking like that. Bullets don't bounce off anybody – they don't even bounce off Kevlar; they get stuck *in* Kevlar. I'm not cowardly for wearing a bulletproof vest – I just want to live!'

'But you have to agree that this – being a superhero – isn't a normal thing to do, right?' I said.

'This is *absolutely* not normal,' Midnight Jack agreed. 'This is some weird shit, bro. Listen, in a world where you have guys dressing up like superheroes and effectively fighting crime – not *saying* that they fight crime but *actually* fighting crime – something is broken with the system.'

'I agree with that statement completely,' Phoenix said.

'What's the broken thing?' I asked.

'We don't know!' Midnight Jack said. 'When we have it figured out, maybe we won't have to dress up like Batman and Spiderman and fight crime, anymore.'

Despite the rain that had begun to fall, Phoenix wound down the window on Midnight Jack's side of the car. Jack looked to his right, staring at the rain that was coming through his window and landing in his suit. Then he turned to face Phoenix.

'Really?' he asked.

'I don't like you, man,' Phoenix joked. 'Out of all of my friends, I hate you the most!'

'Dude, the only thing you need is a pair of aviator sunglasses to go with that Tom Cruise attitude of yours,' Jack told him. Then he leant over the back seat to grab his pepper-spray canister.

'Dude, you reach for your pepper and I'll go for my Phazzer. And I'll win,' Phoenix told him, laughing.

The talk of weapons made me wonder if Phoenix or Jack had ever considered carrying something a little more deadly than pepper-spray and a taser. I wondered if they had ever considered carrying a gun, like Superhero.

'No superhero should be carrying a gun, in my opinion,' Jack said. 'But if you decide that you're going to have guns, then you need to have firearms procedures in place. As far as I'm concerned, that's not what the superhero movement should be about. We made a decision in the RCSM: no guns.'

'I made that decision, Jack,' Phoenix interjected.

'Well, there was a little discussion,' Jack said, shrugging his shoulders.

Phoenix turned to me. 'We got into a big argument over guns,' he said.

'It was over less-lethal munitions, not firearms. Thank you very much,' Jack said, correcting Phoenix.

'You wanted to carry a shotgun with riot-bags in it!'

'Correct. That's what I wanted to carry.'

'And the answer was no. And it's still no!'

'Would anything make you reconsider carrying guns?' I asked.

'No. Absolutely not. Not with the experience I have now,' Jack said. 'I've handled pretty much everything I can run into, including active shooter situations, without a firearm. I don't see why I would need one.'

'Firearms really inhibit my ability to make clear decisions,' Phoenix said.

'Do you think that could be true for the police, also?' I asked.

'I think the difference is what types of crime we fight and what's legal for a civilian,' Phoenix said. 'If we had the same legality as a police officer, I think a gun would make more sense. But then, ethically, I'm not about killing people. I don't think the theft of a purse is worth killing someone for.'

'Not to mention, we don't do the same job as the police,' Jack added. 'Plus, we get to choose what we deal with; the police don't have that choice. The police have to respond to a lot of crazy shit.'

'But don't you deal with a lot of crazy shit too?'

'Sure, but the thing is, a lot of people look at us and think we do what the police do. But no, we don't. We do a very different job. We're just a buffer between people and law enforcement. We handle bar fights and all that and keep a situation calm so the police don't have to work as hard. I tell people to think of us as being like bouncers for the entire city.'

'But I do have a problem with the way the police use their weapons,' Phoenix said. 'There are a lot of unjustified police shootings. A lot. The other day, they shot a guy just up the street from my house. The guy was swinging around a crowbar and he hit a cop with it. The cop opened fire and shot him nine times.'

'Yeah,' Jack said, 'that's unnecessary.'

'When you've got four guys with you as back up, if you can't take down a guy with a crowbar, you shouldn't be a cop. If a guy comes at me with a crowbar, I'm just going to laugh at that shit.'

Jack looked at Phoenix and shook his head. 'You're not going to laugh about a crowbar,' he said, challenging Phoenix's remark.

'The last time someone came at me with a crowbar, I laughed.'

'Well, you might just be crazy then. I'm telling you, right now, as far as improvised street weapons go, it doesn't get much better than a crowbar,' Jack said. 'Personally, I'm partial to a rubber mallet, especially when it comes to home defence.'

Phoenix and Jack were suddenly off, having a whole new conversation.

'I've got a meat tenderiser at home,' Phoenix said.

'A meat tenderiser is good if you're really trying to be nasty,' Jack concurred. 'But a rubber mallet is good for home defence for two reasons. Number one: it really hurts and it will take the teeth out of your mouth. Number two: it's really hard to kill somebody with a rubber mallet. After all, it's rubber! So you can knock somebody unconscious very easily, but you're not going to kill them – most of the time, anyway. That being said, I wouldn't carry one out here. Here I've got other options. I'm actually not even pro-baton any more.'

'Batons are garbage,' Phoenix said.

'I have a lot more confidence in me now,' Jack continued. 'I had no formal fight training, so in the past I just went straight for a weapon, such as a nightstick – the great American equaliser! When you pull a baton, you send one message and one message only. You're saying: *come get you some!* But you don't want to send "come get you some" as a message all the time.'

'Well, sometimes you do,' Phoenix said.

'There are lots of things I thought were awesome that stopped being awesome very quickly – like smoke grenades,' Jack continued. 'When I first started doing this, I thought, "I know, I'll get some smoke grenades and throw them down before I go into situations." No – it's actually dispersing a chemical agent into a crowd and causing a panic. It's a crime. So you can't do that.'

139

'I see. Anything else?' I asked.

'Bat-a-rang type things. I'd have little bits of shit that'd I'd throw at people. That stopped being cool real quick after Phoenix told me how he broke two car windows and had to pay for them.'

'For your information, they weren't bat-a-rangs; they were hockey pucks that had my phoenix symbol on them,' Phoenix said.

'Grappling hooks,' Jack said, after thinking a little more.

'Yeah. That's how I got arrested for trespassing,' Phoenix said. 'Technically I was "detained", but still, grappling hooks are no good in real life.'

'Basically, there's just a bunch of stuff that looks cool in comic books that's not cool in reality,' Jack told me. 'Really, all you need is a bulletproof vest, a mask and a can of pepper-spray. That will see you through most situations.'

'I'm gonna pull over here,' Phoenix said.

'Why? You see something?' Jack asked.

'No, but we're running early for the stakeout, so we may as take a walk and kill some time.'

Phoenix pulled over in a dark, quiet street, lined with short trees and small, independent businesses. As soon as he and Midnight Jack had pulled on their masks, we stepped out of the car

'Hey, you want some ganja?' a slim black man immediately asked.

'It's legal in this state,' Phoenix told me, seeing my expression.

'We once had a guy ask us if we wanted to buy some crack,' Jack told me. 'And we were dressed in our full outfits at the time! This dude comes up to us with a handful of crack and goes, "I've got your superpower right here, man!"'

We reached a street corner, and Phoenix stopped dead.

'Is everything alright?' I asked.

He pointed at a black sports car with dark, tinted windows. The driver's door was open and three men – two black, one white – were standing next to it, in conversation. The group looked odd, like they had just come from another place altogether; they simply didn't fit.

The white guy was wearing a bright green St Patrick's Day t-shirt, even though St Patrick's Day was still several days away. He looked towards us and then leant down to speak to the driver of the car. The other men now looked over at us. My *Spidey senses* began to tingle; something wasn't right.

'They could be muggers,' Phoenix said, sounding hopeful.

'More likely they're dealing drugs,' Jack suggested. 'They're probably cutting up crack in the car.'

The white guy walked away, towards a fast food place. The two black men also walked away but in a different direction. The driver's door was slammed shut but the driver remaining inside and hidden behind the tinted glass.

'The white guy had a knife in his front pocket,' Phoenix said.

I hadn't noticed anything. 'How did you see that?'

'Because I see everything. Do you want to go check him out?'

'The guy with the knife?'

'Yeah.'

'No.'

'I think we should,' Jack said.

'Why?' I asked.

'Because I'm offended by his shirt.'

'His shirt?'

'You didn't see his shirt? It had a leprechaun throwing-up in a bucket.'

'That's what you're offended by? What about the bloody knife!'

Walking straight up to a man suspected of being either a mugger or a drug dealer, who Phoenix believed to be armed with a knife, seemed like a very poor idea indeed, but Phoenix and Jack were already striding towards him. I quickly ran over to join them.

The guy had come to a stop on a street corner, folding his arms as he watched us approach. I looked to see if Phoenix had drawn his Phazzer, but he hadn't. Jack did have one hand placed on his pepper-spray canister, however.

'What's up?' he guy asked, casually.

'Not much,' Phoenix replied. 'Seems quiet tonight.'

'You're those superhero dudes, right? Felix Jones?'

'*Phoenix* Jones.'

'Phoenix. Right.'

The guy lit a cigarette and stared at us. Phoenix and Jack stood next to him, showing no intention of moving away from this spot. For a moment, there was a silent standoff.

'Is it just the three of you out tonight?' he asked.

'Nope,' Phoenix said. 'There are four teams out tonight in different parts of the city. Some of the teams are in regular clothing, undercover.'

This was a blatant lie, but it was obvious why Phoenix had said it.

Then the guy flicked his barely-smoked cigarette onto the ground and reached into his pocket. Phoenix's hand dropped down, towards his Phazzer. But the guy was only pulling out an iPhone.

'Can I take a picture of you guys?' he asked.

'Sure,' Phoenix replied.

After taking a photo of Phoenix and Jack, he walked away, back towards the car. He stepped into it and the car was driven away with an aggressive roar.

'He was feeling us out,' Jack said. 'He took our photograph to send to the rest of his homeys. That picture will be sent to the phones of all the other shit-bags in the area, letting them know that we're out here and what we look like.'

'That's why I told him we were eight deep with four teams,' Phoenix added. 'It might make them think twice before attacking us.'

The black guys, who had previously been standing by the car, now appeared on the opposite side of the road. One of them looked down at the screen on his phone, then back up at us.

'What are we going to do?' I asked.

'We're gonna go stand where they're standing,' Phoenix said.

And that's what we did. But as soon as we approached them, the two men walked away, towards a parking lot.

'What the hell was that about?' I asked.

'They're just clearing the block,' Jack told me. 'They're here to make sure we leave. They won't have gone far.'

'I imagine it's moments like this that you're glad you're wearing a mask,' I said.

'My secret identity was cool in the beginning,' Jack said. 'But when it starts to hinder your effectiveness, that's when you've really got to ask yourself if being mysterious is really more important than a legal conviction or making an arrest. Is the mask and secret identity more important than saving a life?'

Though the attraction of this line of work for many was the actual superhero part, for Jack it had evolved into something more. It was clear that Jack considered all this to be a genuine service to the community.

'I refer to myself now as a "professional crime interventionist",' Jack continued. 'That's what I do – I professionally intervene in crime. I'm trained, I'm extremely professional and I just happen to dress like a superhero. But the superhero part of all this is really the last part that matters.'

'The superhero part matters,' Phoenix said, sounding irritated. 'That's how we're identified. Without it, we're just regular citizens on the sidewalk. For the same reason police wear a uniform, we wear superhero outfits.'

Jack shrugged.

We remained for a while on the street corner. From it we had a good view up and down the street, as well as the nearby parking lot. Then, a moment later, we heard the growl of an engine. The car with the tinted windows was back. It drove slowly through the parking lot and out onto the street we were standing on, eventually coming to a stop opposite us. The windows were rolled up and it was impossible to see into the car. Then the car continued slowly down the road.

'Still checking up on us,' Phoenix said.

'If they come back, we should step behind a wall,' Jack said. 'I don't want to be a victim of a drive-by, tonight. I've got some TV shows I need to watch.'

The car came to a halt at a red stop signal a little further along the street. Then it pulled a U-turn and headed back towards us, fast.

Shit.

'Okay, get behind the wall,' Phoenix ordered.

The car roared at high speed along the street, heading directly at us. As we scrabbled to duck behind a concrete wall, I noticed that the front passenger window had been brought down. Jack's words – "*drive-by*" – rang around my head.

'Get down!' I heard Phoenix say.

Instinctively, I ducked down. Then I heard the sound of the car screeching to a halt, just feet from our wall. Moments later came the sound of wheels spinning and an engine screaming. The car roared away, out of sight.

We stepped back out and stood in a tight trio for a few moments, looking up the street, but there were no more cars, no more people; just the quickly disappearing grey fog of car fumes and the smell of burnt rubber.

'We need to get going,' Phoenix said, whipping off his mask.

Jumping back into his car, we continued on, each of us feeling relieved that nothing serious had come from the men or the car.

'So where are we doing the stakeout?' I asked.

'Capitol Hill,' Jack told me.

'Oh, I've been in that area,' I said, cheerily. 'Apart from the police-hating anarchists, it seemed quite nice.'

'Nice?' Jack said. 'Capitol Hill is enemy territory...'

Capitol Hill was the area where I had first encountered the Rain City Superheroes, at the demo. Despite that, it had seemed to me like an otherwise pleasant neighbourhood. It was full of students, funky bars, burger joints and bookstores. It was just a short, uphill walk, east of downtown and Pike Place Market, and I had previously spent an enjoyable day hanging out in its bohemian coffee houses.

'We believe that the Black Bloc have their headquarters up there,' Phoenix told me. 'And, as you may know, we don't exactly get on.'

'Have you seen the May Day footage?' Jack asked. 'It's those fuckers in Capitol Hill – that's where they hang out.'

I had seen the May Day footage, online, and it explained why Phoenix and Jack considered Capitol Hill to be "enemy territory".

What had started out as a regular Seattle protest against globalisation had quickly turned into a riot after the Black Bloc had arrived. Stores and buildings were attacked as the police struggled to contain the violence, and in amongst it all were three superheroes – Phoenix Jones, Midnight Jack and El Caballero.

'We were lucky to come out of there alive,' Jack told me, shaking his head. 'We got hit with rocks and sticks and everything.'

'And you were wearing your outfits, right?' I asked.

'Yeah. There were statements released saying that the Black Bloc was going to break windows and assault police officers. Well, we felt that we couldn't justify not being there. So me, Phoenix and El Caballero took the day off work and went down. There should have been more of us, but everyone else cancelled at the last minute. But we go and it starts off calm and peaceful – everybody was standing around singing *Kum Ba Yah*. It was like that until the march started.'

It was then that the Black Bloc showed up, wearing black clothing, black masks and carrying poles and flags. Jack estimated that there were around seventy-five of them. As soon as they arrived, the atmosphere changed. As the superheroes walked along with the protestors, they began to notice paint that had been thrown at buildings and businesses. But it was when they reached the courthouse on 6th Ave that things really started to come unstuck.

Some of the most striking footage from that day, footage that made the news, was of the superheroes standing outside that courthouse, attempting to protect it from protestors and anarchists armed with sticks and poles. Most of the glass in the courthouse doors had already been smashed.

'Glass was torn out of the entire building,' Jack told me. 'If there was a window, it was a broken window. So we ran across the street and stood there. The flagpoles the anarchists carried were actually filled with concrete. They were using the poles to bash out the windows. The second we intervened, it was a battle. They started attacking us with rocks. Phoenix took the worst. But it started getting really scary when I saw them throwing hammers. That kind of made it real. Then I heard a popping sound, followed by smoke and fire.'

As a large smoke bomb billowed behind them, Midnight Jack and Phoenix Jones held their ground, arms raised, defensively spraying anyone who came too close, with a generous blast of pepper-spray. El Caballero was lost somewhere in amongst the crowd.

'Then they threw something like a pepper-powder bomb,' Jack told me. 'They were throwing these ghetto teargas grenades at us. At that point, I stopped playing. I had been separated from Phoenix, so I just started spraying people. Anybody who stepped up to me with a weapon got sprayed.'

People screamed and shouted at them, wishing nothing but harm against the superheroes. But, somehow, Phoenix and Jack managed to hold the mob at bay.

'I was just trying to keep them away from the building,' Jack continued. 'There were innocent people inside and the protestors were trying to throw teargas and explosive devices into it. But we were not going to let that happen.'

I could tell that the incident had had a real effect on Jack. The video showed him and Phoenix standing alone, fighting off dozens of protestors. They were terrifyingly outnumbered and in very real danger. As a police officer, I've fought in riots, so I know that feeling. It's anyone's guess how the incident would have played out had it remained that way, but then a cop joined Phoenix and Jack.

'This Homeland Security officer shows up in a damn hurry,' Jack said. 'He showed up wearing riot armour and carrying a shotgun and he stood next to us. At that point, the riot was over; or at least that part of the riot – the protestors moved on to Niketown and did some more damage there, sparring with police for the rest of the day. But that was the end of our part. We were fortunate to come out of there with only a bruised media image. It was a very strange day.'

Jack fell silent, thinking over the incident in his head, perhaps considering what might have happened, because the truth is that a mob of people, caught up in such a frenzy, can quickly lose all sense of right and wrong. As well as the mob itself, there were the incendiary devices and explosives. Phoenix and Jack could very easily have been killed.

'What a lot of people don't know is that I couldn't think clearly after that,' Jack told me. 'I was pretty compromised, emotionally. I was very, very distressed.' Jack stopped speaking for a moment and shook his head. 'We got home and I thought that was going to be the end of it,' he continued. 'And then I watched it on the news – and they showed some of the weapons that had been confiscated. The flagpoles had razor wire wrapped around them and razorblades lined up the sides. The ends of the poles had been sharpened to points. And these were the same poles that they had been charging us with and swinging at me and Phoenix. That made it really scary. It was two weeks before I was cool to talk to anybody. I was angry that I'd been put in that situation. Even though I'd agreed to it, I was still mad.'

'At one point we were facing sixty anarchists,' Phoenix said. 'There was stuff on fire, people throwing rocks. It was intense. We couldn't leave even if we wanted to, so we had to just stand there and defend the building.'

'What happened to Cabbie during all this?' I asked.

'He was there too,' Phoenix said. 'But we lost him as we were fighting outside the courthouse. You'll have to ask him about it.'

Whether it had been wise to get involved or not – and I felt firmly *not* – once again they had been there, actually doing what they claimed they did. They weren't pretending. But still, it had taken a toll, and we sat in reflective silence for a while, two American superheroes and an Englishman.

'So, anyway, there's been some car crime in Capitol Hill,' Phoenix said, breaking the gloom. 'Muggings, too.'

'The best place to mug someone, is Freeway Park,' Jack said. 'Not only is that where I would mug people, it's where I *have* mugged people.'

I stared at Midnight Jack's reflection in the rear-view mirror. 'What do you mean?' I asked.

'What do you mean, *what do I mean*? I mugged people in Freeway Park.'

'What?'

'I robbed people to pay for my drugs.'

'*What?*'

Everything I thought I knew about Midnight Jack changed at that moment. Suddenly, just like that, he didn't seem so funny.

11

The Legend of Midnight Jack

Midnight Jack was the most unlikely of superheroes, and under no circumstances should his destiny have been to become one. He was, in fact, a former criminal. He had been a drug dealer, drug addict, robber and a general nasty, violent piece of work. Yet here he was now, wearing his black and silver facemask and superhero suit. Villain had become hero.

Midnight Jack was in his early twenties. He had grown up in a working class suburb north of Seattle. He described his family as being "half Norse, half Irish".

'I was a good kid when I was a young teenager,' he told me. 'But when I hit eighteen, I really had no idea what I was going to do with my life. I didn't have money for college or anything.'

Having already flunked out of high school, Jack felt that he had no future.

'I started smoking weed,' he said, 'and then I started to do other drugs. From there, it was a downward spiral.'

Jack progressed to cocaine and ecstasy, and started to drink heavily. He began hanging out with others who were equally stuck in this world, including one guy who told him how to make money to fund his addictions. As someone with expensive habits, Jack was interested in what the guy had to say. 'You just rob people,' the guy told him.

So that's what Jack did; he robbed people – often in Freeway Park – to get money to pay for his drugs.

'The reason I robbed people in Freeway Park was because I've then got the whole downtown area for cover,' Jack told me. 'After I mug someone, I can dip right back into the fucking crowd, disappear and be gone with the money. In Freeway Park, people are isolated, they're alone and they're vulnerable.'

Freeway Park was close to my hotel and I often cut through it on my way to other parts of the city. I thought it would be safe as it was in the heart of the downtown area but, after this conversation with Jack, I made a mental note not to use it late at night or when it was quiet.

'Did you ever hurt anybody?' I asked.

'This sounds bad,' he said, hesitating. 'I hit somebody with... this sounds terrible, okay...'

'The whole thing sounds terrible!' Phoenix said.

'I'm gonna tell this story, okay, but I need no judgement.'

'I don't judge people,' I told him.

'I do,' Phoenix said.

Midnight Jack told us the story anyway. 'I had this rusty old woodcutting axe that I had stashed on the back of my belt and up my coat. I followed this dude around; this guy was a low-level drug pusher. I talked some shit to him and I got him to turn around and walk up on me. Then I pulled the axe out and fucking smacked him on the side of the head with the blunt end. Then I took his shoes, his wallet and his coat and ran away.'

I looked at Jack with alarm, trying to stick to my word about not judging him.

'For me, I liked blunt instruments like pipes – stuff that you can bring out of your sleeve,' he said, matter-of-fact. 'Knives are effective as well but, with a knife, you can't just smack somebody if you have to; you have to cut them and that's a whole different fucking ball game. A knife is always the first weapon someone brings to a fight, but for me, blunt instruments were the way to go.'

From using drugs and robbing people, Jack advanced to "enforcing" – working for a drug dealer, making sure he didn't get robbed. He also undertook some "pushing" and "dealing" of his own. I asked him what the difference was.

'*Dealing*, the drugs are yours. *Pushing*, you're selling for someone else – or you bring people to the dealer and the dealer pays you in drugs or money,' he told me.

'How did you get out of that life?'

'I left the state,' he said. 'I ended up getting burnt on a couple of deals, so I had to go into hiding for a while. Then I got hooked on some really bad coke that was cut poorly. I don't want to say that it was *ever* fun, but it stopped being enjoyable, you know? It stopped being, "*Yeah, I'm the boss. I enforce for these dealers. I sell drugs! This is my life and that's how I do things.*" I went from being high on the totem pole to being very low on the totem pole.'

Jack had hit rock bottom and, one day, he found himself at an apartment cutting lines of coke on a coffee table with a bunch of strangers. He wasn't even sure how he had got there.

'That was the trigger,' he said. 'I just had this moment where I asked myself: *how did I get to this point?*'

He put the drugs down and left. He walked out of the apartment and kept walking. He kept walking all the way back to where he was living, and he wasn't even sure how far it was or how long it took but, when he got there, he went into his room and shut the door behind him. He stayed in his room for three days and didn't speak to anybody.

'I just needed to stop,' he said. 'I didn't need to sit and talk to someone about my problems. I just needed to stop. I was done.'

So Jack left the state and didn't return for a year.

Jack made his very real achievement of turning away from drugs seem almost effortless – but, of course, it wasn't that simple. I couldn't imagine the amount of determination Jack must have had to walk away from his terrible addiction, not to mention the utter misery he would have gone through. But that was Jack: he never looked for sympathy; he never sought out pity. Jack had been to hell and back, yet you would never know it. His almost constant upbeat attitude, jokey ways and friendliness concealed a whole other life. But I never felt he was trying to hide this previous existence, nor that he was faking his cheerfulness and covering up the truth about his past. He really did seem to have moved on. It was extraordinary. Perhaps when he was alone, he was different. Perhaps he still had dark moments where the pull and power of addiction would torment him – but that is not a side of Jack I ever witnessed.

By the time Jack returned to Seattle, he was clean. Then, about three months later, as he watched the TV news, he saw the report of Phoenix Jones being arrested. At first Jack had dismissed it as some sort of publicity stunt.

'But I found out that it was real. So I did some research and started to realise that there was a lot of legal leeway open to a person who wanted to stop crime. That's when I started my first patrols, wearing my leather jacket and carrying a flashlight.'

Jack would spend his evenings patrolling his local housing project dressed like a poorly equipped security guard, until one night when he decided to put on a mask – more as a joke than anything else. The police stopped him that same night and wanted to know just what the hell he thought he was doing.

As he tried to think up a reason they suddenly asked, 'Oh, are you doing some superhero thing?'

Jack decided to play along and told them that he was. After that, they left him alone.

'It's a long way from your drug and robbery days,' I said.

'I know, but I really wanted to give something back. I wanted to make up for the things I'd done in my past. This seemed like a good way of doing that.'

As time went on, Jack and Phoenix began to run into each other, and got to know one another. Eventually, Phoenix started calling on Jack to back him up, until Jack inevitably got absorbed into the Rain City Superheroes.

'From there, everything was a huge upgrade,' Jack said. 'I had a track jacket at one point, with a little neoprene motorcycle mask – that was my super-suit. Then I got the black and silver jacket and mask. Phoenix actually bought me my first utility belt. I started to get more appropriate gear.'

After the equipment upgrade, Phoenix began to teach Midnight Jack hand-to-hand fighting and combat techniques. Before that, all Jack knew how to do was punch someone in the face. Or hit them with an axe.

'I'm not saying I'm Bruce Lee, but I've got a little more skills now,' Jack told me.

Even so, at heart, Jack was still an in-the-gutter, dirty, blood, mud and spit, street fighter. Phoenix had taught him some skills but he was still able to fight the old fashioned way. The fighting was where Jack found issue with some of the guys who were trained in martial arts.

'Martial artists are used to fighting a certain way, but it leads to two problems. Firstly, they fight very formally. You can't fight formally when you're out on the sidewalk. Secondly, they want to fight *all* the time. They see it as a challenge. But that's not what you want. What you want is verbal de-escalation. What you want is to appear passive but be mentally aggressive. I want the fight to be over in your head before you even throw a punch. And that's where we run into problems with the martial artists. *"Well, if he wants some, he can come get some!"* No, that's not how you do it.'

As well as these newly acquired skills, Jack's past had brought genuine benefits to Phoenix's team. He was a diamond-in-the-rough when he first joined the Rain City Superheroes, but this *roughness* proved to have great worth and I now understood why Phoenix valued Jack's input so much when they were out on patrol. Jack's criminal background was a unique addition to the skills-set on the team. He had an instinct for criminality that none of the others could ever hope to match. Jack had been there – he had been a criminal – so he was able to think like a criminal.

'I'm the only guy who doesn't fall into the qualifications needed to be on the team,' he said. 'We have police officers and ex-military. You need a background in one of those professions or else hold some martial arts skills. I had none of that. I took drugs and robbed people. And although it's been years since I did anything like that, I still retain those skills and knowledge. I can always spot a prowler. I taught Phoenix a lot of things, too. If he chased someone and if they got away from him, he would just consider them gone, but they're not. You've got to ask the following: Was that person intoxicated? Did they look like they had a car? What are the ways out of the city? You've seen Belltown; you can't just escape and be gone. You've got to come back around. So I taught Phoenix to wait five minutes, watch all the entry points back into the city. Watch the parking lots. They're going to show back up. That's the kind of stuff he likes having me around for. I guess that's my X-factor, my niche.'

Jack had something else, equally as valuable – he was extremely street-wise.

'Common sense is the most important thing,' he told me. 'Lots and lots of common sense. If you don't have that, you're going to run into trouble real quick and you're going to jail. We have issues with military guys on the team, because they're used to doing things a certain way. It's drilled into them. They're not open to interpreting things their own ways. They also have problems with costume design and weaponry. They're the ones you see who want to belt up real hard and carry all this stuff. They have overloading issues with their equipment. They go more *commando* with their super-suit and they end up scaring people. You don't want to scare people as a superhero.'

Jack was right. I thought back to the night when Ratchet had come out looking all "future soldier", with his black, Special Forces-style outfit and anonymous, frightening mask. And Ratchet wasn't the only one. I had briefly met another Rain City superhero, called Pitch Black, who also went for the all black, futuristic, Special Forces look. And Pitch Black really was a soldier – he was with the US Army, but spent his leave patrolling with the RCSM. Compared to someone walking up to you looking like Spiderman or Batman – as Midnight Jack and Phoenix Jones did – these more sinister outfits were confusing and threatening. They certainly weren't in the spirit of how a superhero was expected to look.

So the truth is, I was impressed with Jack. When he wasn't making wisecracks at others' expense, he was an astute, thoughtful, smart guy. His time on the streets, taking drugs, dealing drugs, robbing people, and the life he had fallen into a few years previously had ultimately been one of the best educations a person working the streets could have. I had little doubt that Midnight Jack was the most shrewd and streetwise member of the Rain City Superheroes.

Like many criminals, Jack had a way of thinking that was out-of-the-box, sneaky, devious and useful. And when it came down to the physical, I didn't doubt that he knew how to throw a punch – albeit one that you probably weren't expecting, and one that was going to land on your nose with a sickening, bloody crunch. While other heroes were busy getting into the *flying dove* move or whatever it was that they did, Jack was just going to pummel you into the ground.

He was clearly mentally strong as well. It takes some doing to recognise and then walk away from a drug habit. Yet Jack had done just that. Then, accepting the wrongs he had done, he had set about putting them right in his own way – and without anyone pushing him to do it. All of those things, I thought, were heroic.

The more time I spent with Jack, the more I saw a strong leader in the making. He was smart, thoughtful and brave, and in many ways he reminded me of Urban Avenger from the Xtreme Justice League in San Diego. There were times when I thought he would have made an excellent platoon leader in the army or a superb cop. The knowledge and skills he had acquired in his darker days would be invaluable to one of those professions. But, although he had moved on from his past, I still felt that he was trying to make up for it, that he was still feeling the guilt of what he had become in his teenaged years. Being a superhero certainly wasn't a form of self-punishment, but I doubted he could see past it. Not yet, anyway.

12

The Stakeout

It would be Phoenix Jones' last night out for a few days. He was going to Portland, Oregon to meet a group of superheroes who to join his "organisation". Phoenix had told me that he was planning to start a "Jones Army", spreading his word and philosophy to other superhero groups around the country. It was similar to something Mr Xtreme had mentioned to me – basically, franchising out. At first, I wondered why any independent superhero would need or want to become part of another team, especially when that team was in another city or even another state, but after spending time with Phoenix, it became clear; he was the most famous real-life superhero in America and being associated with him might give another superhero some kudos and perhaps make them feel more legitimate. They could feel that they were part of something bigger, and there would be some kind of support network and friendship there. And, if you believed that what you were doing was important – as Phoenix Jones did – then the next logical step to spread your message and values would be to expand. (This was exactly what New York's Guardian Angels had done in the '80s, when "Chapters" had appeared not just across America but also around the world. The Guardian Angels might have worn berets and t-shirts rather than capes and masks, but their objectives had been basically the same as the superheroes: stop crime.) I had even heard that one hero in New York had grand plans to set up a school for superheroes. Kind of like an X-Men, *Xavier's School for Gifted Youngsters* thing. Only not.

Tonight was going to be different. This wasn't a regular Rain City

Superhero patrol, where they simply looked for trouble and tried not to get arrested (although getting arrested was still a very real possibility). Tonight they were doing a police-style operation, staking out car thieves in Capitol Hill.

'What makes you think something is going to happen in Cap Hill?' I asked.

'One of Purple's friends had their car broken into in that area,' Phoenix told me. 'When we pulled up the crime maps, we could see that the area was teeming with break-ins. So I decided I was going to fix it.'

A stakeout was a serious step up when it came to crime fighting. Walking around, looking for trouble and getting free drinks was one thing, but a stakeout took significant organising and planning. Having studied the police reports and crime maps, Phoenix and Purple had picked the streets on which they wanted to concentrate. Even though Purple had done much of the research, she would be staying home, watching live reports and updates from the police that she could then feed through to Phoenix and the rest of the team.

Phoenix had planned to meet the rest of the Rain City superheroes on the top floor of a multi-storey parking lot, close to where we would be carrying out the sting operation. We were the last to arrive and waiting for us in a dark, quiet corner were Griff Grey, Boomer, Ratchet, USID, Evo and two superheroes I hadn't met before: Scarlet Falcon and Tomahawk.

'Is this everyone for tonight?' Phoenix asked.

'That's it boss,' Evo answered.

'No Cabbie?'

'Nope. Cabbie bailed on us tonight. Not sure why.'

Phoenix seemed disappointed, but he gathered everyone together to discuss team names for the operation. There would be four teams and he wanted each to use the location they would be parked in, for their name.

Someone suggested just calling the teams, 1, 2, 3 and 4 – but

Phoenix was against the idea, as it wouldn't give the team's actual location.

'I have an idea,' Jack said, although the look on his face suggested that what he was about to say wasn't going to be in the least bit serious or constructive. 'Why don't you be Team One and we can be Team A?'

Everyone looked at him blankly as he began to giggle to himself.

'Nobody?' he asked. 'Seriously? Nobody? Screw you, I'm funny. Someone has to be; Mr Sad and Serious over there, dressed in his black rubber suit all the damn time.'

'If I wasn't brooding I wouldn't be having any fun,' Phoenix replied.

'Let me ask you one question,' Midnight Jack said. 'Do you wear your suit in your basement and talk to yourself, when you're alone? Maybe in the living room? The bathroom? Somewhere?'

'Only one question per team,' Phoenix said, batting Jack's teasing comment away before returning to the serious business of the stakeout. 'We'll keep with the street names as our call signs.'

The plan was to cover four corners of a small block. Each team would be in their own separate vehicle on one of the corners, watching one of the streets. At the end of that street would be another team, watching the next street running off to the right of the first street, until the entire square block was covered by the eyes of the superheroes, meaning that no one could move around that block without one of the Rain City superheroes seeing them.

Phoenix showed the team a map of the area that Purple had created. On it she had placed long coloured triangle shapes. Each of these triangles stretched out from one of the corners that each of the teams would be in, indicating the view from that point. Each of the triangles overlapped another one, so in effect, anybody walking around the area would be visible to at least one of the teams. It was a good bit of work from Purple and clearly demonstrated why each team needed to be disciplined and remain in their assigned areas. With everyone sitting in cars, in their positions, they would have the square of streets completely covered. On top of this, Phoenix was going to deploy USID on foot.

Phoenix walked us through the small square of streets we would be staking out, allocating a corner to each team. Scarlet Falcon and Tomahawk would be *Team Union* as they were on Union Street, a fairly quiet, dark road that ran east through Capitol Hill. Jack and Grey would be *Team 10th Ave*, a smaller street running north to south through Union. Phoenix, Evo and myself would be *Team Seneca*, on East Seneca Street, a small, narrow road running parallel with Union, and next to an IHOP (International House of Pancakes) parking lot. Finally, there would be Boomer and Ratchet who would become *Team Broadway Court*. Broadway Court was little more than an alley, but wide and long enough to park half a dozen cars. It was mostly dark and deserted. If a car break-in was going to happen, Phoenix believed it would happen here. Broadway Court was strewn with glass from broken car windows, and nearby, at the intersection with Union Street, there was an entire shattered windscreen.

Turning to me, Phoenix said, 'Mick, I want you as my 911 guy tonight.'

'*Me?*' I asked, surprised.

'Yeah. If anything happens or anyone is hurt, it's your responsibility to call 911.'

This was the first time I had been given a specific role within the group. At first I felt uneasy about it. Having an actual job made me part of the team. But the more I thought about it, the more comfortable I became. Being the person who called 911 didn't make me a superhero – just a responsible member of the public. It was, I felt, a role that was risk-free of arrest. I also liked the feeling of having an actual position with the group rather than just being a hanger-on with nothing to offer.

Phoenix then turned to USID, who was hovering at the back of the heroes, with his grey hood pulled low, over his eyes.

'You know what to do,' Phoenix told him. 'You're really good at just being old and creepy, so I'm going to let you keep doing that.'

Phoenix had originally planned for USID to hang around a nearby bus stop on Broadway – but then thought better of it, deciding that it would look odd for USID to be standing at the stop after all the different buses had come and gone. In the end, it was decided that USID would go to a store and buy a bottle of alcohol, then wonder around the neighbourhood like a drunk. Boomer could see a possible issue though.

'What happens if the cops accost him?' he asked.

'Accost USID?' Phoenix asked.

'Yeah.'

'USID, you know what to tell 'em, right?'

USID stared at Boomer and Phoenix in silence for a moment, thinking about the scenario and what he would say. Eventually he came out with, 'No habla?'

'What about...' Boomer began to say.

'What about what?' Phoenix asked Boomer, getting irritated. 'Sorry, did I come up with the plan or did you come up with the plan?'

Boomer sunk back, into the body of heroes standing around him.

'I'm just asking a question,' he muttered.

'This is not a debate,' Phoenix said sternly.

We continued on. Phoenix pointed out some more shattered glass on the ground, further evidence that this was a good spot to stake out. Then he reminded the team that they were covered legally should they get arrested.

'If you end up in jail, I'll bail you out in seven hours,' he told them, before adding, 'As long as you're current on your dues that is. So think about that.'

The *dues* – twenty dollars a month that each member of the RCSM paid – insured them on legal matters and against injury.

'I'm current!' Boomer quickly said.

The stakeout was a real change of focus for Phoenix Jones and his motley group of superheroes. They seemed to be evolving into more than just a bunch of costumed activists. It was much more the type of operation carried out by police than a bunch of guys in masks, but then I remembered that one of the team was a cop.

I turned to Evo, who was standing next to me. 'Evo, are you a cop?' I asked, outright.

'Nope,' he replied firmly.

We stood in silence. It seemed I had created an awkward moment, but decided to continue along this line regardless, asking my questions in a way that I hoped would lead to something more than monosyllabic answers.

'If you were a cop – I know you say you're not – but if you *were*, what do you think would drive a cop to become a superhero?'

He looked down at me. 'Well, you should know,' he said. 'After all, you're a cop, aren't you?'

'True. But I'm not a superhero. So what do you think would make a cop become one?'

'Hmm... I suppose a cop might be interested in doing something like this if their day-job wasn't satisfying enough,' he replied.

'How wouldn't it be satisfying? Being a cop can be exciting.'

'Absolutely, but the bureaucracy can slow you down. It may not be to your pace or your liking. Maybe you can do more on your own – still within the confines of the law but your own way.'

'Meaning?'

'Assuming you've got a good head for it and stay clear of the vigilante path, and you don't decide to break laws just because you wear a mask, you can actually get a lot more done as a superhero.'

'You think a cop would be able to do things as a superhero that they couldn't do as a cop?'

'Yes. In the interest of time, and... hell, just in the interest of self-satisfaction! Everyone's got their own reason for doing it.'

'Do you think it's easier to tackle crime as a superhero, than as a cop?'

Evo was starting to sound tired of my questions. He huffed. 'I would imagine, yes. I think the biggest differences are probably logistical ones. We have very minimal paperwork, for a start. There's not nearly as much red tape.'

'But there must be real concern for a cop – concern about being found out. Phoenix has been arrested, other team members have been detained...'

'Right.'

'...and had their details taken.'

'Right.'

'So if a cop doing this was detained by the police, they could lose their job.'

Evo huffed a second time. 'I think as long as he's not breaking the law, he could be detained but he would be let go. However, there'd be a conflict of interest, I would imagine. He would have a contract with his department probably forbidding him from doing anything that could be remotely perceived as vigilante – even though we are very clear that that is not what we do. It's not *what* it is; it's what it *appears* to be. This could be very hazardous PR-wise. This kind of work require quite a bit of explanation. A lot of people hear "superhero" and they make a thousand presumptions. I find there's a lot more explaining of what it *doesn't* mean and what we *don't* do. People think we're fighting criminals on the rooftops and stopping bank robbers and taking care of the dirty work that the police can't do because of laws. But no, we're pretty much confined to the same rulebook.'

'But do you think a cop should really be doing this sort of thing?' I asked.

'Do you?'

'No.'

'And yet, here you are.'

Check mate.

Evo assured me again that he wasn't a cop. I decided to leave it there, feeling it wouldn't be fair to keep pushing the matter.

We returned to the parking lot, where each superhero kitted themselves up with their equipment – pepper-spray, tasers and body armour – but no masks or outfits. This was a plain-clothes operation, except for Phoenix Jones, who for some reason had decided to wear his rubber outfit and then wrap a blanket around his body to cover it up.

Ratchet then handed each team a small walkie-talkie. They were new radios that Ratchet had recently purchased out of the team funds, and he attempted to explain to everyone how they worked. It was a simple radio – push a button at the side to talk, and push another button to change channels. There was also a "squelch" button, and each radio had its own unique sound. Ratchet thought this was a useful tool to help identify each team. Phoenix wasn't so sure, worrying that no one would remember which sound related to which team. As the superheroes argued about this, Midnight Jack, who had been silent over the matter, decided to speak up and talk some sense.

'Hey, I've got an idea – how about we just push the button and say who we are? Then we can quit jerking each other off over the radios and get to work.'

Everyone thought that this was probably a better idea, and the matter of the squelch button was put to one side.

'Now, is everybody happy with what they're doing?' Phoenix asked.

'I get it already,' Jack said, sounding impatient. 'Everybody's got it, right? No one needs me to hold their hand?'

'Okay, let's go stop these motherfuckers,' Phoenix said. 'Everybody in.' He placed his hand in the middle of the team circle, inviting the rest of us to place our hands on his. 'Okay, we'll say "Rain City", on three.'

'That seems like a bad idea if we're meant to be undercover,' Jack said.

'Well, we're not undercover at this very moment,' Phoenix told him. 'Now, on three...'

Once everyone was in place, we settled down and began to watch the shadowy streets. They were dimly illuminated by weak streetlights, giving the entire scene a matt grey-blue colour. My only concern was how close we all were. The square we were staking out was small, in a quiet part of Capitol Hill, and I worried that anyone walking through would spot us immediately. But it was dark and murky and we were all parked in deep shadows, so Phoenix and Evo were satisfied that we wouldn't be spotted.

As people started to come through the area, each team put up possible suspects and USID would follow them for a short distance before he was satisfied that the "suspect" was, in fact, an innocent member of the public.

Then Jack put up a man that he had been watching for a while. The guy had walked through the area a number of times and Jack wasn't at all happy about him.

'I've got a black guy, wearing a black hoodie, white shoes, about six foot one, heading your way, Union,' Jack called over the radio.

'We've got him,' Falcon replied.

We sat in silence, waiting for the next transmission. If the man had walked past Jack, towards Scarlet Falcon and Tomahawk, there was a chance he might turn into Broadway Court, the most likely spot for a break-in.

'I'm running camera,' Phoenix told us. Then, speaking to Purple, who was at home, monitoring Phoenix's transmissions, he said, 'My GoPro is going to be shooting black. This is audio only. I have my GoPro hidden under a blanket. I have people in the car with their masks off and their identities exposed.'

Boomer then came on the radio. The man had now turned into Broadway Court, and Boomer had eyes on the guy. As we were at the intersection of Seneca and Broadway Court, we too had a view of the suspect. He walked slowly up the short street, alongside the parked cars. He stopped by the second one – a small, white Ford. The guy had no idea that, at that moment, five pairs of eyes were burning into him, almost pleading for him to smash a window and lean into the vehicle. But then he continued on, until eventually he walked passed us. But Phoenix wasn't happy with the guy and directed USID to follow him.

'Jack is stepping out on foot also,' Grey said over the radio.

'He's doing what?' Phoenix asked. 'Why? Oh my God! Tell him to get back to his fucking post!'

But it was too late – Midnight Jack was already out of the car and following behind USID.

'Wait, if Grey has the radio, what does Jack have?' Phoenix asked us.

'Jack, do you have a radio?' Evo asked over the walkie-talkie.

Silence. Evo asked again, even though we all knew the answer.

'No, he doesn't,' Grey said, eventually.

Phoenix was fuming. 'So, let me see if I understand. Jack left his post with no radio or general communications with the rest of us, and he's chasing somebody who hasn't done anything wrong, is that it?'

'Whoever has contact with Jack, tell him to go back to his post, over,' Evo said calmly but firmly over the radio.

'I'm kind of pissed,' Phoenix said.

Then, as if to rub a bucket of salt into Phoenix's emotional wound, another superhero suddenly moseyed onto the scene.

'Is that Tommy?' Phoenix asked, almost in disbelief.

'Erm... Yes,' Evo answered.

Tomahawk was now out on foot, wandering around Union at the end of Broadway Court.

'What is Tommy doing? What the fuck is happening around here?'

Evo wound down his window and pointed his finger towards Tommy, indicating for him to get back to his car. Tommy quickly turned around, heading back towards Union and Broadway.

Then Jack came walking towards us, across the IHOP parking lot.

'You need to talk to him,' Phoenix told Evo. 'I can't do it. I will beat his ass.'

'I've got it,' Evo replied.

Jack walked up to Phoenix's open window. Phoenix stared straight ahead, refusing to acknowledge Jack's presence.

'Dude, where did you go?' Evo asked, gently.

Jack leant down to look at Evo. 'I walked around, but lost him on Harvard.'

'Okay but we had USID on that. You didn't have to go as well.'

'Yeah but they told me that USID was going to pull back after a block or so, so I wanted to be there to pick up the slack.'

'Okay, but we lost total fucking radio comms with you too.'

'I had one of USID's radios but it malfunctioned. Listen, I'm going to get back to my post.'

'Why did you leave your post?' Phoenix finally asked, breaking his silence.

'I left my post because that guy looked into three cars,' Jack said, starting to sound defensive.

'But that wasn't your job!'

'But I lost eyes on him.'

'We had eyes on him. That wasn't your job to leave your post.'

'I'm going to go back to work,' Jack said, sounding as though he wasn't sure why he was being attacked and criticised by Phoenix.

'No!' Phoenix told him. 'We need to figure this out. I'm a little lost. Remember those triangles on the map? Well, when a suspect leaves your triangle, they walk into ours and we watch them. Then, when they leave our triangle, they walk into USID's triangle. So you don't have to leave your car. If something had happened to you out there, we couldn't have helped you, man.'

'Listen, I was about a block and a half away from this dude – he didn't know I was there. It was all good. I had USID with me too. He was on the other side of the street from me, so I was never alone.'

'Let me rephrase this,' Phoenix said, sounding dictatorial. 'Do you think what you did was the protocol for the mission?'

'Probably not but, to be honest, I thought I had a shot at capturing this dude, so I took it.'

Phoenix stared at Jack for a moment, in silence. 'I guess I have no further questions,' he said finally.

But Jack wasn't done. 'I asked you about this stuff before we started.'

'And I answered it.'

Things were starting to feel awkward. Both Evo and I sat in silence as Jack and Phoenix had their little squabble. Whatever the rights and wrongs of Jack leaving his post, arguing about it in the street wasn't going to catch us a thief.

'You told me to use my own judgement. Well, I used it.'

'Okay,' Phoenix said, and he returned to staring out of the windscreen. 'Return to your post.'

Jack turned around and walked across Seneca towards 10th, where Grey was still waiting in their vehicle. I was pleased the spat was over and felt Evo relaxing a little also. But then Phoenix spotted something in Jack's back pocket.

'Whoa! Whoa! Whoa! Rewind! Rewind!' Phoenix shouted towards Jack. 'Jack! Jack! Wait.'

Jack walked back towards us and looked at Phoenix.

'Jack, what's in your pocket, bro?'

'What's in my pocket? It's fucking self defence is what I have.'

'But what is it?'

'I've got a blackjack in my pocket.'

Phoenix was horrified. 'Dawg! You can't follow a dude and hit him with a blackjack!'

'The blackjack's in case the motherfucker swings at me,' Jack said.

'If he swings at you with his fists, you can't hit him with that!'

'Well, I can't exactly hide a big-ass can of pepper-spray in my coat pocket, can I?'

'Oh my God! Fuck!' Phoenix shook his head in disbelief. 'Just leave,' he told Jack, sounding as though he was half laughing, half crying. 'Just leave me alone.'

Jack couldn't see the problem and walked away without another word.

'Didn't he have one of those before?' I asked.

'Yep,' Evo said.

'Is it even legal?' I asked.

'No!' Phoenix said. 'Not in these circumstances. It's highly illegal.'

'But a taser and pepper-spray *are* legal?'

'It depends on the circumstances. That blackjack is the only weapon Jack has with him. He pulls that out and it totally escalates the situation. Pepper-spray, taser – they incapacitate somebody assaulting you. A blackjack is incredibly inappropriate...'

'It's far more lethal than pepper-spray,' Evo added.

'Yeah, you can kill someone with a blackjack. It's extremely serious. One or two hits with that and the guy's dead,' Phoenix said. 'You ever hit somebody with a blackjack before?'

'No,' I said.

'Well I have and, let me tell you, it's bad.'

Phoenix took the radio from Evo and called Griff Grey. 'Grey, I put you on that team to use your judgement, bro. Do you think that your judgement is good when Jack is leaving the vehicle with no way to communicate with us, when he's chasing a guy who has not broken the law? Over.'

'I tried to discourage him from leaving,' Grey replied.

'Understood,' Phoenix told him. 'Continue discouraging. Only harsher.'

This seemed extremely unfair. Grey wasn't Jack's keeper. If Jack decided he was going to leave their vehicle, there would have been little that Grey could have done about it. I couldn't see how it was his fault that Jack had gone against orders. But Phoenix was still pissed off.

'I'm not bringing Jack next time,' Phoenix told Evo. 'He wasn't listening during set-up and he just left his post. Should I be mad? I feel like I should be super pissed.'

'He's just bringing the enthusiasm he'd usually bring to patrol, to a quiet, laid-back stakeout,' Evo said. 'He made a patrol decision, not a stakeout decision.'

'Well, I feel like crying.'

Things started to calm down. Everyone remained in their vehicle and the streets became quieter. Even the 24-hour IHOP was emptying out.

Myself, Evo and Phoenix had been watching a couple of homeless men who were sitting by a small, boarded-up building, further along Seneca, past 10th Avenue. Evo had called in USID to speak to them to try and find out what they were all about.

'Team Seneca, Team Broadway,' Boomer called, after we watched USID walking away from the men.

'This is Team Seneca,' Evo replied. 'Go ahead, over.'

'Relay from USID. Those men don't know of anyone breaking into cars, but they advised him that, if he was breaking into cars, they wanted a piece of the action.'

'Nice,' Phoenix said. 'Well, if they want a bit of USID's shit, then maybe they *are* involved in car break-ins.'

More time passed. The two homeless men left the area and Phoenix went to the IHOP to get the three of us some food. On his return, he handed me an enormous box containing an entire blueberry pancake pie with whipped cream.

'Can you believe they tried to charge me twice for pancake syrup?' Phoenix complained. 'Charging me for pancake syrup that I've already paid for is not acceptable in America.'

As we tucked into the pancakes and fruit, a light drizzle began to fall, and a cool wind whipped up through the gloomy streets.

Jack, clearly bored, called up over the radio. 'Man, it's quieter than Dick Cheney's house after nine-thirty,' he said.

Phoenix and Evo chuckled at the comment.

'What?' I said. 'I don't get it. Does nothing happen at Dick Cheney's house after nine-thirty?'

'It's because Dick Cheney's a square,' Phoenix told me. 'He doesn't do anything fun.'

Half an hour later, Jack came back on the radio. 'Dude, it's quieter out here than an Anne Murray record.'

'A what?' I asked, confused once more.

'Anne Murray, she's a country singer,' Evo said. 'The sort of stuff your grandparents would listen to.'

Jack came back on the radio.

'Now what?' Phoenix asked out loud.

'Er... Broadway Court, this is Tenth. We've got a woman in a white jacket walking with a white male in a dark jacket. The female's got a flashlight and she keeps shining it into parked cars. They're heading towards you, Broadway.'

We all bolted up straight. This sounded promising.

'This is Broadway Court,' Boomer said over the radio. 'We have eyes on the suspects. They've stopped at the first parked car and the woman is shining the flashlight into the passenger window.'

After sitting up straight, we then slunk back down in our seats, doing our best to remain hidden. The woman and the man were a short distance from us, still peering into the first car, just as Boomer had described. The woman was bending forward, her small flashlight illuminating the inside of the car, as the man in the dark jacket stood a couple of feet away from her, looking up and down the road. I was again worried that we would be seen, but we were in a dark spot, away from any streetlights and, as we ducked down, we were nicely silhouetted against the seats of Phoenix's car.

The woman looked in the rear before the couple moved on to the next vehicle – a dark coloured Toyota. Just as before, she shone her flashlight into the front of the car – but this time she placed her hand against the window and looked as though she were trying to push it in. The man remained nearby, watching.

This was it – the couple were looking to break into a car, there was no doubt.

The pair walked back towards the white Ford, but then continued on, back towards Union, where they stopped at the intersection, looking up and down the road. Then they walked back to the white Ford. The woman shone her flashlight into it again, before walking back to the intersection with Union. The man remained with the

Ford, looking up and down Broadway Court. The woman stood at the intersection, checking up and down Union and then, just as she was about to walk back to the Ford, she stopped. She stood perfectly still, looking west, along Union, towards Broadway. Then she turned to the man and made some urgent hand signals. The man joined her, looking in the direction of Broadway. He said something to the woman and they both hurried away, back along Union, past Grey and Jack, turning into a nearby street, towards the crowded bar area. They were gone.

'What?' Phoenix said. 'What the fuck?'

Something had spooked them.

The radio came on. 'This is Tommy,' Tomahawk called. 'The woman looked straight at me before she started signalling to the man. I think there might have been a compromise.'

'God damn it!' Phoenix shouted. 'She heard your fucking radio!'

'No,' Evo said. 'She wouldn't have heard it at that distance. She must have looked at him.'

'So? Looking at him doesn't mean anything. Why would that have stopped her from breaking into a car on Broadway Court?'

Evo called up Tommy. 'Tomahawk, this is Evo. Was there anything else apart from just looking at you?'

After a moment of silence, Tommy came back on the radio. 'Well, I was filming her with my camera. She looked straight at it.'

'Damn it!' Phoenix said angrily. 'Does he have that big-ass digital SLR camera thing with him?'

'Yep,' Evo said.

'Fuck! That was our moment and now they're bugging out. Damn!'

USID followed the pair as far as Pike, but left them as they disappeared into the Friday night crowds.

Phoenix was pissed off once again and decided to call it a night. Taking the radio from Evo, he spoke to the other teams. 'All units, this is Jones. That was our chance, guys. That was our fucking moment. We missed the witching hour and we're now eight minutes into the safe zone. No break-ins have been reported after one-thirty in the morning. Let's meet back at the parking lot. Jones out.'

Midnight Jack quickly spoke on the radio. 'Do you want to give it another fifteen minutes?' he asked. 'If this couple are desperate to make a bust, they might just hide out for fifteen minutes, switch jackets and then come back through. That's what I would do if I were them.'

Phoenix handed the radio back to Evo. He was in no mood to talk anymore. 'Ask Jack if it's just a hunch or a *Jack feeling*.'

Evo relayed Phoenix's question to Jack.

'This is not a hunch or a Jack feeling,' Jack replied, sounding angry himself now. 'It's a professional criminal thing. It's what I would do.'

'That's what I said. That's a *Jack feeling*,' Phoenix said to me and Evo. 'Evo, give me back that radio. Jack, this is Jones. You're being kind of defensive. What I meant by a "Jack feeling" was just that – is this something Jack would do? Because I trust those feelings one hundred percent. If that's your play, I'll back you.'

'If it was me, I'd wait fifteen minutes, come back and continue with my shit – only more cautiously.'

'Roger that. I'm rolling with Jack on this. Scarlet Falcon, Tommy, roll the fuck out, okay? Go to the top of the parking lot, we'll see you there in fifteen if nothing happens.'

Despite Jack's criminal instincts, the pair didn't return and, at 2am, we started to break away from the small set of streets we had been watching.

'That was disheartening,' Phoenix said as we pulled away from Seneca. 'We almost had them, dude.' He picked up the radio and called to the other heroes. 'This mission was a failure. Jones out.'

13

Time Travelling Racoons

A few nights later, I was back in the University District – or *U-Dub* – where Cabbie was leading a patrol, in Phoenix Jones' absence. It was the first time I had seen Cabbie since the night he'd been chasing the suspect in Pike Place Market. The U-Dub was a neighbourhood that the Rain City Superheroes felt they had been neglecting, so they wanted to re-establish their presence, especially after the run-in Phoenix, Jack and I had with the three men and the car, the night of the stakeout. With Cabbie would be myself, Boomer, Griff Grey and USID. I noticed that Cabbie had made a few modifications to his outfit, including a ballistic helmet – the type worn by police SWAT teams, only it was a sparkly and purple.

'It's class-three armour,' Cabbie told me. 'It's also got foam cushions in it – so, unlike the old helmets where, if you get hit, you'd probably get scrambled-egg brains, this actually protects the skull.'

He also had a large plastic crucifix stuck to the middle of his dark-blue body armour.

'You found God?' I asked in all seriousness, because with Cabbie, you just never knew.

'I got that when I was knighted with the Templars.'

'You're a Knight Templar?'

'Yes. I'm a Mason. And I've travelled to the East, too.'

Then Cabbie calmly lit a cigarette, indicating that the conversation was over. The glow of the orange flame illuminated his mask-covered face and reflected off the cross on his chest. Taking a step back, into the shadow of a doorway, he looked like a character from an old noir movie, watching the comings and goings at a nearby bar.

I wasn't sure what to make of Cabbie's claim to be a Templar. He was a strange one – even by real-life superhero standards, that was for sure. I was even told that Cabbie could travel through time. Yes, *time*. Phoenix explained that he and Cabbie had been delivering a talk to some school children when Cabbie started telling them about a time he had been fighting the Nazis. I wondered if there had been some confusion between actual goose-stepping, Third Reich Nazis and the modern day, but equally abhorrent, neo-Nazis. Regardless, I was assured that he could actually travel through time. Phoenix had once told me he had a rule, and if anyone trying to join the team claimed to have special powers, they were sent on their way. But Cabbie, who could apparently travel through time, was allowed to stay. It was something I had brought up with Phoenix before he left for Portland.

'Our rule about superpowers has always been that it can't be a physical or mental ability that would hinder your decision making,' Phoenix told me. 'Let me give you an example. Cabbie says: "I'm bullet proof." That endangers the rest of us, because the logical pattern of how he makes choices is compromised by him thinking he can't be punctured by bullets, which is crazy. But if he tells me that he travels through time, on his days off, how does that affect his patrol? It doesn't. So I don't care. I need you to think that you have the same weaknesses that I do, so you can make appropriate choices – but, if you want to believe that you can travel through fucking time, knock yourself out.'

The thing is, Cabbie was such a strange and mysterious character that, if there ever was a person who could actually travel through time, El Caballero would be it. There was always something about Cabbie that felt different from the rest of the heroes. Some may call it aloofness but, to me, he really did seem, well, *otherworldly* – as if he had just teleported in from some adventure in another dimension. He was like a cross between a 1970s Japanese science fiction cartoon character and Dr Who.

'Phoenix and Jack were telling me about the May Day incident. You were there too, weren't you?' I asked Cabbie.

'I was there. I ended up being on 911-duty that day. I kind of blended in with the mob.'

'Did you have your mask on?'

'Yeah, I had all my gear.'

'But you still managed to blend in with the crowd?'

'Well, it was really weird, because I couldn't tell who was the press, who were pseudo-terrorists, and who were just people protesting. There were a few people I had to bat off. I ended up jumping away from an incendiary device that someone had thrown. Some people complained that they got pepper-sprayed, or whatever. Yeah, well, they're lucky it was just us and not Homeland Security firing a 9mm bullet through their skull, because let me tell you, those protestors were throwing IEDs into the federal courthouses.'

Unlike Jack, Cabbie was very matter-of-fact when he spoke about the riot, and he didn't seem too fazed by any of it, as if fighting off hordes of maniacs and bomb-throwing "pseudo-terrorists" was a normal, everyday occurrence. Cabbie wasn't trying to avoid talking about the May Day incident, but he didn't really have anything else to say about it. It was just one more chapter in the incredible life of El Caballero – and something that he seemed to have moved on from.

The usual light drizzle had begun to drift down and a cooling breeze travelled along the street on which we were standing.

'Is everyone here?' Cabbie asked. 'Is this it for tonight?'

'This is pretty much it,' Boomer told him.

'No Midnight Jack?' USID asked.

'No, he's taken the night off.'

Cabbie stubbed out his cigarette and gave the team his pre-patrol briefing. It contained none of the warnings about "shooters" and "hostiles" that were common during a Phoenix Jones briefing. Instead, Cabbie was more concerned about how the heroes behaved, and their public image.

'One of my pet peeves is when people on the team don't smile,' he told us. 'Smile at people, be nice. And don't block the sidewalk. I hate it when we walk down the street creating a wall. Let people get past, don't get in their way.'

I got the impression that Cabbie would have been just as happy – if not happier – to have been out on his own tonight. He was always calm and his tone was always soft and mild-mannered, but he looked tired – tired of babysitting others. It was something I had noticed the first time I had seen him. I would see him giving other heroes directions, telling them what they needed to do and how to do it. He was like a superhero puppy-walker – albeit a reluctant one.

We set off along University Way. USID had already gone ahead, to scout around in his usual "hoodie up" way. Cabbie was walking ahead with Griff Grey.

'Mick, you're with me,' Boomer said. 'You have first aid training, right?'

'Yes.'

'CPR?'

'That too.'

'Good. Then there's two of us available tonight should anything happen – or if I get compromised again.'

I looked at Boomer. He was pulling up his black utility belt, which had begun to slip down with the weight of equipment he was carrying. We quickened our pace to catch up with Cabbie and Grey and to get across an intersection before the lights turned against us.

'What do you mean, "compromised"?' I asked.

'That drunk in Belltown. Things like that get to me sometimes.'

We were getting closer to the bar area along University Way. 'Keep up,' Cabbie called out to us.

We picked up our pace. 'Get to you how?' I asked Boomer.

'My dad.'

Boomer had his face covered by his neoprene crash-test dummy mask, but he was staring down at the ground as we trotted along the sidewalk. His eyes looked sad and we had clearly delved into a painful memory.

'It's okay,' Boomer said, sensing my apprehension. 'You can ask.'

'What happened to your father?'

'Actually it started with my mum. She died of lung cancer two days after my thirty-third birthday. My father had been an alcoholic for a few years and, after my mum died, it got worse. Then he got a DUI [Driving Under the Influence], and a week after that he fell and broke his left arm, shoulder, elbow and wrist. He spent seven months in a nursing home, rehab, and detox. He went to court for the DUI and got his licence back – but then he started drinking and driving again. He didn't care. Anyway, my father fell a second time and broke his right shoulder. It flew straight out of the socket. He went in for surgery... but he never recovered.'

Boomer's breathing rate had increased and it was becoming hard for him to talk and move at the same time. I wasn't sure if it was the speed we were walking at or the memories he was bringing up. Perhaps it was a mixture of both.

'The oxygen and the carbon dioxide levels in his body wouldn't normal out,' Boomer continued, after a few seconds. 'The carbon dioxide kept building up until his blood became acidic. Eventually, he died of respiratory failure.'

Boomer fell quiet again and stared at the ground. I didn't say anything. I didn't know what I could say. Then he broke the silence for me, bringing what he had told me about his father back round to the Belltown drunk and his "Fourth of July" problem.

'The way that guy was in the street – his condition – that was how my dad was a week before he died. That's why it knocked me on my ass. I had no clue what to do.'

I felt for Boomer. Here was a guy who had been orphaned in his early thirties (he was also divorced, he told me), and was, for much of the time, someone for the others on the team to poke fun at. He was the team medic, even though there were clearly incidents that were going to emotionally conflict with his past. Despite this, he kept coming out on patrol, weighed down with medical kits, willing to step in and help a person in real trouble. But, for most of the time, he was a medic without a patient, and he was often lagging behind, trying to keep up. I suspected that he needed the Rain City Superheroes more than they needed him.

Boomer told me that he had approached Phoenix Jones after seeing a news report about him, and asked if he could be of use, offering up his medical expertise. Phoenix was quick to see the benefits in having a medic on board and Boomer soon found himself part of the Rain City Superhero Movement. It was an arrangement that suited them both. Boomer needed a purpose and Phoenix Jones needed a medical professional. I considered Boomer and USID to be similar in that way – they both needed something in their lives and they both found it with the RCSM. Each offered Phoenix Jones something he hadn't had before – a medic and an undercover operative.

There was one incident in particular that had expedited Boomer's enrolment onto Phoenix's superhero team: the shooting of Nicole Westbrook. Nicole Westbrook was a 21 year-old Navajo woman, who had recently moved to Seattle, and as she was leaving a club with her boyfriend, a car drove past and someone from within it began to shoot randomly. Nicole was shot in the cheek and, as the bullet travelled through her face, it shattered her spine. A few days later, she died from her injuries. The incident was obviously devastating for her family; already her father had been killed serving in Iraq and her uncle killed serving in Afghanistan.

The shooting of Nicole Westbrook caused further concerns for residents and businesses in the Pioneer Square area, as the neighbourhood was already seeing people leave and vacant stores remaining empty.

Phoenix and his team had been in the area at the time of the shooting and had rushed to help. He and Cabbie had start running in the direction of the shots. As they did, they saw a man in a backpack running away and chased after him. But they were quickly stopped by the police. The man they had chased after was never found. He may have been innocent, he may have been the intended target, but we still don't know what, if anything, his involvement had been.

But the shooting had left an emotional mark on Phoenix and his team. They had felt terrible that they were not able to do more – either in assisting Nicole Westbrook as she lay dying, or in catching the shooter. It was then that Phoenix realised the importance of having a trained medic on the team – someone who could help members of the public, but also someone who could help his own team, should something serious happen to them.

'After Nicole Westbrook was killed in Pioneer Square, I found out that no one on the team had adequate first aid training or knowledge, let alone the gear, to handle a traumatic injury,' Boomer told me. 'Cabbie now carries a ten by twelve Israeli dressing for haemorrhage control, for large, abdominal wounds. I carry a couple of smaller ones, a tourniquet, gauze. Nobody had adequate first aid supplies whereas I had a metric-shit-ton. So I made a trauma kit for PJ, and gave him a first aid book as a donation to his team. It was my contribution to help them save lives. Then I was asked if I was willing to go on patrol with them. And I was.'

But with Ratchet now completing his EMT training, and Boomer carrying a number of injuries, not to mention his weight issues, I had to wonder what his future on the team would be, even though he seemed like a solid, regular and reliable member of the Rain City Superhero Movement.

Just then a guy across the street shouted out to us, calling us "pussies".

'I am what I eat,' Boomer replied dryly and we continued walking.

Boomer wanted to stop and rest. His back was starting to give him trouble. The pace we were walking at didn't help – but neither did the amount of kit he was carrying, not to mention his bulletproof vest. He also blamed it on another reason.

'It's part of the problem with being overweight,' he told me. 'I'm two-hundred and ninety pounds and five-foot-eight.'

'But part of your job as a superhero could be to run and fight,' I said.

'Except, according to PJ – and I agree – me being the Chief Medical Officer in this organisation, I should never see frontline combat.'

Boomer's use of terms such as "Chief Medical Officer" and "frontline combat" again made me feel that he was looking for something more in his life and that the Rain City Superhero Movement was providing that for him.

'Did you become medically trained after your father died? Was that the reason?' I asked.

'No. I did the training before he died, for another reason completely. I was on my motorcycle going to work – I used to work in broadcasting – and, as I'm heading to the TV station, I'm at a four way stop. A car comes up behind me, doing about a hundred mph, and hits the left side of my bike and my leg. A flap of skin was all that was holding my left leg together, below the knee. Tib and Fib were shattered and my foot was next to my knee. It was nasty. It took me a year and a half to walk again. Spent a little time in a wheelchair, a cane, crutches – trying to get my feet back working. But, once I stopped being in a wheelchair, I started learning everything I could about emergency medicine and first aid – advanced and basic. I even enrolled on an EMT course, but I had to drop out because my father had tried to kill himself by downing half a bottle of Zanex and a half a gallon of whiskey. So, EMT course over, I had to go back home and be a son again.'

'Maybe they should call you Lucky?' I suggested. Thankfully, Boomer smiled at my insensitive joke.

Boomer wasn't fishing for sympathy. He was telling me these things simply because he knew I was curious. He knew that I wanted to humanise the superheroes and have people see them as more than just a bunch of guys dressing up in costumes. Of all the superheroes, Boomer was easily the most open and straight talking, although that was something that was occasionally used against him.

As we continued walking, a tipsy black guy in 1980s gym shorts and elastic headband stopped us. 'Hey, you're the superheroes. I've seen you on YouTube,' he said. 'Is Phoenix Jones around?'

'He's around,' Boomer lied.

'Cool. He's roaming the streets?'

'Yeah.'

'Cool.' And with that he walked away.

Boomer turned to me. 'Of course, we never say where PJ is; we just say that he's around. It keeps them in fear.'

I left Boomer with Grey, outside a comic book store called *The Dreaming*, so that Boomer could rest, and headed with Cabbie and USID for a wide, pot-holed alley at the rear of a bar. Cabbie wanted to check it as he had occasionally found passed-out drunks down there. It was near pitch-black and lined with large trashcans. Cabbie shone his flashlight along the path and we suddenly saw some movement on the ground by some bins.

'Is that a cat?' asked Cabbie.

'I'm not sure,' USID said, shining his own flashlight. 'I think it could be a racoon.'

The creature cautiously stepped out into the alley. It was indeed a racoon – a large one. We all stopped moving (including the racoon) and stared. The racoon stared back. I looked around at the group of superheroes and then down at the racoon. It was like a line-up from *Guardians of the Galaxy*.

I looked at Cabbie again, with his facemask, and then back down at the plucky racoon, with its own mask – a thick black stripe stretching across its eyes, looking like a comic book bank robber. It was a small, comic moment that I kept to myself, these two masked characters staring each other out, like two superheroes that had accidentally stumbled across each other's path. Then Cabbie shone his flashlight into the racoon's eyes, which lit up like shiny trinkets, and it shuffled off grumpily, into some scrub.

Cabbie huffed and looked over his shoulder, back down the dimly lit alley. He didn't seem bored as such, just weary, like he had been doing this for all of his life and it no longer held the excitement it once did.

'Do you still patrol as much as you used to?' I asked. 'It's just that I haven't seen you much with the others downtown.'

Cabbie stood still and nodded his head. 'I do a lot of day patrols now,' he answered. 'I call it "being half Cabbed-up". I'll have my utility belt, but I won't have my mask.'

'You patrol alone? Solo?'

'Yeah. I have a camera on me though, so I can still record everything.'

Going solo was against Phoenix's rules for the Rain City superheroes, but I didn't believe for a moment that Cabbie would give two shits about the rules, so I decided not to bring it up.

'You do solo patrols at night as well?'

'Yeah, that too.'

'What's the reason for going solo?' I asked, even though I felt sure I knew what his answer would be – and I was right.

'I get kind of annoyed at having to deal with everyone,' he said, meaning the other superheroes. 'I'm not really in to handholding and all that kind of stuff.'

'Is the team becoming too big?'

Cabbie thought about the question for a moment, perhaps considering how he should answer it, and probably believing that anything he said would get back to Phoenix. 'I've expressed it to PJ before, but sometimes I feel like it's overkill,' he told me, finally. 'I don't mind having new guys out, especially as I can't be out every night – but, I don't know, it's just my nature I guess. Obviously I'm gonna like it how it was back in the day, when it was just Phoenix and I.'

'I take it you see many people just coming and going?'

'Yeah. You see that online too. Two years ago, there were lots of people on Facebook talking about doing this kind of work, and then they come to realise that it's a lot of lonely nights out in the cold and rain, having to deal with shit you probably wouldn't normally have to deal with. So people disappear after a while. And I don't blame them or begrudge them. At least they tried it.'

The talk of lonely nights in the cold and rain made me think about the realities of police work. The non-stop action that is often depicted on TV is such a small part of a much larger reality. This truth was obviously the same when it came to being a superhero.

Cabbie lifted his chin, indicating silently that we should keep walking. We exited the alley and re-joined Boomer and Grey, before continuing on. The bars were still crammed with rowdy drunks. It would be closing time soon and I was mentally preparing myself for the melee that would follow.

'Okay,' Cabbie suddenly said, 'I think we can call it a night.'

Call it a night? The bars would be kicking out at any moment.

Surely this was the time we had been waiting for? I looked at the others. No one said anything and I didn't feel it was my place to throw my opinion in. Instead, we returned to our cars: Cabbie to his, alone, as myself, USID and Grey joined Boomer at his vehicle. Then we left (although I wondered to myself if Cabbie hadn't just dumped us, so he could go solo).

Boomer drove spectacularly slowly along University Way. I guessed the reason for his cautious driving speed and commented on how surprised I was that Cabbie had ended the patrol at the moment he had.

'It's like leaving before the climax of a movie,' Grey said.

'Yeah,' I agreed.

'After all, what's another thirty minutes? We're already here. But I'm not leading patrol, so it's not my decision.'

It was Cabbie's patrol and Cabbie's choice to end it, but there was nothing stopping the others from cruising slowly through the streets, as they were now off duty. As far as they were concerned, should something happen in front of them that they needed to get involved in, they would now be acting only as *good Samaritans*. Samaritans with a police scanner, pepper-spray and masks.

It was the last patrol I would do with Cabbie. I never saw him again. It was a shame, as I liked him. I liked his mellow approach, his cabaret outfit and the fact he could travel through time. There are occasions where I find myself thinking about him and I like to imagine that he's back in 1940s Berlin, hiding in the shadows before jumping out and kicking the shit out of unsuspecting Nazis.

And who knows...

14

The People's Republic of Seattle

Before he left for Portland, I had mentioned to Phoenix that I had arranged to meet with the Seattle police spokesperson to talk about Seattle and the superheroes.

Phoenix's eyes widened like the entrance to the Batcave. 'Do they know you've patrolled with me and my guys?' he asked.

'Sure, I told them.'

'You meeting with Jamieson?'

'Yeah. Mark Jamieson. You know him?'

'He's always on TV talking about me,' Phoenix said. 'I'll be interested to hear what he tells you.'

I too was interested to find out what those in more official positions thought about a group of superheroes operating in their city, although I already had a good idea. The city attorney had once stated, "Phoenix Jones is a deeply misguided individual."

Mark Jamieson, the Seattle Police Department spokesperson, had arranged to meet me downtown, in the reception of the Seattle Police Headquarters, but he didn't plan on talking to me there. Instead, he took me to the tallest building in downtown Seattle – the nearby Columbia Center building – where we rode an elevator to the 40th floor. Here, far above the city, was a Starbucks. Naturally. He ordered our drinks, paid for them and we took a seat in a quiet corner overlooking the busy streets below. The panoramic views towards the cold waters of Puget Sound were spectacular.

I felt uneasy asking Mark about the superheroes, unsure as to how he would react. I was aware that he had given interviews about

Phoenix Jones before but wondered if he was bored or irritated with being continually asked about him. At the same time, there was no denying the fact that Phoenix Jones and his crew were out there doing their thing. So I jumped right into it.

'Someone said to me, either a superhero is going to kill somebody or somebody is going to kill a superhero,' I said, and sat back, taking a long sip of my burning-hot coffee.

Mark placed his coffee cup on the table in front of us. 'Yeah, that's my fear,' he said softly. 'That has been our message ever since Phoenix Jones came to our attention. We have been saying – and we continue to say – that, if you want to dress up as a superhero and walk around the streets of Seattle, you are perfectly within your rights to do that. If you want to go to public events and have your picture taken with tourists – knock yourself out. You know what? If you can make money out of it, all the better. Our only concern is when he inserts himself into these volatile situations where he may or may not know all of what's going on. Wear a costume if you want, but when you cross the line and start doing law enforcement, that's dangerous territory for you to be on. You could get hurt. Other people could get hurt. You could be held liable for anything that happens. Like that time he responded to what he perceived was a disturbance; he used pepper-spray and got arrested. That was totally avoidable. All he had to do – just like any other citizen – was pick up the phone and call 911 and say, "I think there's a fight going on. You need to send the police."'

'So you think it was wrong of him to intervene?' I asked. I was expecting a firm "yes" but Mark was more diplomatic than that.

'I just think he needs to be careful because, if it's two o'clock in the morning and the bars are letting out and somebody runs up to me wearing a mask, I'm not necessarily going to think: *superhero*. I might think he's coming to rob me. And I would be well within my rights to defend myself from somebody running up on me. He's said that he's been assaulted before; he says he's been stabbed, he says he's been shot. Now I don't know about you, but for me, that would be enough. I don't have to be stabbed or shot multiple times to get the message. Once is enough.'

It was a fair assessment and, truth be told, I felt the same way.

I had been unsure at the response I would get from Mark, but he was far more open on the subject of Phoenix Jones than I was expecting. He certainly wasn't putting up barriers at the first mention of his name. He was also open-minded about the superheroes in general, and that's something I wasn't expecting.

'It's sort of admirable what they're doing – going out, the civic engagement,' Mark said. 'We would just caution them and say, "If you see something, call 911 and let our officers handle it. Be a good witness, stick around and give the officers all the information you have." But we would ask that of anybody.'

Mark again cited the incident in the underpass, where Phoenix had pepper-sprayed the group he believed were fighting, resulting in his arrest.

'He did call us but, instead of waiting for the officers to arrive to sort it out, he ran right into the middle of the fray and tried to break it up. You saw the video. He started spraying people.'

'In the UK, pepper-spray and tasers are illegal,' I said. 'But over here citizens can legally carry them, right?'

'People can carry it, yeah, but it's one of those things; you know, a baseball bat is perfectly legal to have but, if you use it on somebody, you're going to be charged with assault. I think the reason for his arrest was because the officer, in his mind, said: *You know what? You can't claim self defence if you ran into the middle of the fight.* Nobody was attacking him until he inserted himself into it. It was totally avoidable. Just call the police.'

Mark also wasn't sure that everyone in the superhero community agreed with the direction that Phoenix Jones was taking the movement.

'There's the National or International Real-Life Superheroes Movement, or whatever,' Mark said. 'And a lot of those guys are not keen on what he's doing. They think he's sort of going rogue.

He's just the one getting all the press because he's the most charismatic.'

I told Mark about the other heroes I'd met around the country and the different views I had heard about what a superhero should be – that some believed in the more *in-your-face crime-fighting* approach, whereas others believed it was about providing charity and giving hope.

'And that's how Phoenix Jones started,' Mark said. 'He would wear the costume and go out and give sandwiches to the homeless and things like that – and then, if he saw something, he would report it to the police. We thought that was great. But then it sort of... I think he got a little taste of publicity and it sort of went to his head. He started getting more and more bold. That's when some of these problems happened. I think – *hopefully* – that he's learnt from that incident where he got arrested.'

'I guess the cops must all know him,' I said.

'Oh God yeah! Our officers downtown and our officers in the U-District, they all know him because they see him and they respond to calls that he's on or that he himself has called us on. When he first started, he would call us, but he wouldn't want to give his name to be a witness; he said that he had to retain his anonymity because he's a superhero.'

Not giving his name, however, had caused the officers problems. The arrest of a perpetrator was only part of the process for a police officer investigating a crime. A successful conviction often requires witnesses willing to give evidence in court. By not giving his details, that process was hindered. But there was little the officers or the department could do about it.

All that changed once Phoenix had been arrested and his true identity was revealed. Mark claimed that the department already knew who he was but, before his arrest, it had been Phoenix's right to keep his identity a secret.

'Are there any officers that actually support what the superheroes are doing?' I asked. (It was a claim that Phoenix Jones had once made to me. I was also thinking about the transit officers we had spoken to.)

Mark looked surprised. 'That actually *support* them? Let me put it this way, I think Phoenix... if he's out there, he's dressed up, he's walking around, he's talking to people, getting his picture taken – that's great. And if him walking around is a deterrent, then that's also great and I don't think any officer would fault him for doing that. He's not a problem until he is, right? As soon as he inserts himself into a situation and makes it worse instead of better, then I think that's where most officers have an issue with it. If it's a matter of life and death, then by all means, go in there and do what you need to do. But these incidents where he inserts himself are not life and death; they're usually drunk guys arguing. Then he'll try and break it up and then it becomes a fight.'

I brought up the mutual combat video I had seen of Phoenix fighting the drunk, and told Mark how surprised I was that the officers hadn't got involved. Mark told me that Phoenix had done the right thing in calling the police, but he believed Phoenix should have walked away once the officers arrived. Even so, I questioned him about the decision of the officers not to intervene.

'The officers couldn't get involved, because Phoenix and the drunk agreed to fight, is that correct?'

'Yeah. If there're no victims and both guys agree to it. I mean, I would suggest that they don't do it on the street. If you guys want to fight, go to a gym or something and put on some gloves.'

'But let's say Phoenix Jones punched this man and killed him, which could happen – he's a mixed martial artist, after all – what happens then?'

Mark nodded his head. 'So maybe he didn't technically break the law or anything, but if this guy decides to civilly sue him – I mean you can sue anybody for just about anything – I guess my point is, why even put yourself in that position? Phoenix Jones is a household name – international, even – there's a chance that some people are going to exploit that, right? "*Oh, he's Phoenix Jones, he's probably got loads of money. I'm going to challenge him to a fight. I'm going to get him to hit me and then I'm going to sue him."* So why put yourself in that position to begin with?' Mark was in no doubt where the buck stopped. 'Bottom line is, we're police officers, we've gone through the training, we have the experience and tools. We know what's a crime, when it's a crime and how to investigate it. I think people recognise Phoenix Jones for what he is – it's cute, it's novel, a guy dressed up in a costume. But if there's a real problem, people call 911. They don't call him.'

'There's no giant bat signal,' I offered.

'Exactly.'

'Have you ever met him?' I asked.

'Nope.'

'Would you like to meet him?'

'Not really,' he replied.

With that, I finished my coffee and prepared to leave.

'You back out with Phoenix Jones again, tonight?' Mark asked, as we headed towards the elevators.

'Actually, I'm going to take a look at the anti-police demo that's happening downtown today,' I told him.

Mark looked at me with a curious, half smile. 'This is a very strange vacation you're on,' he said.

A short, white guy in his twenties lifted up his t-shirt and showed me a tattoo he had inked across his midriff. *FUCK THE POLICE* it read in large, red letters.

'You don't like the police, then,' I said.

'It's not that I hate the police,' he told me, somewhat contradicting what he had permanently scripted across his body. 'I just hate what they do.'

We were downtown, standing in City Hall Park, a small green space shaded by a canopy of trees at the side of the King County Courthouse. Activists had organised an anti-police demonstration and were planning to march through the city to protest alleged police brutality. Two hundred and fifty protestors were expected to turn up but, in the end, only fifty or sixty actually bothered. I wondered if the movement against the police was starting to wane. But there was a second protest planned straight after, this time in Capitol Hill, so maybe more people would be attending that, instead. Maybe even the Black Bloc.

The superheroes had decided not to make an appearance, feeling their presence could inflame the situation. It seemed they had learnt a few lessons from their previous encounters – all except Boomer, that is, who had mentioned to me that he was planning to attend and "keep and eye on things". I hadn't seen him yet, but it wouldn't be difficult to spot him with such small numbers at the demo.

One thing the protestors didn't lack, however, was loud voices and strong views. A woman wearing a blue plaid shirt and Doc Marten boots was standing on a raised, concrete seating area within City Hall Park. She wore a Guy Fawkes mask over her face – the type that had been adopted by anarchists around the world and often seen at protests. Speaking to the assembled crowd through a loudhailer, she was reminding them why they were there and telling them about recent incidents of alleged police brutality. She was also informing them of their rights and how they should not consent to being searched by the police, encouraging everyone to film the police at every opportunity.

'Fuck yeah!' shouted tattoo guy.

Then, without warning, he jumped onto the raised area and took the loudhailer from the woman in the Guy Fawkes mask.

'Firstly, I want to tell you that everything I say is my own opinion and does not represent the opinion of anybody else, individual or group,' he told the crowd, sounding quite reasonable. But then he continued, 'But you know what? We have the right to protect ourselves and each other. If you see a cop attacking someone illegally and you're carrying a firearm, I would say, *shoot that cop!*'

The crowd, who had been whooping and shouting in agreement

at what most of the other speakers had to say, suddenly fell quiet. I looked at the dozen or so cycle cops who were settled in a line behind the seating area. They seemed uninterested in what the guy had to say and were chatting among themselves.

Then the tattooed guy turned to face the cycle cops and shouted down the loudhailer at them, 'FUCK YOU! YOU FUCKING PIGS!'

The cycle cops looked over at him and started to laugh.

'FUCK YOU!' he shouted again. The cops continued to laugh at him.

Some of the crowd, perhaps feeling brave now that the cops had showed little interest in the guy shouting abuse, started to whoop and yell again.

'YOU BITCHES!'

Then the woman in the Guy Fawkes mask snatched the loudhailer from tattoo guy and encouraged him to step down, which he did. The cops continued to laugh.

'IF YOU WANT A WAR WITH ME, YOU GOT IT! WE'LL HAVE A STRAIGHT UP WAR!' he screamed at the cops.

Then he turned to me and said, 'Where were we?'

'You were telling me how you don't hate cops,' I said.

'I'm okay with the whole concept of police,' he told me, seemingly hell-bent on confusing me with where he stood on the subject. 'The police are supposed to protect us, but instead they're shooting innocent people. Our society is being run by psychopaths, literally.' Then he added, 'Listen, if you're an undercover cop, I really don't care.'

I assured him I wasn't an undercover cop. I also decided it was best not to mention that I was an *actual* cop. Then I asked, 'But what's the alternative? What would you have if not the police?'

'We should protect each other.'

It was something other people at the demonstration had spoken about. There was a desire within the group to have a world where communities looked after themselves without a need for police at all. It was a nice idea but utterly delusional. It would simply never work. At some point, people are going to disagree and when people disagree, laws are created to impose one side's point of view. But because some will disagree with the laws, the laws will need enforcing. *Police.*

'What about the Real-Life Superheroes? Could they be an alternative?' I asked.

'No. They think they're something special but they're really not.'

A photographer standing nearby overheard me asking about the superheroes and stepped into the conversation. 'They're fucking assholes, man,' he said. 'We were on a march on May Day, walking past the Federal Building, when someone from the crowd threw a rock at the building. Then these fucking superheroes jump out of the bushes and start pepper-spraying people at random. Who the fuck do they think they are? That's assault. They're not fucking cops. They're just jackasses dressed in costumes.'

'They said that they were attacked. That they had rocks thrown at them and that there were incendiary devices thrown at the building.'

'There were no incendiary device thrown until Niketown – and that was to do with the Black Bloc. Listen, I'm sure their hearts are in the right place but vigilante justice is never a good idea – especially with people who have no fucking clue what they're doing. They've got pepper-spray and tasers. I've even seen them with leather straps before.'

'Blackjacks?' I asked, innocently.

'Yeah, blackjacks. I'm not even sure they're legal in Seattle. It's ridiculous.'

I was going to leave it at that, but he wasn't finished. 'There's an anti-superhero,' he said. 'His name is Rex Velvet. I mean, you've got superheroes, so you need a super-villain, right? You should look him up. He's making a mockery of the superheroes. Have you heard of him?'

I told him I had.

Rex Velvet's videos were becoming increasingly popular, as well as increasingly hostile. The latest video to appear online was particularly nasty and sadistic; it showed an actor playing a "superhero", tied to a chair. The superhero had been "captured" by Rex Velvet's henchmen after falling behind on a patrol. In the video, he was aggressively questioned by Rex Velvet before being tortured, and was later seen covered in cuts and scars. As before, it was made to look silly and comedic – but I also found it rather tasteless. Can torture ever be funny?

Regardless, Rex Velvet had found an audience. And since Rex Velvet, I had found others with a similar anti-superhero drive. There was *ROACH* – the Ruthless Organization Against Citizen Heroes – who were a response to a superhero group operating in Cincinnati, called the Allegiance of Heroes. ROACH, founded by "evil genius" "The Potentate", had a recruitment video stating that "Evil must act". This "Consortium of Evil" had even put a bounty on the true identity of a superhero known as *Shadow Hare*. The bounty, which had been placed on Craigslist, was only worth $10, but still, you got the message.

Rex Velvet was using the heroes to sell vodka. ROACH was trying to flog t-shirts. But the fact was, whether it was just for fun or not, there were people and groups out there who would happily disrupt the activities of the Real-Life Superheroes and who would, given a chance, publicly reveal their identities. It was something that could have serious implications, particularly if a superhero had been involved in upsetting the work of genuine criminals. Whatever a person's opinion of the superheroes might have been, the fact remained that there were dangers and they did have enemies.

With these thoughts in mind, I looked around for Boomer. I still couldn't see him. Perhaps he had gone undercover in one of those Guy Fawkes masks? Most of all, I hoped he wouldn't turn up in his superhero gear. From what I had seen previously, the result would be disastrous.

A young white woman, who looked as though she was a university student, was now speaking through the loudhailer, calling for the abolition of the police and talking of how communities should protect themselves. As she spoke, she became more worked up, almost hyperventilating.

'The institution of the police is to enable white supremacy, patriarchy, genocide and slavery!' she announced, and she continued on for some time about how police were actually a bunch of murderers and rapists.

Eventually, another demonstrator took the loudhailer from her and simply said, 'Shall we march?'

The crowd cheered (perhaps happy to just be getting on with it) and everyone started to move north, up 3rd Avenue. The cops mounted their black bicycles, rolling down the slope through the small park so that they could travel with the demonstrators.

The mostly white group of men and women were a mix of ages. Some carried banners and placards with a variety of slogans targeting the Seattle Police Department: *Police not above the law*; *Honor the dead, fight for the living*; *film the police* and *Hold SPD accountable*.

'Fuck the police! No justice, no peace!' they called out as they walked along the centre of the road.

The police had blocked off the street, to stop vehicles driving along the route and to allow the protest to move quickly through. The protestors stopped briefly outside the Seattle Police Department headquarters building, which was guarded by a dozen cycle cops.

'WHOSE STREETS? OUR STREETS!' the protestors shouted repeatedly.

'If they're our streets, why don't we just take the whole fucking thing?' tattoo guy called out, sounding frustrated and itching for more direct action.

I overheard two middle-aged women, who were both wearing berets and corduroy jackets, talking about tattoo guy. 'I don't like him,' one of them said. 'He always shows up, yelling random stuff.'

A Seattle police car was held across the lanes at the intersection with Cherry Street, preventing the evening traffic from proceeding and, I assumed, to deter the marchers from continuing in that direction. But the protestors walked either side of the police car and weaved in and out of the cars and buses that had come to a stop behind it. The two clowns, who I had seen at the demonstration in Capitol Hill, suddenly rode past on their bicycles, honking their comedy horns. Both were dressed as before, with clown makeup and foam noses. "General Malaise" was wearing his old-fashioned "Keystone Kop" police helmet and the second clown was wearing the green, army jacket with the words "Clandestine Insurgent Rebel Clown Army" on the back. The police allowed the protestors – and the clowns – to continue along this new route.

As we reached Madison Street, a businessman standing at a bus stop shouted at the protestors, telling them to "fuck off" and "get a job". This earned an immediate response.

An older guy, with long, greasy grey hair, charged towards the businessman, incensed. 'Where's *your* job? Where's *your* job?' he shouted back.

'I've got a job,' the businessman told him. 'What about you?'

'I'M SORRY! I'M SORRY THAT YOU'RE AN IDIOT!' the old man screamed into the businessman's face.

'I'm an idiot? Try looking in the mirror, buddy.'

'What's a few dead innocents, eh?' the old man said angrily.

A couple of cycle cops rode over. They didn't get involved, but their presence was enough to encourage the older man to continue with the march. The businessman turned to the other city workers at the bus stop and shrugged his shoulders.

'What's this protest all about?' a woman asked one of the cops.

'Police brutality,' he told her, sounding tired. 'It's not a very good turn out this time, though.'

Nearby, another member of the public stood holding a flyer that he had just been handed by one of the protestors. The flyer claimed the police were murderers. He stared at it, reading the words, and then shouted at the protestors, 'We need the police, you fucking assholes!'

The march continued through the downtown streets until it

reached Century Plaza, which was outside a Macy's department store and just a few blocks east from Pike Place Market. Crowds of locals and groups of bemused tourists stopped to watch the protestors as they gathered in the plaza. Fat sticks of coloured chalk were handed out and the protestors began writing various slogans on the paved ground, such as: *PEOPLE KILL COPS FOR A REASON; SMASH THE POLICE STATE; DO YOU FEEL SAFER HAVING MURDERERS WITH GUNS PROTECTING YOU?* and *YOU ARE 8 TIMES MORE LIKELY TO BE KILLED BY A COP THAN A TERRORIST.*

The cycle cops stood nearby, chatting among themselves as the protestors covered the ground with their provocative writings. A line of cops on Harley Davidson motorcycles were parked outside an Abercrombie and Fitch store and another large group of cops, slurping coffees, stood outside a nearby Starbucks, watching the protestors literally make their mark, like parents watching their children at a playground. But just off the plaza were a couple of large, black SUVs. Inside were state troopers carrying large assault weapons. They wore black clothing, heavy ballistic body armour and wraparound sunglasses. They were an intimidating sight.

At the plaza, most of the protestors mingled around – but a few took hold of the loudhailer again, repeating much of what they had previously said. I noticed the two clowns riding off. They headed up Pine Street, towards Capitol Hill, where the second protest was due to start. I decided to follow their lead and headed that way myself.

Things felt different in Capitol Hill. The atmosphere seemed tetchy. Whereas the first demo had some organisation about it, with speakers, flyers and tattoos, Capitol Hill was more a gathering of angry looking anarchists. City Hall Park had been loud, but seemed somewhat purposeful. Capitol Hill simply felt like a bunch of people looking for trouble. For a start, many of the protestors (who all appeared to be in their twenties) were carrying banners and signs that simply read: FUCK THE POLICE. There was no specific mention of the SPD's apparent brutality. As I hadn't seen Boomer at the first demo, I feared I would see him here – and once again prayed that he wouldn't appear in his superhero outfit.

The protestors had met in Cal Anderson Park, a medium-sized green space, with a small reservoir, in the centre of the Capitol Hill neighbourhood. A line of half a dozen police horses with visors protecting their eyes, stood close by and more cycle cops – some of whom had ridden up from the first demo – were also nearby, both in the park and out on the streets.

For a long time, the protestors mingled and chatted among themselves. I was beginning to wonder if they were planning to march at all. As with the first demonstration, there seemed to be far fewer of them than I – and I suspect, they – had been expecting. There were perhaps thirty altogether, many wearing black masks and balaclavas over their faces. *Black Bloc.*

Without warning, the group rushed out of the park, running along a pedestrian path between two buildings, perhaps in an effort to evade the police or to confuse them. But the cycle cops quickly followed, and there were further police already waiting for them on the other side of the path.

The two clowns on bikes appeared, as did tattoo guy from the first demo. More banners and signs were handed out. Most still read FUCK THE POLICE, but there were others calling for the abolition of borders and prisons.

The protestors marched noisily along Pine Street, high above the busy I-5 highway, as if they were heading downtown. The cycle cops remained with the group, riding slowly behind them, keeping their distance but close enough to move in quickly, should they need to. On occasions the protestors would stop in the road, forcing the evening traffic to come to a halt, or else they would simply jaywalk, ignoring drivers' right of way. Most drivers looked bemused by the sudden appearance of thirty, mostly masked protestors walking in front of their cars, holding up banners and shouting, "FUCK THE POLICE!" and "ALL COPS ARE BASTARDS!"

As we weaved though the streets, we reached the SPD's West Precinct building at Virginia and 8th, where the protestors' chants took a particularly nasty turn.

One protestor shouted at the police, 'Save a life. Kill yourself!' This set off some of the others in the group, who began shouting out comments about police officers who had committed suicide.

'Blow your own brains out like your buddy in the South Precinct!' one woman shouted towards the cops.

Other protestors laughed at this particularly tasteless remark, but then took the chant up themselves, repeating it over and over. The cops simply continued to cycle behind them without responding.

The suicide that the woman was referring to was of a Seattle Police Department officer who had been arrested for possession of crack-cocaine after the department had carried out a sting operation. The officer, who had been on the force for over twenty years, went on to shoot and kill himself.

The march continued past the police precinct and turned into Boren Avenue, where the protestors began to make their way back towards Capitol Hill. Ahead of us was a crossroad where Boren met Howell. Cars were driving up Howell, away from the city – but the protestors continued and, as before, looked as though they had no intention of stopping.

'Mick! Mick!' I turned to my left. It was Boomer. He was driving alongside me on Boren, in his tatty, white car. 'You want a ride?' he asked, excitedly.

'No thanks, I'm gonna keep walking with the crowd,' I told him. 'I wasn't sure if I was going to see you here.'

'I'm just keeping an eye on things and letting the rest of the RCSM know what's going down.'

He had his laptop computer set up beside him and was monitoring the police radio traffic on his scanner.

'Are you on your own?' I asked.

'Yeah. I'm not sure how happy PJ will be about me being here through. But this is my city too and I want to make sure it stays safe. Besides, he's in Portland.'

The line of cars Boomer was sitting in had come to a slow crawl as they travelled behind the protestors, who had now reached the crossroad with Howell and had come to an obstructive stop. I told Boomer that I was going to catch up with the march.

But, just as I started to walk towards them, total chaos erupted.

The driver of one of the cars, perhaps frustrated with the protestors blocking the road, had decided to simply drive through them. The protestors refused to move but the car kept going until bodies began to scatter in all directions. People began to scream and shout. Half a dozen of the protestors jumped onto the moving car, some on the hood, others hanging off the sides. They began thumping and kicking the car as it continued to plough through the protestors.

'Oh shit!' I heard Boomer shout behind me.

I ran towards the car as dozens of cops piled into the mayhem, pulling people off the vehicle and keeping protestors away from the driver, who they were trying to attack. Cops started pushing people back and created a semi-organised barrier between the car and the protestors so that the car could continue on its way. A protestor ran towards one of the cycle cops and kicked out at him, knocking his bike back and nearly toppling the cop. More cops, jumping out from the back of a large van, arrived to re-enforce the cycle cops.

One of the protestors stormed up to a line of officers as the car drove away. 'That's assault with a deadly weapon!' he screamed.

'Why don't you arrest the driver of that car?' a young, female protestor shouted at the cop. 'Why don't you arrest him? Why don't you do something?'

Perhaps because you said, "*fuck the police*", "*go shoot yourselves in the head*" and "*we don't need cops*", I thought to myself.

But then, just like that, things began to calm down and the march continued on, finally reaching Cal Anderson Park, where it had all started an hour before.

The two demos had been noisy, passionate and, at times, downright nasty – but they had also been poorly attended.

As I stood in the park, watching people filter away, one of the clowns approached me.

'I heard you asking about the superheroes,' he said.

'That's right. I was wondering what people's opinions of them were. What do you think about Phoenix Jones?'

'I'm not really hip to what he's doing,' he told me in a slow, monotone voice. 'We have enough problems with police, let alone people who aren't even qualified. We don't need some jumped-up superhero running around thinking he's a cop.'

'But if you don't want police, couldn't these guys be an alternative?'

'I'd rather have nothing,' he said and he cycled off, honking his comedy horn.

15

Number Two in Pioneer Square

'I wasn't supposed to be here tonight,' Boomer said, as he drove Jack, USID and me along 1st Avenue towards Pioneer Square.

'No you weren't,' agreed Jack. 'I was supposed to have some real back-up.'

Jack was livid. With Phoenix in Portland, Jack had been left in charge to run tonight's patrol, but everyone had bailed on him – everyone except for Boomer, USID and myself.

'Weren't you meant to be on a date tonight?' Jack asked Boomer.

'Yeah, but she got sick and cancelled,' Boomer told him.

'She came to her senses, more like.'

'She took a rain check,' Boomer said. 'Hopefully we'll meet next weekend.'

Jack opened his mouth but, before he had a chance to poke more fun, Boomer saved him the effort. 'Some girl asked me if I could dance once. I told her, "Listen lady, the last time I tried to dance, Greenpeace turned up and threw a bucket of salt water on me."'

'Did I ever tell you about my Greenpeace idea?' Jack said. 'What I wanted to do was get a bunch of my buddies together, get hold of some Greenpeace t-shirts, put them on, go to a beach and then roll some fat person back into the water.'

Jack didn't wait for our response and just started laughing at his own joke.

'So why did no one turn up tonight?' I asked, changing the subject.

'Because they're all a bunch of idiots, that's why,' Jack said.

'Everybody went out on Cabbie's patrol the other night,' he added, sounding offended. 'If Phoenix delegates duties to me, people should take that as if the orders that I give are coming from PJ himself. You know what I mean? That's the way I look at it, but it's not the way others look at it.'

'People don't take patrol as seriously if PJ isn't running it?' I asked.

'Correct.'

'PJ is the face of the movement,' Boomer said. 'People know Phoenix Jones – *he's the black guy in the black and gold suit* – whereas no one gives a fuck about the rest of us and no one's going to take us seriously, even when Midnight Jack is leading.'

This was something that I had long believed myself. Others had come to work specifically for Phoenix Jones after seeing him on the news or hearing about him from some other outlet. But anyone thinking that they would find some sort of fame for themselves, simply by hanging out with Phoenix Jones, was probably going to be disappointed – or fired, as had happened previously. Everything about Phoenix Jones – his outfit, his videos, his arrest – had brought him to people's attention. The others were just the sidekicks and wannabes, some of whom were trying to emulate what Phoenix had already become. Some wouldn't care about the fame (and of course some were actually desperate to stay out of the limelight), but I suspected that there were others in the group who would have liked at least a little recognition. It seemed to me that, as far as the public were concerned, there was no "Boomer", "Midnight Jack" or "USID". There was only Phoenix Jones. The rest were simply viewed as his hangers-on.

Jack mulled over the neighbourhoods that were on his list as possible spots for the patrol. There were three up for consideration but, as there were so few of us, he was feeling cautious. The Seattle bars were promoting "St Patrick's Day weekend", so Jack decided against Belltown; it was bound to be an especially wild, riotous night that would require a bigger team. Capitol Hill was out as well, because of the protests that had taken place earlier. That left us with his third choice: Pioneer Square was also a potentially dangerous area at night, but one that Jack was happier to hit.

'It's the only viable area tonight,' he told us. 'I think it's the only place we can safely patrol. But don't get me wrong – I'm still *riot-gearing* up. And let's face it Boomer, you can't even run.'

'Erm...'

'You can't run.'

'Well, the one time I did, there was a damn good reason for it. It hurt like hell for a few days afterwards. In fact, I could barely walk.'

'Like I said, you can't run.'

Boomer parked in a quiet street, under a viaduct. Jack wasn't kidding about the riot gear. From the trunk of Boomer's, car he pulled out his usual kit, along with a heavy, black-coloured body piece that included a chest and back plate along with shoulder and arm guards. Pulling it over his head, he strapped it in place. Written in white on the rear of the armour were the letters RCSM.

'The armour's re-enforced plastic and moulded foam,' Jack told me. 'It's pressure sensitive, so it disperses the impact when something hits it. It's real riot armour. The best shit out there.'

It was the first time I'd seen him in this more aggressive gear, and I questioned why he had decided on it tonight.

'Because it's just us,' he told me. 'If more people had shown up, I wouldn't have needed it. The other reason I grabbed this damn thing is because of the protests that took place today. I don't want to run into people from the protests that are down here drinking and in the mood to start some shit. Having them run into me wearing this is better than having them run into me without this.'

After assisting Jack with the riot armour straps, Boomer began getting his own gear on. He picked up a large black belt with pouches and holsters hanging off it, which he strapped to his thigh.

'What do you think of my new leg kit?' Boomer asked Jack, looking for some approval.

'Yeah, it looks real nice, Lara Croft,' Jack teased.

Boomer handed each of us a small walkie-talkie, which we tested out and ensured were all on the same channel. Then USID pulled up his grey hood and headed into Pioneer Square alone, as we finished getting ready.

'Did Phoenix give you any directions for tonight?' I asked Jack.

'He trusts me to do things my way,' he replied.

'I think his words were, "Don't fuck up and don't die",' Boomer said.

'Okay, let's talk about tonight's structure,' Jack said. 'Boomer, you're the medic, obviously, so you'll be my Three. I'll run as Number One. Mick, I'm going to have you as my Number Two. Number Two means, if something goes down, I'm going to be expecting you to be standing behind me.'

This I hadn't been expecting. Sure, Jack was short of superheroes, but even so. As well as being his backup, I would be expected to step in and take charge if something happened to him. But then what choice did Jack really have? USID was doing what USID does – undercover patrols, separate from us – and Boomer's role was as the team medic. So that left Jack with me – and, just like that, I found myself as the Number Two on a live, superhero patrol, whether I liked it or not. (*Not*, in case you were wondering.)

'You've come a long way, Mick,' Boomer said, grinning, almost proudly. 'Here, take this.'

I looked down at Boomer's hands. He was trying to pass me a canister of pepper-spray.

'No,' I said firmly.

'Oh, okay then. In that case, let's talk about how to defend yourself and fight, should you need to. Open-hand techniques only, okay? It's more defensible in court if you get arrested.'

I stared at Boomer. It was one thing shadowing them as they went about their patrols – but, despite that one time when I had instinctively chased after the guy with the bag, I had always made it clear that I was not going to actively involve myself with the actual *job* of being a superhero. Yet here I was: Jack's Number Two. And although this was not what I had intended, there seemed no other option than to go along with it. I had grown to like these guys. Midnight Jack had started to trust me and saw me as one of the team. Boomer, too, had opened up to me about his life and the RCSM. I was fond of them both and the truth was, if someone did try to hurt them, I would naturally step in and help. So why not run as Jack's Number Two? It was just some made-up title, after all.

Jack stepped in and stopped Boomer from trying to pass on his knowledge of "defensive moves" and "open-hand techniques".

'Mick knows how to play this game, Boomer; he's a cop, remember. We don't need to explain to him how to defend himself or fight.'

A short time later, USID came over the radio to give us the low-down on the area. There were four nightclubs in a close proximity that were well known to the team. USID informed us that all were packed with revellers. A large biker gang was hanging around the entrance to one, and a second club nearby was rammed with hip-hop fans – mostly young black men and women. The other two, a little further up the street, had lines of young drunks standing in the chilly night air, waiting to get in. There seemed to be no police in the area at all, so we made our way towards the clubs.

'Whoa! Are you guys ninjas?' a drunk man asked, doing his best to hold up his even more wasted friend as they staggered past.

'Nope,' Boomer told him casually.

'Power Rangers?'

'Nope.'

We continued past without another word, and cut through one of the wide alleys that ran between the old brick buildings common in this part of town. From here we walked into spacious Occidental Square, with its tall, dark wooden totem poles and even taller maple trees. Outside Trinity nightclub – just a small, black painted, single storey building – was the biker gang, whose members were lined up on their sports motorcycles, all facing the same direction, rear wheels pressed up against the kerb.

'Are they trouble?' I asked.

'No. They're not trouble,' Jack told me. 'They tend to play nice with everybody, as long as everybody else plays nice with them. But they will fuck you up if you don't play nice.'

USID stood on the corner at the intersection of Occidental and Washington, fifty yards away. He was watching us, as well as continuing to keep an eye of the other clubs. At the intersection, where USID stood, was The Last Supper Club, where the hip-hop crowd were gathered. Further along Washington, just past a small parking lot, were the last two clubs – Fuel and Volume. They were also small, single storey, brick buildings. Each had crowds of young, excited revellers outside the doors, just as USID had described.

Jack stopped outside Volume, on the intersection of Washington and 2nd Avenue. A couple of bouncers outside the club were keeping the line orderly. They seemed relaxed and in control. One of them, Mario, was a short black man in a smart, dark suit. He knew Jack and shook his hand. Mario explained that they were having a busy night but, so far, everything was in order. The problems could arise later though, he mentioned. An hour from now, at 2am, they would be closing the club – but only for half an hour. At 2.30am, the club would reopen, this time serving only coffee and soda. It was a way for the clubs to get around the law, which required them to stop serving alcohol. By not serving alcohol, it meant that minors could then be admitted into the club as well.

'Eighteen year olds who are already high,' Jack told me.

Mario was expecting to turn plenty of people away at the door; it was then that he was anticipating issues and trouble.

'We'll be in the neighbourhood,' Jack told him. 'We'll keep an eye out for any trouble makers.'

'Thank you Jack, I appreciate that,' Mario said.

As we walked away, Jack told me that Mario probably wouldn't need our help tonight, and that he was more than capable of handling things himself.

'He can control his own business as well as the club next door,' Jack said. 'All on his own!'

We walked away from the clubs, along 2nd Avenue, towards the International District (the "*I-D*", Jack called it) – essentially, Seattle's Chinatown. It was a shady area, particularly at night. USID had called up on the radio; he had seen two Hispanic guys walking away from the clubs that he wasn't happy about. Drunk and aggressive, they were heading towards the I-D – so went to check them out, while USID remained in the club area, keeping an eye on things there.

As we continued along 2nd Avenue towards Main Street, we spotted the two Hispanic men up ahead. They seemed unsteady on their feet and were facing up to each other on the sidewalk, like they were getting ready to fight.

'Shit!' cried Jack. 'Quick!'

Each of the men began to throw full-blown punches at the other's face. Jack sprinted towards them. He had his hand on his large canister of pepper-spray, ready to pull it from its pouch. I charged up behind Jack, reminding myself that I was his Number Two. Even Boomer had followed behind, doing his best to keep up. There was no getting out of this one, and I could feel a small amount of anxiety creeping in, not at the thought that we may have to fight the men – I was quite confident that myself and Jack could handle them (after all, Jack was armed with his enormous can of pepper-spray) – but because this was the very thing I had been concerned about all along; that I would have to get involved in an incident, as a *superhero* – or at least as part of a superhero team – and this would bring me to the attention of the police and the authorities, with who-knows-what consequences. Even so, there was no way that I was just going to stand back and watch as Jack and Boomer took the men on alone. I was no longer prepared to be a bystander.

As we drew closer, I watched as one of the men landed a hard punch on the other's nose. The second man stumbled backwards a couple of steps but then launched himself forwards and struck the first man around the side of his head, nearly knocking him to the ground.

Mentally, I readied myself to jump into the fray and pull them apart.

'Stop!' Jack shouted at the men. 'Hold it!'

He was starting to pull out his pepper-spray, in case one or both of the men turned on us.

Suddenly both men stopped fighting. They turned to face us. I caught up with Jack and stood next to him, fists clenched, getting ready for what was about to go down.

'Stop fighting!' Jack ordered.

Both men put their hands up in front of them, indicating that everything was okay, as they each tried to catch their breath. For the moment, it appeared that they really had stopped fighting, so Jack began to release his grip on the pepper-spray canister.

'It's okay,' one of the men said as he gasped for air. 'We're friends.'

The other man bent over, clutching his waist with his hands but nodding in agreement.

They waved their hands at us, indicating for us to back down; then they turned and walked away together, up Main Street.

Boomer caught up with us. 'What was that all about?'

'Friends fighting,' Jack told him.

'That strange thing you call *mutual combat*,' I added.

'Weird things like that always happen around here,' Jack said.

We walked back, along 2nd Avenue. As we reached Washington, near to the clubs, Jack told me about a time he and another hero – *Ghost* – had come across two men fighting at the crosswalk in this exact spot.

'We came around the corner and there's this man choking out another man. We ran over and separated them and held them both at pepper-point.'

'Pepper-point?' I asked.

'Like gun-point, only with pepper-spray.'

'Of course.'

'Anyway, it turned out that the guy who was being choked had just tried to rob the other guy. At first both were saying, "Oh we're glad you're here. Help us!" It was really confusing. But the second we find out that this guy is the victim of a robbery, the other guy, who was getting choked, immediately pulls out a broken pair of scissors – and then he's trying to stab us. We backed up and were about to pepper him when the police arrived. But it goes to show you, just because someone is losing a fight, it doesn't mean that they're not the perpetrator of it. It was a good learning experience for us.'

By now, we had passed the clubs and were close to 3rd Avenue, where we checked some of the alleyways. They were covered in water and soap.

'Ah, the familiar smell of green apple and urine!' Jack said as we stepped into an alley.

He was right. The alley did, indeed, have a strange aroma of both apple and piss.

'Why is that?' I asked.

'The city cleans the alleys at night with green apple soap to try and disguise the smell,' Jack told me. 'It makes for an interesting mix.'

As we walked out of the alley, Jack started to feel uncomfortable. It was quiet, other than the odd homeless person or drug dealer wandering about.

'I've got a feeling,' he said.

'A *Jack feeling*?' I asked. 'Something bad?'

'Not bad, just that we should be back at the clubs. I just feel that's where we should be. Has USID called in since that fight?'

'Not heard anything,' Boomer replied.

I hadn't heard anything either. In fact, all I'd heard had been a near constant static over the radio, possibly because of the area we were patrolling. If USID had been calling up, we didn't hear it.

As it turned out, Midnight Jack's *Spidey sense* had been right. When we arrived back at Occidental and Washington, we saw three Seattle police cars parked at various angles, outside Volume nightclub. The car doors were all open and the air around us was alternating in flashes of red and blue, from the police emergency lights. Half a dozen cops were fighting with a man on the ground, in the middle of the road. Something serious had happened.

But where was USID?

I looked about frantically, trying to find his grey hood among the crowds of people who were spilling from the clubs to watch the fight.

I took hold of my radio and pushed the transmit button. 'USID. USID, come in,' I said urgently.

Nothing.

'USID are you receiving?'

Still nothing.

Then, from a crowd of people in the parking lot nearby, USID stepped out. He nodded his head at me. He was safe.

More police cars began to arrive. The cops were struggling to control the fighting man, a large, bare-chested white guy, in jeans. By now, a dozen cops were on the scene, some holding the man down on the ground, others standing nearby, watching the crowd that had gathered.

One of the cops watching the crowd nodded his head and raised a hand in a friendly *hello* gesture. Jack explained that they had once helped the cop during another fight.

'He's one of the good ones who actually likes us...'

Meanwhile, the cops who were fighting the man on the ground had managed to twist his hands behind his back and place him in a set of handcuffs. Jack and Boomer began to speculate about what had happened. Jack thought that a weapon might have been involved due to the amount of police on scene. Maybe even a gun. It got Jack thinking.

'In the event of an active shooter, let them shoot at me,' he told us, in all seriousness. 'I am in command tonight, and that's my responsibility. Let them shoot at me.'

Mario was standing near the trouble. It had happened outside his club –Volume. Jack wanted to go check on him. As it was, Mario was fine and the police now had the man well and truly under control. Mario told us that he had denied the guy entry to the club due to the drunken state he had been in. It was then that the man had become violent. Luckily, the police had been nearby and Mario and his team were unhurt.

As we talked, a police van turned up (Boomer called it a "paddy wagon"). The police loaded the man into it and took him away.

'What do they call paddy wagons in the UK?' Boomer asked.

'A van,' I told him.

'Jack gets upset when I call them paddy wagons. He says it's racist.'

'It is a racist term,' Jack said. 'You're insulting my heritage.'

I looked around at the mix of people dressed in varying shades of green. Many – who didn't look to be in the slightest bit Irish – wore leprechaun outfits, enormous green foam hats, and ginger beards.

'There's nothing worse than a Mexican dude dressed up like a leprechaun,' Jack said, shaking his head. 'It's super offensive.'

As things started to calm down, we moved slowly away from the clubs. The biker gang was still outside Trinity, loudly revving the engines to the delight of a dozen young women dressed as though they were about to do the Riverdance.

As Jack walked across the road to check in with a hotdog seller to ensure he hadn't had any hassle, I took the opportunity to speak with Boomer.

'How do you think Jack did tonight?' I asked, knowing he would tell me exactly what he thought.

'Oh great,' Boomer said sincerely. 'But, like we were talking about earlier, everyone just wants to see Phoenix Jones.'

He was right. We had been stopped numerous times by people

asking if any of us was Phoenix Jones, or asking where he was. More than once, people were told that he was about but operating in a different part of the city – the same "tactic" Boomer had used in the U-Dub, when we had been on Cabbie's patrol.

Jack returned as Boomer continued to tell me his thoughts.

'We've got The Father, The Son and The Oh-Shit!' Boomer said. 'The Father being Phoenix Jones, The Son being Midnight Jack and a very weak third – The *Oh-Shit* – being Cabbie, in my opinion.'

'Why a weak third?' I asked.

'Because Cabbie is more of a free spirit. *I'll do what I want. Fuck the system.*'

'Cabbie's great,' Jack said, interjecting.

'But Cabbie does not have this man's life experience,' Boomer told me, referring to Midnight Jack. 'He does not have this man's drive to better himself.'

'What are you talking about?' Jack asked. 'Cabbie's got plenty of life experience. Me and him just come from different places, that's all.'

'Okay, so he fought neo-Nazis in Texas...'

Texas? I thought it was 1940s Berlin?

Jack interjected again, unhappy about Boomer talking so freely to me about other members of the team.

'Listen, right now you're being sort of unprofessional. I need you to shape up.'

'Okay. Sorry.' But Boomer wasn't finished. 'The thing is, in the time that I've worked with the two of you...'

'You prefer working with me,' Jack finished for him. 'We'll leave it at that.'

As we made our way back to Boomer's car, we passed a crowd of drug dealers and addicts hanging around outside Pioneer Square station.

'Back in my early superhero days, I had a red Ford Taurus,' Jack said. 'I'd drive down here and throw golf balls out of the windows.'

'You threw golf balls at drug dealers?' I asked.

214

'Yeah. Green golf balls. Green – *emerald* – for the Emerald City. I used a highlighter pen to colour them in.'

I looked over at Boomer, who was looking back at me. Then we turned back to face Midnight Jack, who was starting to sound quite nostalgic about the whole thing.

'Do you have any idea how much a golf ball hurts when it's thrown at you at a substantial speed from a moving car?'

USID was waiting for us by Boomer's car and, after de-kitting, we made our way back to the downtown business neighbourhood, with it' modern, glass skyscrapers, now mostly in darkness but reflecting the moody, platinum rainclouds that were gliding past a small, glowing moon.

'I keep finding ginger hairs in my car, Jack,' Boomer said, as we drove away, heading towards 1st and Pike. 'You need to stop moulting.'

'We don't like to be called *ginger*,' Jack replied. 'It's *Redheaded American*.'

As we passed Pike Place Market, Jack mentioned how he had been shopping there earlier in the day. Boomer tried for another dig.

'Out in the daylight? A *Redheaded American*? With your skin?'

'Boomer, you piss sitting down. So shut up, okay?'

'I'm just worried about you,' Boomer said.

'Listen, German redheads can't be out in the sun, because their skin's too pale and they burn like vampires. But Irish redheads are different; we can be out in the sun. We're called "Day-walkers". Now drive me home.'

'Maybe you should change your superhero name to Day Walker,' USID suggested to Jack, laughing gently.

'You know, you really should think about getting yourself a superhero name,' Boomer said, turning to me.

'It's true, Mick,' Jack agreed. 'You were a good Number Two tonight. You're a superhero now. You're one of us. You need your own superhero identity.'

I made some mumbling noises and waved a dismissive hand in the air. But maybe they had a point. Whether I liked it or not, I had been an active part of the team tonight – and the last thing I wanted was for people to call me by my real name and to be identifiable. Perhaps it would be prudent to get myself a superhero identity for situations like this. It might even be a little bit fun.

But what name? Having long ago decided against the Sidekick / Physic Mick thing, I was struggling to find inspiration. A friend had emailed me from back home suggesting "Mick Justice". I liked the sound of that, but had gone off the idea of using my actual name within my superhero alter ego. My friend then proposed changing it slightly. 'How about *Dick* Justice?' he had suggested. But we both decided that the name had some seriously homoerotic overtones to it.

In the end it came to me in, of all places, Starbucks, at 1st and Pike. The following day, after my night as Midnight Jack's Number Two, I had gone in for my morning coffee. Looking up at the board of drinks written in chalk, I spotted a syrupy Earl Grey tea called *London Fog*. And with that I had it. It was perfect.

16

The London Fog

This night would be my last; I was due to fly back to London the following day. Phoenix had returned from Portland and he picked me up from my hotel. He didn't look happy.

'How did your trip to Oregon go?' I asked, probing. 'Did you meet with the Portland heroes?'

Phoenix adjusted his glasses before he spoke. It was the first time I had seen him wearing them. 'I get down to Portland and this dude meets me in the lobby of my hotel,' he started. 'He turns up, he's masked up, dressed with his gear on and I'm thinking: *Okay, maybe it's his secret identity or whatever. That's cool.* But he's got something strapped to his back, right? I'm like, "What's that?" He goes, "Oh, that's a landmine."'

I leant forward and gapped at Phoenix, my jaw plummeting towards the foot-well.

'Yeah, your face exactly!' Phoenix said. 'I'm like "Wha…?" And he's like, "Yeah, it's decommissioned but it can be reactivated." The guy has a decommissioned World War Two landmine! He thinks that shit is appropriate! Let me tell you, that meeting lasted five minutes. Are you fucking serious?'

My jaw was still swinging below my face. 'Did you just say a *landmine*?'

'Yeah. I said to him, "Like, what the fuck are you going to use that for?" And he's all like, "If worse comes to worst, I've got this landmine. You know, if things get hairy." No, I don't know! I said, "What do you mean, *if things get hairy*?" He was like, "You know, if things just get out of control."' Phoenix was shaking his head. 'Like, explain to me where it goes so out of control that you need a landmine! He's like, "I also have my gun." And he whips his coat back and he's got this handgun. I was like, "Dude, we're done. You are not Jones Army material."'

'He had a gun as well?'

'Yep. Oh, and a crossbow. Dude had a gun, a crossbow and a landmine.'

This had started off being ridiculous when it was just a landmine – but now that there was a gun and a crossbow too, it had well and truly plummeted off the side of Crazy Mountain.

'What the fuck has he got a crossbow for?' I asked.

'He thought it was a smart move. He goes, "The problem when people shoot guns is that they can't be silent, but no one can hear me with a crossbow." It was crazy. It was one of those things where I'm thinking: *this dude cannot be serious*. But he really was. He was dead serious. I thought he was kidding about the landmine at first, but then he straight up Googled that bitch in front of me and he's like, "Look, it's a landmine!" And it was. It was a Russian landmine. Then he was like, "Why aren't you going to let me on the team, man? Why are you being such a hater right now?" I told him,

"Because you patrol with a real gun, a crossbow and a fucking landmine!"'

'That is scary.'

'Yeah. They're roaming around Portland with that shit. I asked him, "Have you ever stopped any actual crime?" He was like, "Well, no, because when we show up people just leave." Like, no kidding!'

By this point, Phoenix's pissed-off demeanour and my outraged shock had developed into hysterics. Giggles had turned into loud gasps of joyful horror as we thought about the absurdity of it.

'Where did he get a bloody landmine from?' I asked, still laughing.

'That's what I asked him and he was like, "I don't like to divulge my secrets; you know how that is." I was like, "No, bro, I don't know how it is!"'

'Did you patrol with them?'

'No! I didn't even get out of the lobby. The problem is, they're not doing anything illegal. A decommissioned landmine is considered a replica or a toy. You can carry it, even though it can really fucking work. He also had a concealed weapons permit for his gun, and a crossbow is legal everywhere. So they're not breaking the law. It's just that they're carrying weapons where they can't effectively do anything. I mean, if you run into a crime and you crossbow a fool, it's game over. Nothing good comes from a crossbow. So, yeah, fuck those guys.'

I was pleased – *relieved* even – that Phoenix thought the guy was crazy for having a landmine. Not thinking a landmine and a crossbow was a good idea made Phoenix seem more sane, despite his rubber costume, pepper-spray, Phazzer, stab and gunshot wounds, mutual combat incidents and the whole superhero thing he had going on. But Phoenix was back in Seattle now and he was keen to return to work.

'How did you get on with the Seattle PD? Do they hate me?' he asked.

'Actually far from it,' I told him.

'Really? But Jamieson hates me, right?'

'No. In fact, he had some good things to say about you. They're just worried that you're going to get hurt.'

Phoenix looked confused. He also sounded a little disappointed. It was true that the Seattle police weren't exactly in favour of what Phoenix was doing, but the impression I was left with was that they weren't all out against him and that there was actually a level of professional as well as personal interest in what he was doing.

'I hear you're finally getting yourself a superhero identity,' he said.

'Boomer and Jack thought it would be a good idea.'

'So did you come up with one yet?'

'I have,' I told him. (At any other time, I would have felt like an absolute idiot for having a "superhero name" but having spent so much time with Phoenix Jones and his crew, it felt almost normal. *Almost*. Besides, I had convinced myself that having it was all part of my research.)

'What's the name?' he asked.

'Watford Fog,' I told him.

'Watford Fog? You mean London Fog, like the drink.'

'No, Watford Fog.'

'Not London Fog?'

'I don't live in London, I live in Watford.'

'Well London Fog sounds better. Just sayin'.'

We drove to North Seattle to pick up Midnight Jack. Tonight it would just be the three of us. Jack hadn't wanted to come out on patrol, claiming he had to fill in employment forms and search for jobs in the morning, but Phoenix had convinced him that he would still be back early enough to get some rest.

We pulled up in an alley at the rear of Jack's apartment block – a four storey, grey building close to a busy highway – and Midnight Jack came out through a rear fire door, carrying his utility belt and mask.

'Jack, let me introduce you to London Fog,' Phoenix said as Jack stepped into the car.

'Cool name,' he said, smiling.

'It's *Watford* Fog,' I said.

'Watford? What's a "*Watford*"?' Jack asked.

'Okay, London Fog,' I conceded.

Phoenix drove us to the U-Dub.

'We patrolling here tonight?' I asked.

'No, we're going downtown. We just need to make a quick stop.'

He pulled into a parking spot outside The Dreaming comic book store. Its interior light illuminated a small square of sidewalk outside, in a soft yellow hue. Apart from a handful of nearby bars, it appeared to be the only business still open at this hour.

'Research?' I asked.

'This is where we get changed,' Phoenix told me.

'In a comic book store?'

'Of course. We're superheroes.'

The walls were lined with shelves of comics, t-shirts and toys. Along the centre of the small room, a long table had been set up. Around twenty teenagers were sitting on either side of it, playing some superhero card game. They were a mixed bunch of spotty boys and girls. No one looked up as we walked in. The only person who paid us any attention was a slightly rotund man, in his mid-thirties, wearing black cargo pants, a Spiderman t-shirt and a ponytail. He was the manager. He knew both Phoenix Jones and Midnight Jack, and greeted them as we entered his shop.

'This is London Fog,' Jack said. 'He's a superhero from England.'

'Cool,' the manager said, and shook my hand firmly, welcoming me with a wide, genuinely friendly smile.

'Does Phoenix always come here to get changed into his outfit?' I asked.

'If we're open,' the manager told me.

'But why come here?'

'It's more of an old habit,' Jack said. 'Back in the day, Phoenix didn't want people knowing where his house was, so he came here to get ready.'

Phoenix had taken his jacket off. Underneath it he was wearing a tight-fitting, white V-neck t-shirt.

'You look like Simon fucking Cowell in that t-shirt,' Jack told him.

'Fuck off. I fucking hate you, man.'

I turned to look at the kids' playing cards but, when I turned back around, Phoenix was gone. As I stood there, trying to figure out where he had disappeared to, one of the kids came up to the counter where I was standing.

'I don't want to alarm you but somebody just went into your back room with a large bag,' he told the manager. 'Is that okay?'

'Yes, that's fine. Thanks.'

But there was no back room – just rows and rows of comics lined up on shelves along the walls. Then, as I reached up to literally scratch my head, part of the wall suddenly opened – a hidden doorway that had been built into a bookcase – and out walked Phoenix Jones, in all of his black-rubber glory.

I turned back to the manager. 'So let me get this straight. He walks in dressed normal, goes behind a hidden bookcase into a secret room and comes out moments later dressed as a superhero?'

'Yep. The door leads to what has become known as "The Phoenix Lair".'

'This is just too damn good,' I muttered to myself. It was like Clark Kent running into a phone booth, emerging moments later as Superman, only better.

'Would you mind clipping me in?' Phoenix asked.

He had managed to get his suit on, but all of the clips and ties were hanging loose.

'This is the part they miss out in the comic books,' Phoenix said. 'The part that's in-between the comic book panels, where another dude helps the superhero get dressed.'

'You'll notice that I don't have anybody clipping me up,' Jack said, smugly.

'That's because you're dressed like a giant condom,' Phoenix said.

'I've told you before, condoms prevent lives, they don't save them.'

'Who are you guys going after tonight?' a boy asked.

'Muggers and drug dealers,' Phoenix told him.

'Are you gonna kick their ass when you find them?'

Phoenix adjusted his body armour, twitching his left shoulder. Midnight Jack, who was leaning casually against the shop counter, turned to look at Phoenix with his large, silver-coloured superhero eyes, waiting for an answer.

'Well, I can't legally just attack people,' Phoenix told the boy. 'What I try to do is de-escalate as many problems as possible.'

The boy looked disappointed; this was not the answer that one of his comic book heroes would have given.

'I'm wearing lead-lined gloves though,' Jack quickly added. 'And they're bad-ass!'

The boy's disappointment disappeared. Satisfied, he returned to the card game.

Another boy, who had been sitting quietly at the table, suddenly stood up. 'Wait, are you guys actually going to go out and do your superhero thing? For real?'

'Yeah, this is the real deal,' Jack told him.

A girl – perhaps 12 years old – turned to the first boy and said, 'Let this be a warning: this is what happens when you read too many comic books.'

Out on the street, I quizzed Midnight Jack about his lead-lined gloves. 'Are they legal?'

'Well, they're probably a bit iffy,' he told me. 'It's not a solid lump of lead, though; it's just lead sand.'

He threw one at me to feel. The black leather, fingerless glove was weighty and the knuckle area felt firm but pliable, like a hard cushion.

Phoenix wasn't impressed. 'You can't wear any hard covering over your fist and strike another person,' he said.

'Well, it can be argued in court,' Jack answered, doing his best to defend the barely defensible as he often did. 'Besides, they're not illegal to walk around with.'

'True,' Phoenix said. 'You just can't hit someone with them, so you're kind of limiting your method of defence or attack.'

'It's like lots of things,' Jack continued. 'Are there things that are more effective than a can of pepper-spray? Oh hell, yeah! Is it *illegal* for me to carry most of them? Oh hell, yeah! You just have to find a happy medium.'

I guess the lead-lined gloves were his idea of a "happy medium".

It was well past midnight, and on the way to the city, Phoenix received an unexpected phone call. It was his young son, *Freedom*. Freedom was upset that his dad hadn't been to visit him that weekend, and he began to shout at Phoenix. Phoenix stayed calm, explaining that he'd been working in Portland, then telling Freedom that he loved him and that he would do his best to spend even more time with him the following week. After the phone call, Phoenix became quiet. Jack and I tried to make him feel better, but Phoenix had sunk deep into his own thoughts.

We drove into the underground garage in a residential building in Belltown, where the locals had apparently provided Phoenix with his own parking space. Phoenix hadn't said a word since the call. Jack was doing his best to crack jokes and say funny shit but it was clear that Phoenix was extremely upset. Then Phoenix said something that neither Jack nor myself were expecting.

'Jack, I'll run as your Number Two tonight. You run as One.'

'Me?' Jack asked, sounding genuinely surprised. 'Screw that, we never swap roles when we're together.'

'If it's just us, you should run One,' Phoenix told him.

'Oh, it's because you're compromised, isn't it?' Jack said, suddenly understanding Phoenix's reasoning.

Phoenix didn't answer.

Jack continued, 'I'll agree to it, but only if you admit that you're compromised.'

Jack was trying to push Phoenix into showing vulnerability, but Phoenix wasn't prepared to admit to anything.

'Okay, I'll be One,' Phoenix said, reluctantly.

'I guess it must be hard for your son sometimes,' I ventured. 'Imagine if your own father had been a superhero when you were little.'

Phoenix snapped his head around, and looked at me. 'My father?' *Had I said something wrong?*

'I've never told you about him, have I?' he said.

'No, I don't think you have. Why? *Was* he a superhero?'

'No, man. No. Let me tell you about my family. We were living in Texas. My mum had five kids and, out of all of them, I was the one put up for adoption – and I was the middle kid. So I lived down the street in an orphanage while my family lived down the block.'

Phoenix told me that he was adopted by a lady who had taken in – and continued to take in – many children. He told me that he had thirty brothers, making his foster mother, in her own way, superhuman. He loved his foster mum but had little time for his birth mother and father.

'The guy I thought was my dad wasn't my dad,' Phoenix continued. 'My real dad was some dude that my mum had cheated with; that's why they got rid of me. Then my dad – at least the guy I thought was my dad – put me in his car one day and drove to a convenience store. He got out but he left me in the car. He never came back.'

'Where did he go?'

'He didn't go anywhere.'

I stared at Phoenix, confused.

'My dad walked into the store and robbed it,' he explained. 'The thing is, the convenience store owner had a gun. He shot my dad and killed him. I sat in that car and didn't go anywhere until the police found me. I was seven years old.'

It was a shocking revelation. I looked at Phoenix's reflection in the rear-view mirror. There was absolutely no emotion on his face. Everything I had previously felt and believed about Phoenix Jones – the whole "superhero" thing – changed at that moment. I was no psychologist, but lots of things about Phoenix started to make sense. I now understood that there was far more going on. His heart-breaking past explained so much.

'You don't rob a store in Texas – that's just dumb,' Phoenix said. 'He was a bad criminal. If you're going to do something, be good at it – even if it's being a criminal. So I'm disappointed in my father emotionally. He made the wrong choice.'

'Do you ever worry that what you're doing – being a superhero – is the wrong choice?' I asked. Midnight Jack, who had remained unusually silent, looked over, interested in how Phoenix would answer my question.

'No. It can't be wrong. Going after criminals is never wrong. It's not even controversial. People have always hunted bad people.' He turned briefly to face me. 'Mick, ask me your difficult questions, I don't care.'

'Okay then, do you think that indulging in this fantasy is selfish? After all, you have kids.'

'It has selfish moments, yes.'

'But do you care more about this than your family?'

'No.'

'So if Purple or your kids told you to stop doing this, because they were worried about you, would you stop?'

'Not if that was the reason. No one can stop me. If their argument is that they're worried about me taking on criminals, I'd be insulted. They should respect my physical abilities and training. I'd be insulted if my son didn't think that I could take on a regular street punk.'

'But you can't stop a bullet. You can't...'

'I've been shot twice,' he said, stopping me mid-sentence. 'I'm still here.'

I decided to leave it there for the time being. Besides, it was now one o'clock in the morning and time to patrol. Before we left the building, I decided to wear my body armour, just to be safe. The more I hung out with Phoenix and Jack, the more I felt that I was putting myself on offer. I also decided to wear a mask. Earlier that day, I had purchased a black rubber facemask at a costume store. The mask covered the top my head, and dropped down, below my eyes and onto my nose. It had a silver-coloured lightning bolt printed on the forehead and was utterly ridiculous – but I wanted to feel a sense of what Phoenix, Jack and the other superheroes felt. I still wouldn't have been happy to walk around with any weapons but the mask itself felt okay. And, being just the three of us, it made me feel less of an outsider, less of an observer. Plus, any concerns I previously had about being stopped by the police were rapidly waning. The more time I spent with the superheroes, the less concerned I became. So I slipped the black rubber cowl over my head and pulled up my grey hooded top.

The London Fog had arrived.

I realised, almost immediately, that the rubber was a mistake; my head began to sweat like an Italian fountain. But I decided to leave it on, all the same. Now, our patrol could begin.

Almost as soon as we had stepped onto the streets of Belltown, an old black man with a wispy grey beard, wearing tatty dark clothing, stopped us. He looked like a wizard from some apocalyptic, dystopian future. Phoenix seemed pleased to see him – like they knew each other. Then the man began to speak. He told us that he wrote a new song every single day but how he had never written about his father. Today was different, though; today he had written a song about his father and he wanted to recite it for us. What happened next was profound, perhaps even spiritual. Considering what Phoenix had just told me about his own father, and the call he had taken from his son, the timing of the man's words was uncanny. They transfixed Phoenix. They transfixed us all.

It was a long song that described the man's absent father, who had left home before he had been born – and how, if the man's father died, it would be hard to even cry for him, as he never knew him. The song went on to question if all the problems in the old man's life were due to his absent father and his mother's wandering ways?

After the man had finished, Phoenix took hold of his hand, and shook it. 'You'd be surprised how much we have in common,' Phoenix told him softly.

The wizard walked away without another word, disappearing into the hyperactive crowds of Belltown, which was full of sketchy looking people, and the usual collection of drunks and drug dealers.

Something had changed in Phoenix. Now, he was happy. He'd had a complete emotional turnaround. 'Belltown is just an example of awesome cooperation that you don't get anywhere else in this city,' he told me. 'If I could just patrol Belltown, I'd never leave. The problem is, we cleaned it up. I don't mean that we stopped all the crime, but the police are aware of the danger times and danger zones now.'

Phoenix had previously claimed that the mayor of Seattle had ordered the Seattle police to patrol Belltown on foot, having been inspired by Phoenix Jones. Phoenix told me that these police foot patrols had become known as "Jones Patrols". It was quite the claim. (It was also something that I had brought up with Mark Jamieson, of the Seattle police. His reply was, 'God, no!' Mark explained that these "directed patrols" were just part of a larger police strategy. It was "basic policing", and had nothing to do with Phoenix Jones, who he dismissed as making "lots of claims".)

'Okay people, it's Monday night. It's time to go home,' Jack called out. 'Thank you for choosing Belltown,' He had his thumbs hooked through his utility belt like a Sheriff in some Wild West movie.

A few people came up to us with the usual photo requests and Phoenix happily obliged, posing with his fist up in a fighting position and putting on a faux stern face before smiling and joking with the people who had stopped him. Then, as we continued on, two cycle cops rode towards us.

'Hello Benjamin,' one of them said to Phoenix, as he passed by.

Phoenix stopped walking. Suddenly he was furious.

'IT'S PHOENIX JONES!' he shouted angrily at the officer. 'PHOENIX JONES!'

Phoenix pulled his iPhone from his utility belt.

'What are you doing?' I asked.

'Sending a tweet.'

'About what?'

'That officer. He's always fucking with me.'

'That? Seriously? Phoenix, let it go. All he said was *hello*.'

'But you heard the way he said it, right? He was being sarcastic. That cop is always being an ass towards me and my crew. Some cops are like that. They picked a team, and it's not my team. Fuck them. If they're going to come at me, they'd better be ready for a war,' he said, sounding scarily like the "fuck the police" tattooed guy I had met at the anti-police demo.

'But don't you want the Seattle police on your side?' I asked.

'No, I don't,' he responded sharply. 'I want them to do their job. Whether they're on my side or not is completely irrelevant. Whether I like a person or not has nothing to do with how I treat them. The SPD should be the exact same way. And there's no way to change my mind about that because I'm right and they're wrong. If we wanted to make everybody happy and have everybody like us, we would have picked a different profession.'

Phoenix's attitude, his expectations and his intense self-belief, left little room for conversation or debate. As I had seen previously, it was often his way or nothing. Phoenix was always open to questions and had always encouraged me to ask what I liked – but, ultimately, he saw himself as being right and anyone who disagreed with him as being wrong.

Phoenix quickly typed out his tweet, which I looked at just before he sent it. It described the officer as being "rude and unprofessional."

'Don't send it,' I told Phoenix. 'It doesn't mean anything. At least think about this before you send it.'

Phoenix did think about it. Curiously, considering what he had just written, he then added that the officer was "very good at his job". Then he sent it, tagging in the Seattle police and a local radio presenter, for their attention.

Continuing through the city, we headed towards Pioneer Square, where the usual collection of characters were gathered around the rear of Pioneer Square station. Most were shuffling around, passing things to each other, whispering and giving us solid, hard looks.

'Be careful around these guys. This is the area where Nicole Westbrook got shot,' Phoenix said, referring to the murder that Boomer had previously told me about.

'Did you bring your golf balls?' I asked Jack, only half joking.

'No,' he said, smiling through his mask.

'Okay, let's fuck with these guys,' Phoenix said.

We followed him towards a wide alley that ran parallel with 3rd Avenue, between James Street and Jefferson Street.

An old black homeless man stopped to look at us. He smiled and pointed at Phoenix. 'Hey, watch out America! He's gonna kick your ass and you ain't gonna like it!' he whooped, cheerily.

Phoenix gave the man a friendly tap on the shoulder and we continued on, running along the alley until we reached the Jefferson Street end. Phoenix, who was leading, lifted his hand in the air, silently indicating for us to stop. He peered around the corner of the alley towards the area where most of the dealers and users had gathered. Then he waved us on and we crept up Jefferson Street to the doorway of a building where we stopped. As we stood there, half a dozen black men looked around from 3rd Avenue and stared at us. For a few moments, both their team and ours stood still, each waiting for the other to make a move. I wondered what the hell was going on, suddenly glad that I had decided to strap on my body armour.

'What the hell are we doing?' I whispered. 'Let's not fuck with these guys.'

'Shh!' Phoenix ordered.

Then the men stepped back into 3rd Avenue and out of our sight. 'Run!' Phoenix suddenly said.

I chased after Phoenix and Jack, who were sprinting back along the alley towards James Street, still not knowing what we were doing or what was going on. Were those men coming after us? Did they have a gun? What the hell? Imagining the worst, I quickened my pace and sprinted past Jack, who was holding onto his belt rig as he ran, to prevent it from banging around his waist and legs. At the opposite end of the alley, we carried out the same routine, creeping up James Street, ducking into a doorway and waiting for the men to come looking for us. About a minute later, they appeared on the corner before ducking back into 3rd Avenue.

Phoenix explained his "plan" to me: he wanted to keep appearing at both ends of the street, basically pissing off the drug dealers so, no matter which direction they went in, we would be there watching. It seemed like a hazardous technique to me. Any one of those men could have been armed and we were intentionally interfering with their business. How long would it take before one of them simply got bored with our silly games? Phoenix and Jack may have been armed with pepper-spray and tasers (not to mention Jack's lead-lined gloves), but it was likely that some of those men would be armed with something more immediately life threatening. It was also three against thirty. These odds didn't seem to bother Phoenix or Jack, though – and, in the end, it was us who got bored and decided to move on.

Strolling toward Occidental Park and the International District, Jack pulled up his mask, revealing his mouth and chin. My own mask had become extremely hot, so I took the opportunity to whip it off. A fresh, cool air immediately sunk into my exposed head, as heavy drops of sweat and moisture dripped onto the ground from the mask.

In this historic part of Seattle, most of the buildings were old, low level and made from brick. It felt a long way from the modern, downtown business district. We looked around ourselves. The streets were utterly deserted. Tumbleweed wouldn't have looked out of place. But it was also a dangerous neighbourhood late at night. As we stood at 2nd Avenue and Washington Street, three black men came towards us. As they got closer, they shortened and slowed their pace.

'Ah, look at the pigs, dawg,' one of the men said. He was carrying a walking cane and he swung it around threateningly, in front of our faces.

Jack wished them a good evening, then told them that we weren't looking for any trouble. As they approached closer, almost nose-to-nose with us, the largest of the three grabbed hold of the bottom of his t-shirt and pulled it down, covering something in his waistband. He made a show of the movement and I got the impression he was doing it for our benefit – a warning, perhaps. Then they continued on their way.

'I think he's got something,' I said.

'That's what I thought,' Phoenix replied.

'Probably a knife or something,' Jack added.

'Okay, let's call it in,' Phoenix said.

Jack pulled out his phone and warned us not to follow the men, which I had already started to do as I wanted to see the direction they were going in. The men had stopped at the intersection with Yesler Way and they turned to look back at us, watching as Jack made the call. As the 911 call connected with the operator, the men continued up Yesler.

'Yes, hello ma'am, my name's Jack, I work for a local security company. I was doing my patrol and I came across three individuals who are heading north on Yesler. One of them seems to have something concealed under his shirt. I believe it may be a weapon,' Jack told the operator. He spoke calmly and professionally, as though he made these types of calls every day.

Soon, the men appeared again at the intersection of Yesler and 2nd Avenue, watching. If they came for us, we would be in serious trouble. Once again, I doubted that pepper-spray, a taser or lead-lined gloves were going to be enough if it all went a bit *High Noon*. Besides, I was armed with absolutely nothing.

Jack continued to talk to the operator. 'They were hostile at first. I was able to talk them out of doing anything to me – but, as I was conversing with them, one of them tucked his shirt down, concealing something.'

The operator wanted Jack's last name but he coolly explained that he didn't give it out when he made these types of calls. He did, however, tell her that he was with Phoenix Jones and the Rain City Superhero Movement. With that revelation, I wondered if the police would even respond. As Jack completed the call, one of the men shouted something incomprehensible at us before continuing to walk up Yesler.

As it turned out, the police did stop the men. The man Jack had described to the operator was searched. A police officer later called Phoenix to tell him that no weapon had been found, although it was believed that he had handed it to another person or else ditched it before being stopped. In addition, the officer told Phoenix that the man had previously been arrested for aggravated assault with a weapon. In some ways, it felt like a satisfying outcome.

We ended the patrol on the top floor of a deserted, four-storey parking lot, looking down on the street below.

'It's amazing the amount of real superhero shit that we don't get to do,' Jack said.

'How do you mean?' Phoenix asked.

'I mean, this. Standing on a rooftop watching the street for trouble. It's pure comic book.'

'Yeah, but if something happens, it's going to take us five minutes to get down.'

We were all feeling tired, so Jack suggested that we go grab a coffee.

'Why get coffee?' Phoenix asked. 'It'll keep us up all night.'

'I'm wanting to sit down and talk,' Jack told him.

'About what, bro?'

'I don't know, man. We can shoot the shit. We've been business all day. We never just hang out. I get offended. I don't have any other friends.'

But Phoenix just wanted to get back home to Purple.

It had been an interesting night. Phoenix had revealed sides of himself that I hadn't seen before. There were demons in his past. He was vulnerable and he could lose his cool. I felt as though I had finally seen the real Phoenix Jones, the real Ben Fodor. No longer were his emotions impenetrable. He had used the negatives from his past to try and create a positive future for himself – but also for everyone around him. He seemed more human, and was more likeable for having flaws and problems just like the rest of us. Behind that rubber mask was a superhero, but there was also a real person.

As for myself, I needed to get back to my hotel, to pack and prepare for my flight home. I said my good-byes but, before I left, Phoenix had one request.

'Mick, I've been thinking: I want you to head up my London chapter. I want the London Fog to lead the Jones Army in London.'

I didn't know what to say. No, really, I didn't know what to say. I blubbered something or other but figured that it didn't really matter what I said as Phoenix Jones was never going to come to London, anyway. And with that final, incoherent blathering – but certain that Phoenix Jones was never, ever going to set foot in the UK – the London Fog left Seattle and hung up his mask for good. My superhero adventure had come to an end.

Only it hadn't.

17

Superhero International

As I sat on my sofa in Watford, watching the latest episode of Marvel's Agents of S.H.I.E.L.D. (actually, that's a lie, I was watching Glee), my home phone rang. It was Phoenix Jones, calling from Seattle. There was nothing unusual about that – we spoke on the phone every now and then, catching up and talking *shop*. What he said to me, though, was unusual. It was also a tad unsettling.

'Mick, I'm coming to London.'

I wasn't sure, at first, if this was just some over-excited, *maybe* coming to London, thing.

'Actually coming to London?' I asked, doubtfully.

'Yep.'

'When?'

'Next week, the flights are all booked.'

This I wasn't expecting. *Next week?* Then Phoenix explained how a Chinese phone company were flying him and Purple Reign over to the UK for a promotional campaign – the campaign being centred round a superhero theme. They were coming for a week and the phone company had a bunch of interviews and appearances set up for them. But Phoenix had other ideas; as far as he was concerned, he was coming to fight London's criminal underworld.

'What weapons can I bring?' he asked.

'Weapons?'

'Yeah, we're gonna go on patrol in London when I'm over – Phoenix Jones and the London Fog.'

'PJ, you can't bring weapons with you. This is London; the laws here are different to the US. Very different!'

'No Phazzer?'

'No.'

'Pepper-spray is okay though, right?'

'No. It's legally classed as a firearm over here.'

'Really? Oh. What about Jack's weighted gloves? I can bring them, right?'

'No.'

'Not even weighted gloves? Really?'

'Really! They're filled with lead. You could kill someone.'

'What about my bulletproof vest? What's the best way to bring that over? And what about a net? I can carry a net, right? If someone is going to commit a crime and I throw a net on them, that's legal, right?'

It turned into a very long conversation. But PJ and Purple were coming, so I – and London – needed to get ready.

I switched off Glee.

PJ and Purple were in London to promote a phone, but PJ wasn't happy about how little time would be left for him to patrol. However, there were some advantages to being brought over by the phone company, not least the London pad that he and Purple had been put up in.

I pulled up outside an address in fashionable – and expensive – Mayfair. A heavy, black door faced the street, with solid brass accessories shined to perfection. I looked up at the clean, white, Georgian townhouse. It looked plush, even from the outside. This couldn't be it, surely? But it was, and Purple buzzed me in.

'Mick!' PJ stood, open armed, in the centre of a huge living area, which was filled with antique furniture, stylish fittings and several enormous sofas. A large, oak dining table set with blood-coloured, velvet chairs and a large fruit bowl sat between us – but he quickly skipped around it, grabbing my hand and chest-bumping me.

'What do you think of my London Batcave?' he asked, smiling.

'Batcave? PJ, this is more like Bruce Wayne's mansion.'

Phoenix was actually in the middle of squaring up a shit-storm back in Seattle and returned to taking the telephone call he was already in the middle of before I arrived. The previous evening, as someone armed with a knife had been attacking a man, Midnight Jack had thrown a pepper-grenade. Naturally, the media had gotten hold of the story and Phoenix was trying to calm things down. He had concerns that the incident was going to "fuck up" his life and his "legacy" and he was attempting to control the words used by Jack and the other Rain City heroes – "crowd control device" rather than "grenade", for example. Phoenix wasn't at all happy that Jack had even used a grenade. Phoenix himself didn't carry them. He didn't need to, he said. He was a "skilled, trained fighter and he used his brain." I couldn't help but smile. It seemed that all was pretty much the same back in Seattle. PJ was out of town and Jack was running the show in his own, special way.

Purple gave me a hug and, after she had shown me around their palatial apartment, Phoenix wanted to get down to business: patrolling London.

'You have to understand, the violence in London can be particularly vicious,' I warned him. 'It's nasty, dirty and dangerous. People here will beat you to death.'

'No they won't.'

To be fair, the violence in the US could also be vicious – but I had always felt an extra edge in London. Perhaps it was the level of alcohol consumption that went with a good night out here in comparison to the States. That level of drunkenness had always made me a little bit more wary. The street fights I had witnessed in the UK were always far nastier and deadlier than anything I had ever witnessed in the States. And there was something else that Phoenix needed to take into account.

'You have to remember that you don't have pepper-spray or a Phazzer, here. Also, there's no *mutual combat* laws.'

'I'm not worried about that. We're going to stop crime. We're going to fight criminals.'

Purple was watching our exchange anxiously. She, more than Phoenix, seemed to appreciate the differences between London and Seattle. She accepted that they were in a foreign country with different laws. Phoenix, on the other hand, simply didn't care. More than anything, he wanted to patrol the streets of London. The only thing that was stopping him (other than me trying to put him off) was the schedule that the phone company had arranged. There were interviews, corporate events and photo-shoots around the city (in a red telephone box, on the tube, by Big Ben – every cliché – with some of the images later appearing in a double-page spread in The Sun newspaper). So, for a few days, I mostly left them to it, occasionally showing up at events and helping myself to the free drinks and nibbles.

Towards the end of their stay in Mayfair a last minute request came through for Phoenix and Purple to appear on the BBC program, Newsnight.

'Do you know the show?' Phoenix asked.

'Yes. Are you sure it's Newsnight?' I asked.

Purple showed me the email. It was.

I assured them that Newsnight was not like appearing on some fun, friendly, daytime chat show in America. This was a serious news program. I explained that there could be some aggressive and difficult questions, but Phoenix brushed it all off in an unconcerned and uninterested manner. His bravado just troubled me all the more. The last thing I wanted was for them to appear on Newsnight and be torn to pieces by the presenters – I couldn't even imagine what Jeremy Paxman would make of them. Purple was a little more interested in having a heads-up as to what to expect, but Phoenix was completely sure in himself that, whatever questions they were asked, he could answer them. Newsnight meant nothing to him and he wasn't in the slightest bit concerned.

The BBC sent a car to Mayfair the following evening and we were driven a short distance to the studios at the top of Regents Street. I was a total hanger-on, but there was no way I was going to miss this. Standing in the green room, we discussed whether Phoenix should or shouldn't wear his mask. The BBC wanted him to wear it, no doubt thinking of the visual impact, whereas Phoenix wanted to leave it off. He didn't want to hide behind his mask on a national television show (which was a total contradiction of what he had said previously to Purple, when she had decided that wearing a mask conflicted with her message about domestic violence). However, I confess that I was siding with the BBC, trying to imagine viewers at home watching a Newsnight presenter interviewing a pair of fully outfitted comic book superheroes. The mask completed that look and I argued that it was what identified Phoenix Jones as *Phoenix Jones* (again, something he had told me himself, back in Seattle). But Phoenix had made up his mind; the mask was staying off.

At the last minute, I made a suggestion. 'How about if you take the mask in with you but hold it in your lap, so that people can still see it?'

Purple thought that this was a good compromise and Phoenix agreed.

Then it was time; Phoenix and Purple were led to the studio. I remained in the green room, watching the interview on a large TV screen, as I helped myself to the free drinks and snacks.

Kirsty Wark carried out the interview (sadly, Paxman wasn't there. I say *sadly* because, well, could you imagine?). It was the last segment of the show and, after a pre-recorded bit showing Purple and Phoenix dressed in their outfits, shopping for comic books in London's Forbidden Planet store, together with a few clips from YouTube, the actual interview began. At times, Kirsty Wark seemed unsure – or perhaps, unconvinced – by the rubber-suited couple sitting opposite her; moments before she had been speaking to a lady about women's rights in Afghanistan, and now here she was talking to two American Real-Life Superheroes. She looked down at some notes on her lap and suggested that Phoenix and Purple were little more than vigilantes.

'No,' Phoenix says.

'Yes,' Kirsty Wark replied.

Phoenix argued his case and Kirsty Wark moved on to London and whether there were any superheroes here. I held my breath. Phoenix admitted that he had been hanging out with superheroes in London but mentioned no names. Then Kirsty Wark questioned if their reasons for doing what they did was as a response to things that had happened to them in the past.

There would be no time on this short television segment to go over their histories, but Phoenix took the opportunity to make a statement. 'We decided to stand for something," he said. 'We tell citizens, "It's time for you guys to go out there and defend each other and to believe in something."'

Kirsty Wark cut Phoenix off and ended the interview. In all, the segment lasted about five minutes. I thought it went well; neither Purple nor Phoenix had said anything controversial, they were calm and professional and Kirsty wasn't too hard on them. But Phoenix didn't see it that way. He was fuming. As far as he was concerned, the interview did not go well at all. He felt that he didn't have time to get across his message and views. I disagreed. Kirsty Wark made some observations that were only slightly challenging – things viewers might have been thinking themselves, such as why they don't just call the police when they see something happening (Purple had explained that they do call the police), and how, in his mask, Phoenix must appear quite threatening – but she had also given Phoenix and Purple an opportunity to reply.

'I didn't get to say the things I wanted to say,' Phoenix complained. 'That presenter made four negative comments and I only got the chance to say three positive comments. Therefore she won. I'm not happy dude. I'm seriously pissed.'

Phoenix and Purple returned to Mayfair. I took a train back to Watford.

The phone company were paying for the apartment in Mayfair only for the time it took Phoenix and Purple to complete their obligations. But this would leave next to no time for Phoenix to do what he wanted to do, which was patrol; not to mention what Purple wanted, which was to at least try and see some sights before they returned home. So, though they had to vacate the plush apartment, they extended their stay by a few days.

I had made Phoenix and Purple a number of promises back in Seattle about how they were welcome to stay with me should they ever come to the UK, and here they were now, about to be turfed out of luxury and made homeless. As it was, my place was upside down due to an imminent house move – and, although both Phoenix and Purple said that they didn't mind, I know that they would have been extremely uncomfortable. I too would have been extremely uncomfortable, not least because Phoenix would no doubt want to patrol Watford town centre. London, being huge and anonymous, was one thing; my relatively small hometown was another. The last time I took an out-of-town friend there, he got kicked in the face.

In the end, I convinced them both that they would be far more comfortable in a hotel, but with central London hotel prices being what they are, we settled on a room in a chain hotel just off the busy A40 trunk road, in Acton, west London. It was soulless and remote and I felt awful, but at least they would be comfortable and wouldn't get kicked in the head.

I picked them up from Mayfair and, as we drove towards Acton, I attempted to paint a picture so that they realised how very different it was to Mayfair. On the way, Phoenix asked to stop at a Burger King. It was very much a pit-stop type of place as you drove out of London and not somewhere you would bring your family for a treat. We walked in and ordered our food. As we took our trays to a window seat, Phoenix asked if I had locked my car.

'Around here? Of course I have,' I told him.

'Well unlock it,' he said.

'But someone will steal it.'

'Exactly. Leave your car unlocked. I want someone to rob it.'

'Thanks, but no thanks.'

Phoenix was bored and desperate to do some *superhero-ing*. So far, this journey had been nothing but press events, interviews and being told what to do and where to be. Now he wanted nothing more than to do what he does best; I just wasn't prepared to sacrifice my car or its contents to satisfy his crime-fighting cravings.

'I'm going to get some ranch dressing,' he said, and returned to the counter.

'I don't think they do ranch dressing here,' I said to Purple.

She looked concerned.

Phoenix returned to our table looking utterly depressed. 'I can't believe this! They don't have ranch dressing! What sort of country is this? Who doesn't have ranch dressing?'

'It's just not something you see much over here,' I told him.

'That's ridiculous. Everywhere does ranch dressing.'

'Not here. PJ, you have to remember, you're in a different country. Things aren't the same here.'

'I know, and I hate that. Why can't everything be like America? I'm fed up with all these differences. Why can't I just get what I want?'

Purple tried to calm Phoenix down but it was no use. I didn't know what else to say. It was just ranch dressing – but, when I tried to explain to him that there were bigger issues in the world than sauce, he simply wasn't prepared to see it. Then he got up and walked outside. He did everything other than stamp his feet and rip the arms off a teddy bear. But I realised that he was tired, and that he was in an unfamiliar place. I also appreciated that he didn't travel as much as I did, so I tried my best to understand his frustrations. Even so, it was just salad dressing.

After a couple of minutes of personal rage-time, he returned.

'You're acting like a bit of a diva,' I told him.

'No I'm not.'

'You're having a tantrum because they don't have ranch dressing!'

'I'm just fed up with not being able to get what I want. I'm fed up with things being different to home.'

'But you're in a different country. *Embrace* the differences.'

'I'm never leaving America again.'

'Well, if you do, bring your own condiments.'

'I bet this burger doesn't even have growth hormones injected into it,' he said, picking up his Whopper. 'I need growth hormones and chemicals. And I don't like you two laughing at me about the ranch dressing. I don't like being out of my comfort zone. I just want what I want.'

'Well, you can't always get what you want,' I said, now getting seriously annoyed. 'There are far worse problems than not getting the sauce you want.'

'Like what?'

'Cancer.'

'I don't believe in cancer,' he said.

There was nothing further I could – or was prepared – to say.

I felt horribly disillusioned with PJ, but I had to wonder if he didn't feel that same about me. I was hardly the *London Fog* he was expecting me to be. I suspect that, before coming to the UK, he had imagined that we would be out patrolling the smog-filled streets of London looking to prevent crime and help people. But his schedule with the phone company had been keeping him busy and I had my own life to be getting on with. I also had no intention of putting on a rubber mask and walking through the streets of Soho looking like a fucking *gimp*. Still, I couldn't help feeling bad about the way things were working out. I wasn't so much a fallen hero, as a *failed* hero. But, honestly, I was okay with that.

I dropped Phoenix and Purple off at their cheap hotel and left. Phoenix posted a tweet later that evening: "Going on patrol in a place called Acton. According to local police [*I guessed that meant me*] I might die."

Happily Phoenix didn't die and, the following day, Purple and Phoenix went on a bus tour to Windsor Castle, Stonehenge and

Bath. As far as Phoenix was concerned, Purple had now had her way by going on the tour and now he wanted what he wanted – what he had wanted from the very beginning – to patrol London. Purple was still unsure but Phoenix was determined.

As I sat at home that night, watching another episode of Marvel's Agents of S.H.I.E.L.D., I got a message on my phone from someone who had been handling Phoenix's PR while he had been working for the phone company. The message was to meet Phoenix and Purple at Piccadilly Circus at midnight.

I arrived slightly early but, despite the late hour, central London was still buzzing with tourists and opportunists. Under the huge, bright screens of Piccadilly Circus, people were gathered in a large circle around a street performer on a unicycle. Mixed in with the tourists were several young gang members, who were swearing loudly, chasing each other around and generally looking nasty and dangerous.

There was a police car parked on Regent Street, close to the famous Eros statue, and I noticed two police officers looking indifferently towards a man wearing black and gold rubber, who was giving them a friendly wave.

PJ and Purple approached me, striding through the swarms of people. Walking behind Phoenix were three young men, who were all wearing white, Phoenix Jones t-shirts that had been especially printed for this London trip. They had a bright-yellow flaming phoenix printed on the chests and the words "Rise With Me" printed on the back. The tiff between myself and Phoenix went unmentioned. We were friends again.

'You bring your London Fog mask?' he asked.

'Erm... no, the mask's being repaired. It got torn.'

'Torn? In a fight?'

'Something like that,' I told him.

Then he introduced me to the others. I shook their hand and asked them in turn what their names were.

'Haemo-Boy,' the first one said, sounding nervous and unsure.

'Excuse me?'

'Haemo-Boy. I came up with the name because I have too much haemoglobin.'

Haemo-Boy was a five-foot-five, scrawny looking white youth.

I turned to a slim Filipino-looking man who was taller and appeared slightly older than Haemo-Boy. He was perhaps in his early thirties.

'And you?'

'I'm Lone-Don,' he told me quickly, seeming eager to spit the name out, as if he wasn't entirely sure about it.

'London?'

'Lone-Don. As in London but *lone*. Alone – like a lone-wolf type thing, but in London. Hence, Lone-Don.'

I turned to the final guy, who looked like a student with long, shaggy hair and denim shorts. He was carrying a large, digital SLR camera.

'I'm Will,' he said. And before I managed to question him further, he added, 'Just Will.'

They were a strange looking trio; nothing like the superheroes I had met in America. None of them knew each other, but they were all big fans of Phoenix Jones, having seen him on television and online, and they were in complete awe of his presence. I stood back and looked at the group. They didn't have to be here. They didn't have to come out late at night to potentially put themselves in danger and help strangers, but they did. Sure, they may have had some weird-ass fantasy about being a superhero, but if I was having a night out and I was in trouble or getting hurt, or someone was breaking into my car, wouldn't I hope that a member of the public would step in and help? Of course I would. And, if that member of the public just happened to be wearing a superhero outfit, so what? And that was perhaps what my investigation into Real-Life Superheroes had come down to: I was simply grateful that there were people out there who were willing to help others.

But there was no time for self-congratulations. We had work to do. We walked across Piccadilly Circus, quickly skipping over the busy road to avoid the on-coming double decker buses and black taxis, and entered the narrower, darker, more Phoenix-Jones-appropriate streets of Soho. Finding a quiet, Victorian, brick alley, which would have been pitch black had it not been for the single cold grey-glow of an old street lamp, Phoenix mustered his team for a pre-patrol briefing.

He clapped his gloved hands together and began. 'I'll go into any altercation first. I'm not expecting you guys to come into an altercation at all. The best thing you can do for me is to get good video footage, because when the police show up, I want to be able to tell them that I'm not fucking nuts. Okay?'

I turned to see the reactions of the London heroes – they all appeared slightly stunned, but each nodded their head obediently.

Then, completely contradicting himself about the London heroes staying out of any "altercations", Phoenix said, 'You, Haemo-Boy, you're fast on your feet; if worse comes to worst and I take off running, you need to keep an eye on me in case there's a moment for you to jump in or do something. If anyone drops a weapon of any kind, make sure you get to where the weapon is so I can tell the cops. As for you, Lone-don, you're my martial arts backup. If a fight breaks out that I can't control, I'm gonna call you in. The key is not to win the fight; the key is to stop them from whooping my ass. Let's say eight guys jump me and I'm on the floor, you come in and push-kick one guy off of me. But the goal is not to keep fighting. If the victim's out of the crime, then we're out of the crime. If we get people arrested, cool. If we don't get them arrested, no big deal. The key is to actively prevent crime, not to get killed.'

Haemo-Boy, Lone-Don and Will, Just Will, stared at Phoenix, wide-eyed and silent. I knew that feeling. Phoenix had taken their comfort level and phazzed the shit out of it. They seemed utterly overwhelmed. To be fair, I wasn't feeling too good about this London patrol myself. It was good to see PJ finally happy – but he had confided in me earlier how he had plans to force entry into one of the brothels in Soho, in order to "rescue" the girls who he assumed were being held there against their will and forced into the sex trade. I wasn't sure his London team were ready for such an ambitious mission. Haemo-Boy, Lone-Don and Will, Just Will were no Midnight Jack, Evo or Boomer. Looking at them made me realise just how far ahead the Real-Life Superheroes guys in the States were. And London wasn't Seattle – something I had been attempting to drum into PJ all week. Things were very different here. But regardless, PJ was hyped up and itching to hit the streets.

'Okay,' he said, switching on his GoPro camera, 'let's stop some crime. Ready?'

Afterwards

Despite Phoenix Jones contacting me about getting the team back together, things never quite worked out that way. In fact, Phoenix Jones' life went from bad to worse. He and Purple Reign broke up. Phoenix then got himself a new girlfriend. There was talk of a TV show, but nothing seemed to come of it. Phoenix's wiki page showed him being semi-retired. He then began to pop up at MMA – Mixed Martial Arts – events. He fought under his real name – Ben Fodor – although he also kept the Phoenix Jones persona; no doubt it was good for promotion and publicity.

I left the London police and moved to Canada. I lived close to the Washington State border and decided to arrange a meeting with Phoenix Jones, to see how things were going. He was keen to meet up with me. Then, just as I was about to contact him to arrange a date, I saw a news report that completely knocked me: "Real-life superhero 'Phoenix Jones' in super trouble, facing drug charges." During a sting operation, Phoenix Jones had met with undercover police officers and apparently arranged to sell them MDMA (or ecstasy). Officers had arrived at a Seattle hotel, where the meet had been arranged, and after identifying themselves as police, took Phoenix away in handcuffs. His female accomplice was also arrested. It was also alleged that he was found to be in possession of several bundles of cocaine and some other unknown white powder. Local news reported that the police had been working undercover against Phoenix Jones for some time, and that he had previously sold undercover police officers several bags of MDMA at a Starbucks in downtown Seattle.

Meeting up with Phoenix Jones was now out of the question. Members of the Real-Life Superhero community, as well as the MMA community, expressed everything from shock to glee at the news of his arrest. Many quoted a line from the Batman movie, *The Dark Knight*, about either dying a hero or living long enough to become a villain.

Speaking of villains – after Phoenix's arrest, super-villain Rex Velvet, who had been quiet on social media, suddenly sprung back to life, tweeting thanks to the Seattle Police department for their "ongoing efforts to clean up Seattle's streets".

When I later caught up with the former Rain City Superheroes, I would hear how some of them had far less faith and belief in Phoenix Jones than they had previously let on. Not all the superheroes expressed surprise at Phoenix's arrest, and not all were unhappy to witness his public fall from grace. But Phoenix Jones's arrest for alleged drug supply came as a genuine shock to me. I thought back to all those times we had been out patrolling the streets of Seattle when he went out of his way to disrupt and interfere with drugs dealers. Someone more cynical may suggest that he was simply trying to get rid of the competition, but I don't believe that was the case at all. The times I had been with him, he seemed to be genuinely against the activities of drugs dealers. He despised what drugs, and those who dealt them, were doing to his city and the people of the city. However, I was told that others had been far less surprised by his arrest, and had suspected – or even *known* – about Phoenix Jones's apparent involvement in drugs.

There were other allegations made about Phoenix Jones. I was told that the monthly dues paid by members of the RCSM, for what Phoenix claimed was insurance, should they get hurt on patrol, or bail money, should they get arrested, was in fact going straight into his own pocket. How the heroes found out about this, I don't know. There were further allegations that money handed to Phoenix to purchase equipment such as body armour for the heroes was believed to have gone the same way as the dues. I was also told that

Phoenix Jones had set up a GoFundMe campaign to purchase equipment, reaching out to his many fans and followers around the world, but again, there were doubts about where that money actually went. Whether there was any truth behind these beliefs and allegations, I do not know. Then there were accusations of threats made against former friends of Phoenix Jones. All of this had led to what some were calling "The Fall of Phoenix Jones".

The case against him for supplying drugs to undercover police officers was ongoing at the time of writing (April 2020). As it currently stands, it seems almost impossible to believe that Phoenix Jones will come out of this in any positive way. Evidence from undercover officers can be damning.

Ever since I first heard the name Phoenix Jones I was aware there were people – including Real-Life Superheroes – who were against him. Some considered him a joke. Others disapproved of his hands-on, crime-fighting approach to superhero work. But I also detected jealousy. Phoenix Jones had work hard on his public image. He seemed to enjoy the attention he got from the media. He had cultivated a large following of fans around the globe. Phoenix Jones was, without question, the most famous (or perhaps, infamous) Real-Life Superhero in the world. Even with his latest troubles, he remains an inspiration to many. If you want to become a Real-Life Superhero, or you want to learn anything about them, it is impossible to do so without some contribution or influence from the life and times of Phoenix Jones. Whatever comes next for him, he will remain the one big name that will forever be most associated with the Real-Life Superhero movement.

How – or why – he had arrived to where he now was – on bail for serious drug offences – is a unclear. He had a tough upbringing, that's for sure, but in his early years he stayed away from crime, made something of himself, found employment and then began to help others. But despite the following he had gained as Phoenix Jones, I always felt that he wanted more. He always seemed to be tantalisingly close to really breaking through, finding genuine fame and making real money from his activities. He had appeared on many TV news and chat shows around the world. There was a comic book created (although this had been criticised for including real-life events, notably the shooting of Nicole Westbrook). His image had appeared on computer games. And then there was the almost constant talk of potential TV shows or movies that he was to appear in, or that would be made with, or about him. But despite it all, he just never quite made it. A true level of fame was always just out of his reach. When speaking with him over the years his frustration was obvious. There is perhaps another tale here, a story of someone who almost made it. A story of what happens to a person who gets so close, is promised so much, but ultimately finds nothing more than disappointment and crushed dreams.

Whenever I met with a superhero, I was never really sure what was truth and what was fiction. This is also true with Phoenix Jones. But at the time, it never really mattered to me. They could make-up all the wild stories they wanted, whether that was claims of time travelling abilities, or superpowers given by long-dead voodoo queens. It was all part of the wonderful colour that came with these eccentric men and women. They wore outlandish outfits, gave themselves fantastic names and hit the streets, for real. They were *interesting*, and that had been enough for me.

When I heard about Phoenix's arrest, mostly I was just sad. But his arrest and the negative publicity that inevitably followed it, is to me just the latest chapter in the astonishing tale of an orphan from Texas who grew up to become the world's most famous Real-Life Superhero. Where he – and by that I mean Ben Fodor *and* Phoenix Jones – goes from here, I do not know, but I doubt it is the last we will hear from him. Maybe he'll find some inspiration in the mythical beast he named himself after. As I once told Midnight Jack, I don't judge people. I also believe in second chances. I hope Phoenix Jones – or Ben Fodor – finds a way back to the light.

The Rain City Superheroes had disbanded long before all of this. After another May Day protest that the team attended, I was told that some members of the RCSM were unhappy with how the protest was handled, from a safety and leadership point of view, blaming Phoenix Jones. It resulted in the break-up of the RCSM and led some to leave the superhero life behind them completely, although others continue on.

Since my days with the RCSM, Purple Reign has re-married and no longer has anything to do with the superhero movement. I have not spoken to her since I saw her in London.

It seemed, too, that I had got it completely wrong about Evo – he wasn't a cop. Never had been. He is, in fact, a disabled Iraq War veteran, who now volunteers at a local veterans' hospital. He is married, lives outside Seattle and doing well. He is no longer a superhero (of the caped variety, anyway).

However, I did eventually find out which person on the team had been a "cop", and here's the twist: it was Boomer. Well, not exactly a *cop*. Boomer told me that he had spent almost two years working as a reservist state trooper in a different part of the country before moving to Seattle.

But what about everything that Phoenix had told me about there being a cop on the team, and that cop being "extremely concerned" about being found out? Was that just bullshit? Boomer assured me that, other than himself, and the time he had spent with the states troopers, there had never been cop in the Rain City Superhero Movement.

When I spoke with Boomer, to catch up and to find out where he was now, he spent much of the time coughing down the phone, as he was having issues with one of his lungs. Since my time patrolling with him, health problems have continued for Boomer. He told me that his "years of superhero-ing had taken its toll" on his body. He had also broken both of his feet after stopping a "sexual assault in progress" in Capitol Hill, and falling about 35 feet after he tackled the suspect off the side of a building. The injury meant he was unable to patrol as much as he had previously, and as a result had put on more weight.

However, he has had some good news. Boomer is now married and has kids. So I was pleased to hear that he has found some happiness in his life.

USID still keeps in touch with Boomer, his old school friend, but after retiring from the military, he left the state and is no longer working as part of a superhero group.

Ratchet, meanwhile, was kicked off the RCSM after going against one of the main RCSM rules, and apparently bringing a handgun to a stakeout in Capitol Hill.

Griff Grey ended up falling out with Midnight Jack. I was told that they had got into a physical fight. As far as I know, Griff Grey is no longer a superhero.

Midnight Jack started his own superhero group – *The Nightshift*. Boomer still helps out when he can. Boomer told me that sometime he and Jack go out together on what they call "Jack and the Fat-Man" patrols. Scarlet Falcon is also part of The Nightshift.

Cabbie also started a new team of superheroes – the Emerald City Hero Organisation, or *ECHO* – though I have been told that he has handed many of the leadership duties to a superhero called Red Ranger. Somewhere along the way, there was a falling out between Cabbie's team and Midnight Jack's team, during yet another May Day event, and the groups have nothing to do with one another.

Elsewhere in the United States, Mr Xtreme and the Xtreme Justice League continue to patrol the streets of San Diego, although it appears that Urban Avenger is no longer part of the group. Master Legend has had a TV show made about him, by Amazon – *The Legend of Master Legend* – that was inspired by a Rolling Stone magazine article. For some reason, they got an actor to portray Master Legend, and relocated the action to Las Vegas.

In 2018, at the age of 50, Superhero – real name Dale Pople – hung up his super-suit and retired from the superhero-ing business. Age had caught up with him. His knees and back weren't up for this line of work any more.

The President of Sudan – Omar al-Bashir – was eventually arrested; not by a certain New York Superhero and the London Fog, but by the Sudanese army, who it seemed had heard of Khartoum and even knew where it was. He was handed over to the International Criminal Court in The Hague to face trial.

Acknowledgements

I would like to start by thanking the Real-Life Superheroes of America for welcoming me into their lives and allowing me to accompany them as they went about their nocturnal activities. As well as the superheroes that appear in this book, there were others that I reached out to and either met, patrolled with or spoke to. I would like to thank: Superhero / Dale Pople, Master Legend, Mr Xtreme, Urban Avenger, Grimm, Divine Force, Rouroni, Radnor, Phoenix Jones / Ben Fodor, Purple Reign, Boomer, USID, Midnight Jack, Evo, El Caballero, Griff Grey, Ratchet, Scarlet Falcon, Tomahawk, Night Sabre, Tothian, and Amazonia. Thanks also to Peter Tangen for his assistance.

I would like to give a special thank you to Mark Jamieson and the Seattle Police Department for being so open with me about this most unusual of subjects.

Thank you to Ira and his father Norm, for giving me a place to stay in Florida. And thank you to my friend Ben, who suggested I call myself Dick Justice.

I would like to thank Humfrey Hunter at Silvertail Books for actually publishing this and, for some reason, always going along with my weird ideas. Thanks also to Ollie Ray for the cover image. My gut isn't that big. And thank you to Rob Dinsdale – a great editor and also a genuinely great person.

Hello – and *KA-POW!* – to Nathan, Jake, Evie, and Dexter. And also to Ethan, whose superpuissance is being my filleul. And a big *Eh?* to Naomi, Ethan, Bennett and Clara.

Most of all, I would like to thank my amazing wife Lisa. Always my biggest supporter, she is truly a superwoman. I love you.